The Oxford Dictionary of
Local
AND
Family
History

David Hey

Oxford   New York

OXFORD UNIVERSITY PRESS

1997

Oxford University Press, Great Clarendon Street, Oxford OX2 6DP

Oxford New York

Athens Auckland Bangkok Bombay Bogota
Buenos Aires Calcutta Cape Town Dar es Salaam
Delhi Florence Hong Kong Istanbul Karachi
Kuala Lumpur Madras Madrid Melbourne
Mexico City Nairobi Paris Singapore
Taipei Tokyo Toronto

and associated companies in
Berlin Ibadan

Oxford is a trade mark of Oxford University Press

First published by Oxford University Press 1997

British Library Cataloguing in Publication Data
Data available

Library of Congress Cataloguing in Publication Data
Data available

ISBN 0-19-860080-1

10 9 8 7 6 5 4 3 2 1

Typeset by Alliance Phototypesetters
Printed in Great Britain at
Caledonian International Book Manufacturing Ltd
Glasgow

Contents

Preface

The Oxford Dictionary of Local and Family History is designed as an aid for the numerous amateurs who are actively pursuing their own research. It incorporates some of the material that has been assembled in the much larger work, *The Oxford Companion to Local and Family History*, but its purpose is different, for it does not seek to be a complete in-depth guide to the subject. It is intended instead to serve as a handbook which can be taken to record offices and libraries or used at home as a quick means of reference.

The *Dictionary* provides definitions of most of the technical terms that a local and family historian is likely to encounter. It also offers brief guidance on the whereabouts of records, their use, and interpretation. It includes various lists: regnal years, prime ministers, major saints' days, weights and measures, and the addresses of record offices, and has a bibliography of the most important publications in the subject, arranged by topic. The essay in the appendix section (reprinted from *The Oxford Guide to Family History*) is a detailed practical guide to using records in family history research. Many of the topics touched on in the text entries are explored in greater, discursive, depth here. The whole of the British Isles is covered, from prehistoric times to the present day, though the emphasis is on the period from the Norman Conquest onwards, when written records become available in bulk.

The *Dictionary* is therefore conceived as a research tool. The beginner will find guidance on a whole range of matters. The experienced researcher will turn to it to check the meaning of a term or to get basic information about records with which he or she is unfamiliar. The *Dictionary* serves as a starting point. The reader who wishes to pursue a topic in greater depth should turn to the *Companion*.

DAVID HEY

September 1996

abbey. A major monastery, ruled over by an abbot. The *Cistercian and *Premonstratensian foundations were abbeys, whereas the *Cluniac and *Carthusian houses were *priories dependent on the original monastery of their order. The *Benedictines, *Augustinians, and *Gilbertines had both abbeys and priories.

abstract. A summary of a document.

accompt. Archaic form of 'account'.

accounts, medieval. The survival rate of annual accounts for medieval estates varies from one part of the country to another. For Norfolk alone almost 2,000 accounts are extant for the period 1238–1450, representing some 219 different *demesnes, 60 per cent of them with fewer than five *compotus rolls. On the other hand, in the remote north-west and south-west of England hardly any accounts survive.

achievement of arms. The complete representation of the heraldic insignia of a family, including the *coat of arms, crest, helmet, mantling, torse, and motto. The achievement of a peer also includes chapeau, coronet, supporters, and compartment.

acre. Originally an approximate measure of land which a yoke of oxen could plough in a day, it was standardized by Edward I (1272–1307) as a unit of 4,840 square yards. However, in northern and western England, and in Scotland and Ireland, the customary acre remained much larger.

act books. Records which summarize the procedure in a case before an *ecclesiastical court, particularly during the second half of the 16th century and much of the 17th century.

Acts of Parliament. Statute Rolls, which contain all Acts of Parliament since 1500, are housed in the *House of Lords Record Office. Acts which have not been printed may also be seen there. Public Acts from 1485 to 1702 have been printed as *Statutes of the Realm*, and from 1702 as *Statutes at Large*. Local, Personal and Private Acts from 1797 are kept among the Parliament Rolls in the *Public Record Office. Printed sets of Local and Personal Acts are available at the *British Library. Many local *record offices and libraries have printed copies of local Acts, e.g. those relating to parliamentary *enclosure, *turnpike roads, etc.

Adams, John: *Index Villaris*. A list of the market towns of England and Wales, compiled by John Adams (*fl.* 1680). The second edition, published in London in 1690, is the more useful.

administration, letters of and bonds. When a person died without making a *will, or if the named executors were unavailable, the next-of-kin, a friend, or a creditor could apply to a probate court for letters of administration of the estate. The applicant had to swear that he would discharge all funeral expenses and debts and would submit a true and perfect *inventory and an account of his stewardship. He was sometimes required to enter into a *bond.

Administration Acts (the records of the above, known as Admons.) are kept with wills in diocesan *record offices. They were written in Latin until 1733. A probate inventory is often attached.

Admiralty, High Court of. The court with jurisdiction in cases involving piracy, privateering, and other offences committed on the high seas. It developed into the court which heard all matters relating to the high seas and business abroad. Its records—especially for the period from 1525—are kept at the *Public Record Office under HCA 13 (examinations), 15–20 (instance papers), 23 (interrogatories), 24 (libels and answers), and 30 (miscellenea).

adoption. A register of adoption from 1927 onwards is kept at the *General Register Office, St Catherine's House, London. No formal mechanism was available previously, unless the parties drew up a *deed. Birth certificates obtained via the Adopted Children's Register at the General Register Office give the dates of birth and adoption and the names of the adopting parents, but not the child's original surname or the names of the natural parents.

The Children Act, which came into force on 12 November 1975, allows an adopted person over the age of 18 to apply for his or her original birth certificate at the General Register Office or by writing to the General Register Office (CA side), PO Box 7, Titchfield, Fareham, Hampshire PO15 5RU. An applicant who was adopted before 12 November 1975 will be interviewed by an experienced social worker before a certificate is issued. A person adopted after that date can decide whether or not to be interviewed.

Adoption was not recognized in Scottish law until 1930. Records of adoption in the Court of Sessions and Sheriff Court are kept in the *Scottish Record Office, but information is supplied (by order of the court) only if the adopted child has reached the age of 17.

Advent. In the ecclesiastical calendar, the season immediately preceding the festival of the Nativity, including the four Sundays before Christmas.

Because it was regarded as a time for fasting and repentance, this was a prohibited season for marriages.

advowson. The right to appoint a priest to a *benefice, especially a parish church.

affeerers. The officers appointed by a manorial court to fix the amount of the fines for offences.

affinity. Relationship through marriage, not through blood, e.g. son-in-law, stepdaughter.

aftermath (agricultural). Grass that sprouts anew after the cutting of a crop of hay, suitable for grazing.

agger. The raised foundations and drainage ditches of a Roman road.

agistment. 1. The right to graze livestock on the *commons in the summer.
  2. The rate levied or profit made on the grazing of pastures.

agnate. A relative descended from a common male ancestor.

Agrarian History of England and Wales. An eight-volume survey under the general editorship of H. P. R. Finberg and Joan Thirsk, published by Cambridge University Press.

Agricultural Depression, the. This term may refer to the 1930s but more usually relates to the late 1870s.

agricultural labourers. The distinction between a farm labourer and a *farm servant was that a servant was hired on a yearly basis from about the age of 14 and lived on the farm, whereas a labourer was usually a married man, employed on either a regular or a casual basis, who lived elsewhere. In the Tudor and early Stuart period the labouring population of England and Wales probably formed about one quarter or one third of the entire population of the countryside. The figure varied considerably from region to region. As the population recovered to its medieval level, so the proportion of labourers grew.

The term 'labourer'—the 'ag. labs' of *census returns and *parish registers—covered a wide variety of conditions. The labourer was usually far removed from the 'Hodge' stereotype of his social superiors, for he had to possess a variety of skills.

agricultural statistics. The 1801 *crop returns, which are housed in the *Public Record Office under HO 67, are responses on printed forms to government enquiries sent to local clergymen. They are arranged by dioceses and parishes and note the acreages devoted to specific crops, often including general remarks. From 1866 to the present day annual summaries of the livestock kept and crops grown in each parish have been returned to the central government. Those from 1866 to 1963 are kept at the PRO under MAF 68.

ague. Archaic term for acute fever, with cold, hot, and sweating stages. It is also used for malaria, caught in fens and marshes.

aid. 1. A tax or subsidy paid to the Crown.
   2. A feudal due paid by a tenant to a lord. It was limited by *Magna Carta (1215) to ransom, the knighting of the lord's eldest son, and the marriage of the lord's eldest daughter. Feudal aids were abolished in 1660.

aisled hall. A superior form of medieval open hall, where the roof-truss is extended to the wall-plates of aisles so as to provide extra space.

alabaster. A translucent white or nearly white form of gypsum (sulphate of lime), sometimes flecked with red, and much used in the past, particularly in England, for statuary and other decorative purposes. It was quarried mainly in the Trent valley.

alderman. 1. The *Old English title (*ealdorman*) for a royal official comparable with the post-Conquest *sheriff.
   2. A senior member of a medieval *guild or, by extension, *borough, elected by his fellows. This system was also used by 19th- and 20th-century *county or borough councils.

alehouses. The licensing system began in 1495, but most licences were issued after the passing of another Act in 1552. Amongst the records of *quarter sessions are those of special sittings known as *brewster sessions, when each *constable had to present a list of the names of licensed innkeepers and alehouse keepers in his *township. In these records, alehouse keepers are often listed as 'tipplers', without the modern connotation of the word. An Act of 1753 required all *clerks of the peace to keep registers of licensed victuallers. The term 'alehouse' was gradually replaced by 'public house' during the course of the 18th century. The Beer Act (1830) brought free trade to the brewing industry.

ale-taster. A manorial officer responsible for the taste and correct measurement of ale.

alias (Lat. 'otherwise'). Aliases were used in cases of illegitimacy, upon the remarriage of a parent, upon inheriting property from a female relative, etc. In some cases the alias form was inherited for several generations and was thus similar to a double-barrelled surname. See also DEED POLL.

alienation (legal). The transfer of ownership.

aliens, returns of. The *Public Record Office Records Information leaflet no. 10, 'Immigrants: Documents in the Public Record Office' gives full details of the available public records concerning aliens.

allegations, marriage. A statement made on oath, or affidavit, in order to obtain a *marriage licence.

allotment. 1. A piece of land awarded by commissioners under the terms of an Act of *Enclosure.
   2. A plot of land for growing vegetables. A few allotments were provided for *agricultural labourers in the late 18th century, but the impetus to provide such plots grew after the *Napoleonic wars. An enquiry in 1833 showed that 42 per cent of *parishes had some allotments. The Allotments Act (1887) enabled local authorities to purchase land for allotments. By 1900 there were nearly half a million allotments in England and Wales. The number increased during the First World War and reached one and a quarter million in the 1920s.

almanac. Almanacs were very popular from the 17th century onwards. They included a calendar, information on *fairs, *roads, and posts, advice on farming, historical and scientific information, comments on political and religious matters, sensational news, and astrological predictions. In Victorian times, many small towns published their own annual almanac, keeping much of the old format but adding short articles and poems, often written in dialect. Some of these were published into the second half of the 20th century.

almshouse. A charitable foundation for the care of the poor, especially the elderly. In the Middle Ages almshouses were known alternatively as hospitals or *maisons dieu*. They were supervised by a warden or master and contained an infirmary hall and a chapel. Many were dissolved at the *Reformation. The Elizabethans re-established some of the old almshouses and founded many new ones by private benefaction. Many examples survive from the 17th and 18th centuries. Many more almshouses were founded on traditional lines during the 19th century.

altar. The focal point of a church for the celebration of the mass or communion. The altar took the form of a stone slab, with four small incised crosses in each corner, and another in the centre, supported on a rectangular stone base. Other altars were placed in *chantry chapels. At the *Reformation it was ordered that altar stones should be removed and destroyed; nevertheless, a considerable number survive.

alum was used by dyers and tanners as a binding agent.

Amateur Historian. The journal for local historians set up by the *Standing Conference for Local History, and first published in August–September 1952. In 1968 it became *The *Local Historian.*

amercement. The fine for an offence at a manorial *court leet. The jurors presented the offender, the steward declared him to be 'in mercy' of the court, and the amount of the amercement was then decided.

Anabaptist. Originally, a name given to several unorthodox *Protestant sects in Europe, who shared in common a rejection of infant baptism. In the British Isles the term was used in a derogatory way in the 16th and 17th centuries for a *Baptist and, more loosely, for other Protestant dissenters.

ancient demesne. Manors which belonged to the Crown during the reigns of Edward the Confessor and William I, which retained certain privileges.

angel (monetary). A gold coin bearing the image of St Michael the Archangel slaying the dragon, introduced in the reign of Edward IV (1461–83), and valued at 6s. 8d. It was known originally as the angel-noble, being a new issue of the *noble. It ceased to be legal tender in the reign of Charles I (1625–49). It was the coin given to those who were touched for the *King's Evil.

annuity. An annual sum of money, payable for either a fixed term, or for life, or in perpetuity. The first state life annuities were granted in the 1690s. The records, which are kept at the *Public Record Office under NDO 1–3, give names, addresses, ages at entry, and the dates of last payments, together with some marriages, deaths, and wills. Most of the annuitants who are recorded as such in *census returns, *parish registers, etc. received their annuities from private settlements.

apothecaries. The London Company of Apothecaries, incorporated in 1606, was empowered in 1815 to license apothecaries throughout England and Wales and to enforce a five-year *apprenticeship. The records of the Company date from 1670 and are kept at the *Guildhall Library, London. The apothecary may be seen as the forerunner of the general practitioner in medicine.

apparitor. The messenger who summoned people to appear before an *ecclesiastical court.

appraiser. A valuer of property, e.g. one who drew up a probate *inventory.

apprenticeship. The Statute of Apprentices of 1563, which forbade anyone to enter a trade without serving an apprenticeship, remained on the statute book until 1814, though it was modified by later Acts and by legal judgments. The apprenticeship indenture was a legal document which bound a boy to a master, with a premium paid to the master by the boy's parents (or, in the case of paupers, by the overseer of the *poor).

Large numbers of apprenticeship indentures survive in assorted collections in county *record offices. At the Society of *Genealogists 'Crisp's Bonds' lists some 18,000 apprenticeships between 1641 and 1888.

An Act of 1710 made stamp duty payable on indentures of apprenticeship. Registers of money received were kept from 1710 to 1811. These 'Apprenticeship Books' may be consulted at the *Public Record Office, where they are classified as IR 1. They record the names, addresses, and trades of the masters, the names of the apprentices, and the dates of the indentures. Until 1752 the names of the parents of the apprentices are also given. Indexes of masters' names, 1710–62, and of apprentices' names, 1710–74, are available at the Society of Genealogists, and at the Public Record Office under IR 17.

appropriation (in church documents). The transfer to a monastic house or other religious institution of the *tithes and other endowments of a *parish.

appurtenances. The rights and duties appended to an agreement over holding land, especially within a *manor.

apse. A semi-circular or polygonal recess, with an arched or domed roof, especially at the eastern end of the *chancel of a church.

archdeaconries and deaneries. The large *dioceses of the medieval church were subdivided into smaller administrative units, some of which survive to this day. A bishop delegated administrative authority over parts of his diocese to a number of archdeacons. In turn, an archdeaconry was subdivided into rural deaneries, each of which comprised a group of *parishes. The archdeacon was charged with visiting each of his parishes from time to time in order to ensure that churches were kept in good repair, that services were being conducted upon approved lines, and that scandalous behaviour was being punished.

archery. In late medieval England practice with the longbow was a statutory requirement. Fear of French invasion prompted the revival of the statute in 1543. Men in every town and village were required to practice at the *butts after attending church on Sundays and holidays. The statute fell into abeyance during the 17th century.

Arches, Court of. The provincial court of appeal of the Province of Canterbury. The records of this court are kept at *Lambeth Palace Library.

archive. A historical document. The plural form is also applied to the place where such documents are housed, e.g. a county *record office.

armiger. Someone who is entitled to bear a *coat of arms, an *esquire.

armory. *Heraldry; armorial bearings.

Arms, College of. The corporation of heralds, founded in 1483–4. The College is situated in Queen Victoria Street, London EC4. Its registers include grants made or confirmed to English and Welsh families from the 15th century to the present day.

army records. See the *Public Record Office Records Information leaflet no. 59, 'British Army Records as Sources for Biography and Genealogy'.

Personal information about officers should be first sought in the published *Army Lists*, which are available from 1754 in the larger public reference libraries. Manuscript lists of army officers from 1702 to 1752 (with an index) are kept in the Public Record Office under WO 64. Genealogical information about officers was seldom recorded by the army before the early 19th century, from which time several series of records, especially those kept under WO 25 and WO 76, are more informative. These give date and place of birth, and the dates of marriage and the births of children.

The attestation and discharge documents in WO 97 provide a detailed record of service, nearly always with the place of birth, age on enlistment, and a physical description. From 1833 they also note details of next-of-kin, wives, and children. Three series deal with soldiers discharged from 1756 to 1872, 1873 to 1882, and 1883 to 1913. Unfortunately, the records of soldiers who died whilst serving have been destroyed. Regimental pay lists and *muster rolls are available in annual bound volumes from 1732 to 1878 under WO 12 and from 1878 to 1898 under WO 16. Description books, which give a physical description of a soldier, together with his age, place of birth, trade, and length of service, are available for the period 1756–1900 under WO 25, though many regiments have records only for the first half of the 19th century.

Soldiers who completed their term of service or who became invalids received a pension or institutional care in the Royal Hospitals at *Chelsea and Kilmainham. Admission books for out-pensioners in the 18th and 19th centuries are housed under WO 116 to 118. Records of in-pensioners are kept under WO 23. See the PRO Records Information leaflet no. 123. See also leaflet no. 84 for court-martial records.

The *General Register Office at *St Catherine's House, London stores the regimental registers of 1761–1924, which record the births, marriages, and deaths of soldiers who were stationed in the United Kingdom. The marriage records also note the names, births, and baptisms of any children who were born to a given marriage. The Army Register Book (1881–1959) notes genealogical details of the families of those serving overseas. From 1959 the entries of births, marriages, and deaths of the members of the families of those serving in all three forces— Army, Navy, RAF—are combined.

Array, Commission of. In the late 13th century, in order to raise an army from each *shire in times of emergency, Edward I appointed commissioners from the ranks of the *barons, *knights of the shire, and officers of the royal household to choose from the *muster rolls the required number of men from each *township. Musters of males aged between 15 and 60 were held twice a year in every *hundred or *liberty. Wages were paid to men who had to serve abroad, but each man was expected to provide his own equipment. This system of providing against emergency survived until 1551, when the commission was replaced by *lords lieutenant.

Artificers, Statute of (1563). An Act which ordered that the level of wages should be determined by *Justices of the Peace, that the hours of labour should be limited to 12 in the summer and to daylight in the winter, that servants should be hired for at least a year, and that *apprentices should serve seven years. Some of its provisions were difficult to enforce.

artisan. A skilled craft worker. The term was used particularly in the 19th century. Artisans provided the leadership of working-class political reform groups.

Ashkenazic Jews. Those Jews who came from Germany and other parts of eastern, central, and northern Europe. They spoke Yiddish, a form of German written in Hebrew characters.

ashlar. Freestone; smoothly cut stone for building purposes, introduced into Britain by the Normans.

assart. A piece of land, often of irregular shape, brought into cultivation from the waste, especially woodland. The term is usually applied to a medieval clearance.

assembly rooms. By the middle of the 18th century most towns of a reasonable size had their assembly rooms. The regular assemblies formed the weekly basis of the social round, but others were held on special occasions, e.g. at the meetings of *quarter sessions, or during race week.

Assize, Courts of. Sessions of courts presided over by judges on circuit in England and Wales which tried capital and other serious offences, including homicide, infanticide, rape, robbery, burglary, *larceny, and arson, offences which were too serious to be tried at *quarter sessions. The assize judges also tried a variety of civil cases.

The assize circuits that remained in use until 1876 had been defined by the 14th century. England was divided into six circuits beyond London and Middlesex: the Home, Midland, Western, Oxford, Norfolk, and Northern. These were modified between 1876 and 1893 but were subsequently unaltered until the merger of assize and quarter-sessions courts in 1971. After the Union with England in 1536, Wales was divided into four assize circuits: Chester, North Wales, Brecon, and Carmarthen. The records of the assize courts are held in the *Public Record Office under Assi. 44, etc.

Assize of Mort D'ancestor. A court for determining a claim to inheritance, founded in 1176 and abolished in 1833. Most cases were brought by manorial lords in order to repossess property upon the death of a tenant.

Assize of Novel Disseisin. A procedure established in 1176 and abolished in 1833, whereby a tenant who had been removed from his holding could have his case dealt with speedily.

Association Oath rolls. After a plot to assassinate William III in 1696, an Act of Association required all office-holders to take a solemn oath of association by which they vowed to help preserve King William III's person and government. The names of the oath-takers in each *parish, and in the *livery companies of the City of London, are recorded under C 213 at the *Public Record Office.

asylum, lunatic. The earliest asylums were private or charitable institutions. An Act of 1828 empowered *Justices of the Peace to erect and maintain asylums from county rates; another Act of 1845 compelled them to do so. Records of this period will be found amongst those of the *quarter sessions. In 1888 responsibility was transferred to county and borough *councils, until the establishment of the National Health Service in 1948.

For England and Wales few records of a personal nature appear to survive; others are unavailable until they are 100 years old. If the approximate date of admission to an asylum is known, it is worth searching the registers compiled by the Lunacy Commissioners, and from 1913 the Board of Control, for the whole of England and Wales. These are arranged chronologically from 1846 to 1960, and are housed at the *Public Record Office under MH 94. Correspondence and papers under MH 51 include files on individual asylums and gaols with insane prisoners. Class MH 83 contains the building records of the county pauper asylums which were erected under the terms of the 1845 Act.

Scotland has few records of asylums before 1858, though the Aberdeen Sheriff Court records include registers of lunatics in asylums between 1800 and 1823 and between 1855 and 1857. From 1857 Scottish asylums were regulated by the General Board of Commissioners in Lunacy, whose archives are kept at the *Scottish Record Office. These are available only after 75 years. The general register (MC 7) of all lunatics in asylums notes name, date of admission, which asylum, date of discharge or death, and whither removed (if relevant); an index is provided. Notices of Admission (MC 2) record name, age, marital status, previous place of abode, nearest relative, and observations on the mental and physical health of the patient.

attainder. A person condemned to death or outlawry for treason or *felony forfeited both his real and personal estate and, by 'corruption of blood', his right to inherit or transmit property. Attainder was ordered either by judicial judgement or, from 1539, by an Act of Parliament (an Act of Attainder). For most crimes attainder was ended by the Forfeiture Act of 1870, but for outlawry it lasted until 1938. Inventories of the goods and chattels of attainted persons are found in the *Public Record Office, mainly under E 154.

attorneys. By the second half of the 17th century attorneys were found occupying important positions in British towns. They were able to make a handsome living from drafting and executing *wills, drawing up deeds and *settlements, arranging mortgages and loans, giving advice on investments, and by acting as stewards, estate managers, and rent-collectors. Since 1875 attorneys have been called solicitors.

auditor. The Office of the Auditors of Land Revenue formed a sub-department of the *Exchequer from the abolition of the Court of *Augmentations in 1554 until 1832. Its records are kept at the *Public Record Office under E 299 to 330 and LR 1 to 16.

Augmentations, Court of. Formed in 1536 upon the *dissolution of the monasteries to administer the monastic properties and revenues confiscated by the Crown, the Court was amalgamated with the *Exchequer in 1554. Its records are housed in the *Public Record Office under E315 and E321. Some of these have been calendared by the *List and Index Society.

Augustinians. Religious communities of regular canons organized according to the rule of St Augustine of Hippo (354–430), which emphasized poverty, celibacy, and obedience. The order was founded in Italy and France in the mid-11th century; the first community in Britain was that of St Botolph's Priory, Colchester, established in 1103. The order was known in Britain as the Austin Canons (after St Augustine) or the Black Canons (from their black outdoor cloaks). They were popular in lay society and had over 200 houses in England, Scotland, and Wales by 1350, and many others in Ireland. The Austin Canons sometimes shared their church with the parishioners. Some canons were seconded to be *vicars of parish churches that were under the patronage of the priory. The order also founded hospitals, including St Bartholomew's and St Thomas's in London.

aulnage. Edward I (1272–1307) appointed aulnagers to give their seal of approval to cloths manufactured to standard sizes and quality. Aulnage was extended to knitted goods in the 16th century. The regulations on size were repealed in 1381, but those on quality remained in force until 1699. The earliest surviving rolls at the *Public Record Office give the names of clothiers and the numbers of cloths produced.

average. The three most commonly used averages in the statistical analysis of historical data are the mean, the median, and the mode. The mean is the arithmetical average; the median is the middle value when all items in a distribution are arranged in order of size; and the modal value is that for which the frequency is greatest.

back-to-back housing. Once the typical working-class accommodation in the industrial towns of northern England. They consisted of one room on the ground floor and one room above. Their walls were shared by three other houses.

badger (historical). A dealer in meal, malt, dairy produce, eggs, etc. Badgers had to be licensed at the *quarter sessions under an Act of 1563, though those who lived in the northern counties of England were exempt. In time, badgers became general dealers or middlemen.

badging. Under an Act of 1697 those in receipt of poor relief were supposed to have a letter P and the initial of the parish sewn on to their clothes. Many parishes did not insist on this humiliation. Badging was abolished in 1782.

bailey. An enclosure within a *castle, beyond the *keep, containing accommodation, service buildings, etc., and defended by a ditch, rampart, and wall. The larger castles had both an inner and an outer bailey.

bailie. In Scotland, originally the chief magistrate of a *barony or part of a county, equivalent to an English *sheriff. Later, a municipal magistrate, equivalent to the English *alderman.

bailiff. 1. The holder of a public office in a certain district, e.g. a *sheriff or mayor.
2. The agent of the *lord of the manor responsible for administering the estate, collecting rents, etc.
3. A court official responsible for executing writs and distraining goods.

bailiwick. A district or place under the jurisdiction of a *bailiff or *bailie.

balk. An unploughed piece of land which formed a boundary between, and provided access to, the *furlongs of *open-fields. Grass balks did not serve as boundaries between individual *strips, as historians once believed, but were sometimes valued as grazing.

ballads. A high proportion of surviving ballads can be dated, on internal evidence, to the second half of the 16th century and the first part of the 17th century. Thousands of ballads were enrolled by the Company of Stationers during this period.

Band of Hope. Founded in 1847 as a temperance organization for children.

banking and finance. Between 1640 and 1670 the City of London developed the three essential functions of the banker: to take deposits, to discount bills, and to issue notes. This movement culminated in the foundation of the Bank of England in 1694, the foundation of the Bank of Scotland in the following year, the emergence of the Stock Exchange, and the reform of the coinage.

bankruptcy. Records of bankruptcy proceedings are housed at the *Public Record Office. From 1571 some conveyances of bankrupts' property can be found in the *Close rolls. The Court of Bankruptcy's records are available from 1710, under a 75-years rule. Class B 3, which has been indexed by name, place, and occupation, contains the files of examinations and depositions from 1780 to 1842. B 1 contains the order books from 1710 to 1877, B 6 contains the registers from 1733, and B 7 the minute books from 1714. Some *Chancery and *Exchequer records contain information about bankruptcy in law cases. Notices of adjudications were, and still are, published in the *London Gazette and advertised in local *newspapers.

In Scotland, bankruptcy papers prior to 1839 are among the Court of *Session records in the *Scottish Record Office; a 'Guide to Scottish Sequestrations, 1839–1913' is available in the Search Room. In 1883 the Government created a Bankruptcy Department with responsibility for investigating and administering the affairs of insolvent individuals and firms; its records are housed at the Public Record Office under B 11 and 12.

banksman. The man in charge of the winding gear at a *coal mine.

banns of marriage. The proclamation in church of an intended wedding, in order that those who know of any impediment may object. The banns are read on three successive Sundays in the parish churches of both the bride and the bridegroom. The procedure can be avoided by obtaining a *marriage licence.

Between 1653 and 1660, when marriages were civil contracts under the authority of a *Justice of the Peace, banns were read either in church on three consecutive Sundays or in the market-place on three successive weekly market days. These banns were sometimes recorded in a separate book and sometimes in the *parish register, with the letter M (for market) added.

Lord Hardwicke's *Marriage Act (1753) regularized the keeping of registers of banns, but only a few books survive. The registering of banns was stopped in 1812 by *Rose's Act.

banqueting-house. In Elizabethan times, a place for an intimate meal. These were special-purpose buildings, sometimes in the form of rooftop towers, sometimes as garden buildings.

baptism customs. Baptism was held to be essential to salvation in the Middle Ages and was therefore performed as soon as possible after birth. After the *Reformation the *Book of Common Prayer recommended that baptism should be performed upon a Sunday or holy day, unless it was feared that the infant might die. The interval between birth and baptism varied from parish to parish and over time, but was normally only a few days and rarely more than a fortnight. In the early modern period the custom grew up amongst the *gentry of private baptism at home.

Baptists. The English Baptist movement was founded in exile in Amsterdam in 1611 by a group of Separatists from the *Church of England led by John Smith. The following year Thomas Helwys returned to London to establish the first Baptist church in England.

In 1633 a group in Southwark who believed in Calvinistic predestination broke away to form the Particular Baptist Church. Those who remained with the original body became known as the General Baptists. By the late 17th century the Particular Baptists had become the more numerous body. Many General Baptist churches eventually became *Unitarian; those that remained formed the General Baptist New Connection in 1770. Splinter groups like the *Scotch Baptists continued to form and reform. In 1891 the General and Particular Baptists united in the Baptist Union of Great Britain and Ireland.

The Baptist Union Library, 4 Southampton Row, London WC1, incorporates the Baptist Historical Society Library. Other relevant archives are kept at Dr *Williams's Library, Gordon Square, London WC1. Registers before 1837 are kept with other *Nonconformist records at the *Public Record Office.

barbican. An outer fortification or first line of defence, especially at an entrance to a walled city or a *castle, or a temporary wooden tower or bulwark. These structures strengthened defences at weak points, served as watch-towers, and were intended to dictate the approach of enemy forces. They usually date from the 13th or 14th century.

bargain and sale. A 16th-century method of conveying property by a private agreement drawn up by a lawyer, which was gradually replaced by that of *lease and release.

barge board. A board which covered the end of the rafters in the gable of houses. Such boards were often decorated.

barmote court. In the Peak District of Derbyshire all *lead mining in the King's Field was controlled by barmote courts, which date from at least the 13th century.

Barnardo homes, Dr. Thomas John Barnardo (1845–1905) founded his first home for destitute children at Stepney in 1870. The archives of this and many subsequent foundations are kept at the University of Liverpool, where those over 100 years old may be consulted, by arrangement. Between 1874 and 1905 the photographic department of Dr Barnardo's Homes took over 55,000 photographs of nearly all the children in the homes, many of whom emigrated to Australia and Canada.

baron. The lowest rank of the peerage; originally, a rank held by military or other honourable service from the king. The term was introduced after the Norman Conquest to signify a *tenant-in-chief of the king below the rank of *earl. By the 13th century it was applied only to those lords who were summoned to Parliament. The Great Barons attended the king's Great Council. Most modern titles are not ancient; in 1956 only 144 of the 550 baronies went back beyond 1832. Since 1958 non-hereditary peerages with the rank of baron (or baroness) have also been conferred.

baron and feme. A legal term. In common law, a man and his wife were considered as one person. (Feme is derived from French *femme*.) Thus, upon marriage, a woman's personal property became her husband's.

baronet. The hereditary rank created by James I in 1611 to raise money for troops in Ulster, the fee being £1,095. Baronets are styled 'Sir' and take precedence over *knights. Separate baronetcies of Ireland (1619) and Nova Scotia (1625) were also created.

barony. The domain of a *baron. In Ireland, the division of a county. In Scotland, a large *freehold estate or *manor.

baroque. The term is used on the Continent for a florid architectural style that originated during the late Italian Renaissance and which became widely used, particularly for churches, in Catholic Europe during the 17th and 18th centuries. In Britain, the term is used in a more restricted sense and is applied particularly to country houses erected between 1685 and 1715. English baroque was never a unified style, but embraced a variety of individual designs that were classical in their inspiration.

barton. The word is used especially in south-west England, to mean either the home farm of a *lord of a manor, a monastic farm or *grange, or simply a barley farm. In modern times the word normally means a farmyard.

16

bastardy papers. Parish records of the 16th to the 19th century kept by the overseers of the *poor concerning the parentage of illegitimate children and efforts to make the fathers responsible for maintenance.

bastides. The medieval planned towns of France, which have many points of comparison with those of Britain. These include grid patterns, town walls, market squares, and *burgage plots.

bastle. A fortified farmhouse of a type found in the Scottish borders, especially Northumberland, dating from the 16th and 17th centuries, and providing protection from raiders for livestock and people. Cattle were accommodated on the ground floor and the inhabitants occupied an upper room which was reached by an outside staircase.

battlement. An indented parapet along the top of a wall, used originally in fortified buildings, but by the 15th and 16th centuries for ornamentation in major houses and *Perpendicular Gothic churches. The fashion was revived in the 19th century.

bawn. A fortified farm or walled cattle enclosure in Ireland, especially one in the Ulster plantations of the early 17th century.

bay. 1. The area between two sets of principal posts or dividing walls in a building. Early *surveys record buildings as being of so many bays.
    2. A recess in a room with a projecting window. In large houses these were often attractive architectural features.

beacon. In the age before modern communications technology the most rapid means of alerting people to danger from invasion was by the lighting of hill-top beacons. These were not simply bonfires, but were often stone-built structures which were maintained regularly through county rates. A network of beacons was developed in the Middle Ages. The Tudors maintained beacons along the south coast and the Severn estuary to guard against invasion from France and Spain. The method was also used to alert the *militia and volunteer companies during the *Napoleonic wars. Many hill-top sites are commemorated by the place-name 'Beacon'.

beadle. 1. A town-crier or a crier in a law court.
    2. A minor parish official responsible for keeping order; sometimes the equivalent of the *constable.
    3. Someone who walks in front of dignitaries in a procession.

beast gate. The right to pasture an animal on the *commons and wastes was regulated by the manorial *courts, which imposed a stinting system of so many 'gates' per holding.

beating the bounds. See PERAMBULATIONS.

bederoll (also bead-roll). The list of persons to be specially prayed for, which was read out from the pulpit each Sunday and at Christmas and *Michaelmas; these persons usually comprised the benefactors of the church.

bedesman (also beadsman). A man who prayed for the soul or spiritual welfare of others, usually in a paid capacity. The term might be applied to the inmate of an *almshouse who was charged with praying for his benefactor.

bees were the source of the main sweetener in cooking until sugar-cane was grown more abundantly in the Mediterranean in the 16th century and imported into northern Europe. In the early modern period bees were kept on estates in bee-boles, which are recesses built into a south-facing wall in which a straw hive could be protected from rain.

beggars. The Elizabethan *Poor Law Acts of 1597–1601 ordered that beggars should be punished by whipping. Examples of such punishment being meted out can be found in *quarter sessions and *parish records. In the second half of the 17th century strident complaints about beggars ceased to be heard.

Beguines. The lay sisterhoods which began in the Low Countries in the 12th century. They pursued a religious life but did not bind themselves to a strict vow, and sometimes left upon marriage.

bell-founding was an urban craft in the early modern period, when it was often combined with that of the brazier or potter.

bell pit. A pit for the extraction of *iron ore and *coal. Although the technique was a medieval one, it was still used in the 19th century where coal or iron ore were found near the surface. A vertical shaft was dug to the seam, which was then worked in all directions, thus producing a bell shape. Fear of roof collapse would then lead to the pit being abandoned and the digging of a new shaft alongside. Pits are thus arranged in rows, marked by the spoil which was deposited around the head of the shafts.

belvedere. A turret-room, often glazed on all sides, at the top of a house or tower, providing distant views across the countryside; a summer-house. The name is derived from Italian words for a pleasant view or fair prospect. Introduced into Britain during the 16th century, the fashion flourished in the late 18th and early 19th centuries.

bench end. Benches were introduced into the *naves of parish churches towards the end of the 15th century. The earliest ones were very simple, but in time it became the practice to carve bench ends with tracery designs or with heraldic or allegorical subjects.

bench mark. Mark used by surveyors of the *Ordnance Survey to provide a 'bench' or support for a levelling staff in order to determine altitude above mean sea-level. Below the horizontal notch is the broad arrowhead that was used from the Middle Ages onwards to mark the property of the sovereign.

Benedictines. The largest monastic order in Britain, based on the rule of St Benedict (d. 543). The early foundations of the black monks were destroyed in the 9th century by the *Vikings. The Benedictines were re-established in southern England in the 10th century. By the middle of the 12th century southern England had about 50 Benedictine monasteries and 12 *nunneries, most of which were wealthy. In the later Middle Ages the Benedictines had 245 houses in England, Wales, and Scotland, but the movement had lost its impetus before the Anglo-Norman settlement of Ireland. In the 19th century new Benedictine houses were established at Ampleforth and Downside.

benefice. An ecclesiastical living.

benefit of clergy. In the Middle Ages the Common Law courts substituted a minor punishment for the death penalty for some of the less serious capital crimes when the convicted person was a clerk (clergyman). In 1305 this benefit was extended to secular clerks who were able to read and understand Latin. The first verse of the 50th Psalm in the Vulgate version of the *Bible was used as the test. After the *Reformation this was replaced by the ability to read, in English, the same verse in the Authorized Version of the Bible (where it was the 51st Psalm). It became known popularly as the 'Neck Verse'. Anyone convicted of a capital offence who could read this verse was not hanged, but merely branded on his thumb. In practice, benefit of clergy had become a useful legal fiction to mitigate the severity of the law for first offenders. The formality of the test was abandoned in 1705. Benefit of clergy was abolished in 1827.

berewick. A dependent settlement within a *manor. The term is used in the *Domesday Book.

betrothal. Up to the early 17th century a betrothal before witnesses, followed by consummation, was considered a valid marriage. This explains why some *baptisms recorded in early *parish registers follow shortly after a church wedding. Betrothals gradually declined in status to that of the engagement, which could be broken.

bibles. The Vulgate bible, which was based on that prepared by St Jerome *c.*400, and revised in 1592, is the official text of the Roman Catholic church. It takes its name from the Latin *vulgare*, 'make public'. The first translation of the Bible into English was made in 1382 by John Wycliff and his associates. The first printed English bible was that translated by William Tyndale, starting with the New Testament in 1526 and followed by the Pentateuch and the Book of Jonah in 1530–1. A complete English bible, edited by Miles Coverdale, was published on the Continent in 1535. Various other editions extended Tyndale's work. The Geneva Bible of 1560 was popularly known as the Breeches Bible, for it translated the aprons of Genesis 3: 7 as breeches. It became immensely popular during the reign of Elizabeth and ran to over 150 editions. The Authorized or King James Bible was published in 1611. The revised version of the King James Bible was published in 1881–5. It has been largely replaced in *Protestant churches in Britain during the later 20th century by the New English Bible (1961–70).

bidding. A custom which survived in Wales until the late 19th century, whereby close friends and relatives of a bride and groom were bidden by word of mouth or letter to a festivity at which they were expected to make a gift of money towards the setting-up of the new home. The contributions ranged from 6*d*. to 2*s*. 6*d*., the most common being 1*s*. These payments were regarded as 'marriage dues', for the contributors had received, or would hope to receive, such gifts themselves. In effect, the bidding acted as a sort of savings club.

bierlow. The *Viking word for a *township, retained in some place-names.

bill, hedging. The hook-shaped tool with a sharp cutting edge, used by hedge-layers in the late 18th and 19th centuries.

bill of exchange. A method of payment much used to obtain *credit before the system of bank cheques was devised. It took the form of a written order by the writer (the 'drawer') to the person to whom it was addressed (the 'drawee') to pay to the 'drawer' or to a named third person (the 'payee') a stated sum of money on a certain date. Over time it aquired a looser meaning of a promissory note.

birth-rates. The 'crude' birth-rate is the number of births in a given year, expressed as so many per thousand. Since the only evidence in quantity of births before 1837 is the record of baptisms in *parish registers, such figures have to be converted to birth-rates corrected for under-registration. Birth-rates can only be approximations before reasonably accurate population figures are available from *census returns.

bishops' registers. Volumes recording the administrative acts of bishops in their *dioceses. They date from the 12th and 13th centuries onwards, but are less useful after the *Reformation. Such registers record the ordination of clergy and their institution to livings, the *appropriation of *benefices to religious houses, etc.

bishops' transcripts. In 1598 it became the practice for each parish in England and Wales to copy the entries made the previous year in the *parish register and to forward this transcript (signed by the incumbent and the churchwardens) to the bishop of the *diocese or to the head of the relevant *peculiar jurisdiction. These records are now kept in diocesan *record offices or the National Library of *Wales. They are invaluable where an original register has been destroyed or where there are gaps or passages that are difficult to read. On the whole, the transcripts have not been as well preserved as the originals. The copyists frequently lacked care.

Few transcripts were made during the *Commonwealth period, but the practice was revived at the *Restoration. It petered out during the 19th century at times which differed from diocese to diocese.

Black Death. In Britain, its main effects were felt in 1348–9. A third or more of the population died as a result of this epidemic. Further epidemics occurred in 1360–2 and 1369, and plague remained endemic in Britain until the mid-1660s.

Blome, Richard. 17th-century mapmaker. His world map, *Cosmography*, went through various editions from 1669. His *Britannia* (1673) was a series of county maps and included a map of Ireland. The maps have little geographical merit but are decorative.

bloomery. A *forge in an ironworks where the melted ore is hammered into bars of *iron known as blooms, so as to remove the slag. Sites are often located by the presence of slag and by place-names such as Cinder Hill or Smithies. Units of production were small and often short-lived. From the 14th century water power was used for bellows and hammers. Powered bloomeries remained important in many parts of the country until the middle of the 17th century. On average, a bloomery produced 20 to 30 tons of iron a year.

blowing house. The term used on Dartmoor and in Cornwall for the water-powered smelting works of the *tin industry. The technique was well established by the end of the Middle Ages and continued in use into the 19th century, even though the reverberatory *furnace had been introduced by 1702.

blue books. The official series of *parliamentary papers from the late 18th century onwards. The most important ones have been reprinted by the Irish Universities Press and are available in large public libraries, university libraries, and the official publications room of the *British Library. They are often difficult to locate because their lengthy titles are cited in different ways and they are unindexed. They include House of Commons Sessional Papers and Reports of Select Committees and Royal

Commissions. The evidence of witnesses called before committees and commissions can provide vivid local detail, e.g. on the employment of children in *coal mines or *factories. The local historian needs to be aware that the questions that were asked were often designed to lead a witness to the answer that was wanted, and that replies were not necessarily recorded verbatim.

Board of Agriculture. Founded in 1793, with Sir John Sinclair as President and Arthur *Young as Secretary, and an annual parliamentary grant of £3,000. Its founders hoped that it would become a department of state, but it was never more than a private society which spread useful knowledge and encouraged agricultural improvements. Its earliest and most important task was to commission a series of county reports, known as the *General Views of Agriculture*. The government grant was withdrawn in 1820. Attempts to keep the Board in operation by private subscription failed, and it was dissolved in 1822.

board schools. School-board districts were set up by the Education Act (1870), and elected boards were empowered to build new schools and to take over existing ones. The system was changed in 1902; see COUNCIL SCHOOLS.

Bodleian Library. Copyright library at the University of Oxford, which contains thousands of rare volumes and large manuscript collections in the Department of Western Manuscripts.

Boer War. The war in South Africa (1899–1902) between Great Britain and the Afrikaner republics of Transvaal and the Orange Free State. 'Boer' is the Dutch word for countryman or farmer.

bole hill. *Lead-smelting site on the Pennines and the Mendips dating from the period before the adoption of bellows-blown hearths in the 16th century. The sites, which occupied windy escarpments, are often commemorated by the place-name Bole Hill, but remains are difficult to identify. The bole consisted of a stone-walled enclosure up to 5 or 6 yards in diameter, open on the side of the prevailing wind. The ore was stacked in the hearth and covered with brushwood and thicker wood. The molten lead was directed into a pig-mould.

bona notabilia. These Latin words ('considerable goods') are noted in the records of probate courts of the 16th to the 18th centuries when an estate was valued at £5 or more.

bond. 1. A deed by which a person binds himself to pay a certain sum of money, or a document issued by the government or a public company promising to repay borrowed money at interest. Bonds recorded as credits in probate *inventories were of this sort.

2. An agreement with a penalty for non-performance. A bond deed consists of two parts: the *obligation* (which before 1733 was in Latin) states the penalty; the *condition* (written in English) describes the commitment. These bonds could be private agreements or a necessary response to the law, e.g. to obtain a licence as a *drover, *badger, etc.

bond, marriage. An obligation entered into by a groom or someone acting on his behalf that the particulars in a marriage *allegation were true and that there was no impediment to the marriage. The practice was discontinued in 1823.

bondage system. A system of tenure with defined services, common in Northumberland and south Scotland in the 18th and 19th centuries, designed to provide casual labour in times of need. *Farm servants who were hired annually were provided with a house, specified quantities of food and coals, and the keep of a cow or a pig. In return the servant contracted to supply a woman labourer (usually his wife or daughter) to work for his employer for cash wages when required. These female workers performed all the jobs on the farm except ploughing and ditching. The system had virtually died out by the 1890s.

bonding. The arrangement of *bricks in distinctive courses in a wall. As continuous vertical joints are structurally unsound, various types of bonds were evolved. The normal method in the Middle Ages was the English bond, by which courses were arranged alternately in stretchers (bricks laid at length along the face of the wall) and headers (bricks laid at right angles to the face of the wall). Flemish bond (alternate stretchers and headers in the same course) became popular in the 17th century. There are several variations on these two basic types.

bondman. A *villein or *serf.

Book of Common Prayer. This prayer book, which was the sole legal form of worship in England and Wales from Whit Sunday 1549, was the first to set out the liturgy of the *Church of England. Written in English and largely the work of Archbishop Cranmer, it was revised in 1552, 1559, and by James I. The final text is that of 1662.

bookland. The *Old English name for land obtained by 'book' or written *charter, hence the place-name Buckland.

boon work. A manorial duty to do such seasonal work as ploughing and harvesting. The original sense of the word was 'favour', but such tasks became compulsory.

bordar. A term frequently found in the *Domesday Book, meaning a smallholder who farmed *assarted land on the edge of settlements.

Border marriage. Lord Hardwicke's *Marriage Act, which came into force in 1754, made marriages in England and Wales legal only if they were performed in a building licensed for that purpose. Runaway couples therefore crossed the border into Scotland, where marriage could take place by mere consent, in the presence of witnesses, without even a priest. Gretna Green is the best-known of these places, but businesses whose sole purpose it was to perform such ceremonies were set up by men in various border settlements, including Alison's Toll Bar, Lamberton Toll Bar, Sark Toll Bar, Springfield, and Coldstream. Some of the marriage registers of these places have survived.

Lord Brougham's Marriage Act (1856) made it necessary to obtain a licence to marry if neither partner had been resident in the proposed place of marriage during the preceding 21 days. From 1878 marriages in Scotland could be performed only in buildings licensed for that purpose. Marriage by consent was abolished in 1940.

borough. Many English boroughs were recorded as such in the *Domesday Book. The major medieval towns and cities obtained royal *charters which granted or confirmed their privileges. These are kept at the *Public Record Office, mostly in the *Charter rolls or *Patent rolls. Many old boroughs took the precaution of renewing their charters during the reigns of Charles II and James II.

A great number of towns were *seigneurial boroughs, which had a certain amount of independence from their *lord of the manor, but which did not have corporate status. The leading townsmen were called *burgesses, but they administered their affairs through an institution (often a *guild) which was recognized by the lord, but which did not have the same powers as a corporation. The lord of the manor usually retained his manorial courts.

The mayor of a corporation was normally the *ex officio* *Justice of the Peace for the borough. The mayor and corporation were sometimes lords of the manor and usually had jurisdiction over markets and fairs. Borough records, therefore, are often not confined to minutes of corporation meetings, orders, by-laws, lists of admissions to the corporation and mayoralty, etc., but contain *deeds to land, the records of the *quarter sessions, and a great deal of information about the sites of markets and fairs and the attempts to regulate the commercial activities there.

Corporate towns had the right to elect Members of Parliament. Where a borough decayed, the owner of the site retained the right to choose MPs. Such 'rotten' boroughs, together with many 'pocket' boroughs which were under the control of a landowner because the electorate was so restricted in size, were disenfranchised by the Parliamentary Reform Act (1832).

Borough English. The *inheritance custom in certain medieval *boroughs and *manors, notably in the south of England, whereby the youngest son was the heir to his father's lands and tenements.

Borthwick Institute of Historical Research, York. A department of the University of York, specializing in the ecclesiastical history of the province of York, with search facilities (by appointment only) for members of the public in the medieval St Anthony's Hall. The institute houses the diocesan archives, including *wills and *inventories, *parish registers, *bishops' transcripts, *tithe awards, and *ecclesiastical court records. The records of most of the *peculiar jurisdictions within the province of York are also kept there. The parish registers and some other records are on microfilm.

bote. The common right to take timber from the manorial wastes in order to repair houses, hedges, or fences, or for firewood and the making of tools.

bothy. A hut or cottage in Ireland or Scotland with stone or turf walls and roofs, used as a summer residence by farmers pasturing their livestock or as a one-roomed communal dwelling for servants or other workmen.

bourgeoisie. The prosperous middle class.

Bourne, George (1863–1927). The pen-name of George Sturt of Farnham (Surrey), author of *The Bettesworth Book* (1901), *Memoirs of a Surrey Labourer* (1907), *Change in the Village* (1912), *The Wheelwright's Shop* (1923), and other sympathetic accounts of the lives, work, and thoughts of the people of his village during a period of profound change.

bovate. An oxgang, one-eighth of a ploughland or *carucate, varying in size from 10 to 18 *acres according to the condition of the land.

Bowen, Emanuel. 'Engraver of Maps' for both George II of Great Britain and Louis XV of France. With Thomas Kitchin, he produced some of the finest county maps of the 18th century, between 1750 and 1780. These were unusual in devoting a great deal of space to a descriptive text in the form of historical notes.

Boyd's Marriage Index. Percival Boyd's compilation of marriage entries in English *parish registers for 16 counties from the beginning of registration in 1538 up to the year 1837. The entries are copied mainly from printed registers and the coverage is not complete. The index may be consulted at the Society of *Genealogists (which has published a *Key*) or at the *Guildhall Library, London.

The counties included in the index are as follows: (the number of parishes covered, at least in part, is given in brackets): Cambridgeshire (169), Cornwall (202), Cumberland (34), Derbyshire (80), Devon (169),

Durham (72), Essex (374), Gloucestershire (121), Lancashire (101), London and Middlesex (160), Norfolk (146), Northumberland (84), Shropshire (125), Somerset (120), Suffolk (489), Yorkshire (174).

brace. A curving support timber in a roof-truss.

brass, memorial. About 7,500 memorial brasses survive in England alone, more than in any other country. The earliest English brasses were imported from Flanders, but by the 14th century workshops had been set up in London, Norwich, and York. Purchasers normally chose from a series of standard designs, to which was added a personal inscription; but a few were special commissions to the customer's specifications. Brasses were not intended to be accurate portraits. The fashion disappeared during the second half of the 17th century but was revived in the 19th century.

breweries. The early history of brewing was much associated with immigrants from the Low Countries, especially to London. The rise of the 'common brewery', as the large production unit was known in order to distinguish it from the numerous domestic breweries, began in the 18th century. The Beer Act (1830) created a free trade in the sale of beer.

brewster session. A special meeting of the *quarter sessions at which *Justices of the Peace licensed the keepers of *inns and *alehouses. The parish *constable had to provide lists of the names of applicants for licences. The names of inns and alehouses are not recorded.

brick was much used by the Romans, whose forts and villas were quarried by later builders. It was once thought that the art of brick-making was unknown to the Anglo-Saxons, but detailed investigations of major churches have revised that view. Brick was not widely used by the Normans, though examples of 12th-century brickwork are known. The example of the Low Countries led builders in East Yorkshire to use brick extensively in the 14th century. Brick became a prestigious building material in the 15th century, particularly in the Humber basin and other parts of eastern England where no local building stone was available, and sometimes further west because of its rarity value. It was used for *colleges, *castles, gate-towers, and bishops' palaces. *Perpendicular churches in eastern England used brick extensively, particularly for new towers and porches.

Brick was much favoured for the great houses of the Tudor period. Fantastic brick chimney-stacks became popular, even in smaller houses. During the 17th century curved and stepped Dutch gables became fashionable in East Anglia and the south-east. The fashion spread down the social scale during the 17th century, as *yeomen and *husbandmen in districts devoid of suitable stone rebuilt their old *timber-framed houses in brick, often with *pantile roofs. The Great Fire of London (1666), and provincial fires in towns such as Warwick and Blandford Forum (Dorset), convinced urban authorities that brick was safer than wood. Brick became a very fashionable material for the houses and public buildings of Georgian towns.

Bricks were almost invariably made close to the building site. Their variety of colours arises not just from the nature of the local clays but from the firing process that was adopted. The *canals, and then (especially) the *railways, enabled mass-produced, machine-made bricks of regular size to be transported from large brickfields, e.g. in Bedfordshire, to all parts of Britain.

Bridewell. A *house of correction for prisoners, originally *vagabonds who were set to hard labour. It was named after Bride Well in London, which was made into a house of correction in 1552. By the 1630s every county in England and Wales had a similar institution for petty offenders.

bridges. A large number of medieval bridges survive. They can be recognized by their pointed, ribbed arches, but are difficult to date precisely. They are marked on Christopher *Saxton's county maps of the 1570s. These medieval bridges normally had a chapel attached. They were rarely more than 12 to 15 feet wide, and most have been widened to cater for an increased volume of traffic in later centuries.

During the 16th and 17th centuries the *Justices of the Peace took over responsibility for the major bridges, which were designated 'county bridges'. *Quarter sessions records note the money spent on repairing them from time to time. They also note the smaller 'packhorse bridges' which were in need of repair, when local overseers of the *highways were admonished for not performing their duty. Packhorse bridges are not as old as the larger 'county bridges'. They date from the second half of the 17th century and the first half of the 18th.

brief, church. A royal mandate authorizing a collection for some deserving cause, addressed to the incumbent and churchwardens of a parish and read from the pulpit. The collection was made at the end of the service by the *parish clerk, who handed the money to the official travelling collector. The brief was endorsed with the amount raised and the sum entered in the *parish register or *churchwarden's account.

Britain, Great. The whole island, including England, Wales, and Scotland. The term was used by the early antiquarians only in a historical context, with particular reference to *Roman Britain (Latin *Britannia*). Scotland was referred to as North Britain. Upon the accession of James I (James VI of Scotland) in 1603 he was proclaimed 'King of Great Britain'. The two kingdoms were united as Great Britain in 1707. In

1801 the *United Kingdom of Great Britain and Ireland was formed. Since 1922 the Irish part of the UK has consisted only of Northern Ireland.

British Association for Local History. The society which was founded in 1982 to promote the interests of local historians at national level continued the work of the *Standing Conference for Local History. It organizes conferences in various parts of Britain and publishes *The *Local Historian*, handbooks, and *Local History News*.

British and Foreign School Society. Founded by Joseph Lancaster in 1810 to promote elementary schools, provided by *Nonconformist churches, and using the monitorial system of teaching. The society had been known in the previous two years as the Royal Lancasterian Society.

British Library. A group of libraries that was formed in 1973 out of a merger of the national lending, patent and science reference libraries with the collections of the printed-book and manuscript departments of the British Museum.

The manuscript collection includes about 75,000 Additional Manuscripts and a similar number of Additional Charters. For the local historian its greatest riches, however, are perhaps the Cotton and Harleian collections: the former comprises about 1,000 volumes, including many medieval *chronicles and more than 150 medieval *cartularies; while the 7,600 Harleian manuscripts include many heraldic volumes besides more chronicles, cartularies, and a wide range of historical and other texts.

For the early stages of an enquiry involving manuscripts, the most useful starting-point is likely to be the amalgamated index to persons and places, the *Index of Manuscripts in the British Library*, 10 vols. (1984–6). A subject-based approach is best begun through the multi-volume Class Catalogue (comprising catalogue descriptions, cut up and mounted on a subject basis), of which the sole copy is in the Department's reading room, the Students' Room.

The collections of the former Department of Printed Books can be accessed via catalogues in printed form, compact disk, or on-line computer. They comprise about 12 million volumes.

Among the printed-book collections is that of official publications, which has its own reading room in the British Museum building. This contains an exceptionally full set of all British official publications—notably the HMSO's Command Papers and printed parliamentary bills and statutes, including the various governmental commission reports and the like that are often known as *blue books.

The map library has been a separate unit since 1867, and has its own reading room: it contains the fullest sets in existence of *Ordnance

Survey and other published maps of the British Isles as well as a major collection of early printed maps.

Newspapers are divided between the former Department of Printed Books' collections in Bloomsbury and a separate reading room and store at Colindale, in Hendon, north-west London.

British Record Society. Founded in 1888 as the Index Society, it publishes indexes of historical records, such as *Chancery proceedings, *inquisitions post mortem, *wills, and marriage licences.

broadcasting (agricultural). The casting of seed by hand from a basket, alternatively to the right and to the left.

broadcloth. A fine woollen cloth of the Middle Ages and early modern period.

broadside. A printed, popular *ballad of the 16th to the 19th century.

Bronze Age. The prehistoric era between the *Stone Age and the *Iron Age, lasting from *c.*2,500 BC to *c.*800 BC. This was the era of the great *henge monuments.

brother. The term was often used to mean a brother-in-law.

Brown, 'Capability'. Lancelot Brown (1716–83), the most famous landscape gardener of the 18th century and the designer of numerous schemes for British country houses. He swept away the formal gardens of previous generations and provided instead an open, 'natural' look, with rolling pastures, clumps of mature trees, and wide expanses of water.

Buck, Samuel and Nathaniel. As a young man, Samuel Buck (1696–1779) was commissioned to draw views of towns and country houses in Yorkshire for an uncompleted project of John Warburton's. His sketchbook of 1719–23 has been published as *Samuel Buck's Yorkshire Sketchbook* (1979). He and his brother Nathaniel later achieved fame through their prints, made over a period of 30 years, which they assembled in their *Antiquities* (2nd edn., 1774). These careful engravings are now a major source for the study of urban topography and of buildings.

buckwheat. Known alternatively as French wheat, it was grown on barren, sandy ground and was prized as fodder for pigs and *poultry.

Builder, The. Founded in 1834, this journal contains numerous articles which provide information about public buildings and houses erected in many parts of Britain during the Victorian period. It is particularly useful for the period 1844–83, when George Goodwin was editor.

building societies were originally small clubs of 20 to 50 people who paid regular subscriptions which enabled the society to build houses. These were then allotted by ballot. Such societies were formed from the late 18th century onwards, especially in northern industrial towns.

burgage plot. The property owned by a *burgess in a medieval town. As burgesses congregated around the market place and main streets, space at the front was at a premium. Burgage plots are therefore characteristically long and narrow, with a row of outbuildings stretching to the rear of the house and shop. The pattern of burgage plots is often evident from old maps and sometimes can still be discerned on the ground.

burgess. 1. A citizen or *freeman of a *borough, especially a member of the governing body of a town.

2. A member of parliament for a borough, corporation, or university.

burgh. A Scottish town which had a measure of self-government and defined trading privileges. The most important were the royal burghs which were founded by royal charter and whose lands were held directly from the Crown. A large number of 'burghs of barony' were created in the 16th and 17th centuries, but most remained very small.

Burghal Hidage. The date of this document is debatable, but it is generally agreed that it refers to the defensive system created by King Alfred of *Wessex at the time of the Danish invasions. The document lists the *burhs, or fortified places, in a clockwise order, starting in the east.

burh. A fortified place of the late 9th and 10th centuries, constructed by the kings of *Wessex to resist the Danish invaders. As the kingdom of Wessex expanded, so new burhs were erected well north of the former boundaries.

Burke, John (1787–1848). Burke's *Peerage* was first published in 1826. It was an annual publication from 1847 to 1940, except for the years 1918–20. Occasional editions have appeared since 1949. Burke's *Landed Gentry* was first published in 1837. In 1877 Professor E. A. Freeman dismissed the pedigrees published in Burke's *Landed Gentry* as 'much wild nonsense'.

John Burke wrote several other books on heraldry and genealogy. He was succeeded as editor of the *Peerage* and the *Landed Gentry* by his son Sir John Bernard Burke (1814–92) and his grandsons.

butt. 1. A shooting target, a mound for *archery practice. Edward IV (1461–83) made shooting practice compulsory on Sundays and feast days. Every man between the ages of 16 and 60 was expected to own a bow of his own height, and every township was ordered to set up its own butts.

2. Grouse butts, a hideout from which *grouse are shot.

3. A shorter or irregularly shaped *selion, in an *open-field, or one that abuts at right angles upon other selions.

button-making. Buttons were made of a variety of materials, including silver, alcomy (a base metal that resembled gold), brass, horn, and cloth. Button-making originated as an urban craft that required no *apprenticeship and was therefore attractive as an occupation to the poor.

by-employments. The occupational descriptions of people in the past often obscure the fact that they obtained their living in a variety of ways.

bylawman. Alternative name for a *constable.

by-name. Before *surnames became fixed and hereditary, many people had a by-name as well as a personal name in order to distinguish them from other people with similar names. These took similar forms to later surnames, but they were not necessarily passed on to descendants.

byre. A term used in some regions for a cow-shed.

cadet. A younger son or brother; a younger branch of a family.

calendar. 1. In 1752 Britain changed from the inaccurate *Julian calendar to the *Gregorian calendar, which had been used in Catholic countries since 1582. The eleven days' discrepancy between the two calendars meant that 2 September 1752 was followed after the change by 14 September. At the same time the old custom of starting the official year on *Lady Day (25 March) was abandoned in favour of the year beginning on 1 January.

As 1 January had long been regarded by most people as the true beginning of the year, regardless of official reckoning, dates between 1 January and 25 March were often written as e.g. 1688/9. To avoid confusion, it is a useful practice for local and family historians to follow this convention and to refer to dates before 1752 as Old Style and those after 1752 as New Style.

Before 1752 September, October, November, and December were often referred to in written records as 7ber, 8ber, 9ber, and 10ber. *Quakers called all the months by numbers; before 1752 March was their First Month, afterwards it was the Third Month. This Quaker practice continued into the 20th century.

In the Middle Ages documents were dated not by calendar years but by regnal years starting from the time that a monarch ascended the throne. In the early modern period documents give regnal years alongside calendar ones.

2. A catalogue summarizing what the editor deems to be the essential data contained in a series of documents.

Cambridge University archives. The Cambridge University Library, Department of Manuscripts and University Archives, West Road, Cambridge CB3 9DR houses the archives of the University. The various colleges also have archive collections. The older colleges often have *estate records that are of interest to local historians in the various parts of the country where the colleges were landlords.

Camden, William (1551–1623). Author of *Britannia* (1586), a milestone in the development of historical studies. Additional material, including the first study of the etymology of *surnames, was brought together in his *Remaines of a Greater Worke Concerning Britaine* (1605).

Camden Society. Named after William *Camden, the antiquary, the Camden Society was formed in Cambridge in 1839 to further the cause of ecclesiology. It was enormously influential, through its journal, *The *Ecclesiologist*, in determining the style of church building and restoration. The society also published edited historical texts, with introductions. In 1897 it was amalgamated with the Royal Historical Society and represents their series of edited historical texts on extremely varied subjects.

Camping Closes. Field names such as Camping Close indicate the places where the game of camping (a mixture of *football and handball) was played from the Middle Ages through to the 19th century. It was particularly popular in Norfolk, Suffolk, Cambridgeshire, and Essex.

CAMPOP. The Cambridge Group for the Study of Population and Social Structure. This group of researchers, based at Cambridge University and drawing on the labours of local historians throughout England, has since the 1960s placed the study of historical demography on a sound footing. They were the first to use *parish registers to reconstitute families.

canals. The first important British canal was that which brought *coal from the Duke of Bridgewater's mines at Worsley (Lancashire) to Manchester. This was completed by 1761. Within two generations the industrial districts of Britain were connected by a system of canals that involved some amazing technical feats. Canals gradually declined with the coming of the *railways.

The passage of the private Acts of Parliament which authorized canals can be followed in the *House of Commons and the *House of Lords Journals. *Parliamentary papers include the Report of the Select Committee on Canals (1883), the returns made to the Board of Trade of canal statistics (1888), and the 12-volume Report of the Royal Commission on Canals of 1906–11, which contains a great deal of information, including maps. The *Public Record Office has papers and correspondence concerning individual canals.

Candlemas. The feast of the Purification of the Virgin Mary (2 February; 14 February *old style), traditionally celebrated with a display of candles.

canons. 1. (historically). Priests who lived according to a strict, almost monastic rule. The *Augustinian and *Premonstratensian orders arrived from France in Britain during the early 12th century. The *Gilbertines (founded 1131) were the only native order. The canons preached in local parish churches and were expected to combine manual labour with their devotions and studies.

2. (present-day). Member of a cathedral *chapter in the *Church of England.

cantrev. The Welsh equivalent of the English *hundred or *wapentake.

cap money. A statute of 1571, repealed in 1598, enforced the wearing of caps of English wool on Sundays and holy days. Cap money was the fine of 3*s*. 4*d*. for non-observance.

capite, tenant in. The holding of land in *feudal tenure direct from the monarch.

cardmaker. A maker of a wooden instrument which was shaped like a square bat with raised iron spikes and held in the hand in order to card wool in preparation for spinning.

carrier. The long-distance professional carrier operated in the Middle Ages under a variety of names, e.g. salter or *jagger. The numbers of long-distance carriers grew in the later 16th and 17th centuries, by which time regular services to London had been established from all parts of the provinces.

Information about local carriers is hard to come by until the publication of trade and commercial *directories in the late 18th and 19th centuries, which show that a network of routes linking the whole of the country was well established by that time. Directories normally give full details of carriers' services, including starting points and destinations, times of departure and arrival, and connections with distant places.

Carriers' Cosmographie (1637). A publication of John Taylor naming the London *inns which were the destinations of provincial *carriers, and giving the days and times of arrival and departure.

Cartae Antiquae rolls. A series of 46 rolls at the *Public Record Office, containing transcripts of documents from 1189 to 1327, which renewed or confirmed privileges, e.g. *charters.

Carthusians. A monastic order, The Poor Brothers of God of the Charter-house, founded in 1084 in France, but not officially an order until 1142. The Carthusian monks modelled their way of life on that of the desert hermits of early Christian Egypt. This was deliberately harsh, involving the wearing of rough hair shirts and the eating of coarse food in slender portions. The monks were housed in separate cells with a small garden to the rear, arranged around a central courtyard. They accepted a vow of silence, except during the singing of offices.

cartouche. A panel on early maps, containing the title, dedication, etc. They were often in a highly decorative form.

cartulary, or chartulary. A register of the *charters, *deeds, grants of property, etc. of a monastery.

carucate. The term used in the *Danelaw, comparable to the Saxon *hide, for a unit of taxation, originally the amount of land that a team of eight oxen could plough each year. This varied according to the quality of the land but was about 120 *acres. The carucate or hide was the basic unit of taxation in the *Domesday Book.

Cary, John (*c*.1754–1835). A prolific maker of high-standard maps, which rank in accuracy with those of the *Ordnance Survey.

castellany. A large *lordship centred on the castle of one of the Norman *barons, especially in the border areas of northern and western England.

castle. The term 'castle' is used by historians to refer to fortified buildings erected after the Norman Conquest. Hundreds of *motte-and-bailey castles were erected in Britain by the Normans. They were a recent invention which had spread rapidly in Normandy. Others may date from the civil wars of Stephen's reign (1135–54). Most motte-and-baileys were subsequently abandoned, but during the second quarter of the 12th century the most important ones were converted into stone castles, surrounded by huge ditches, ramparts, and a curtain wall, and entered by a *gatehouse.

Major changes in the design of castles came in the later 13th century, particularly with the building of Edward I's castles in north Wales. By the 1380s such castles were becoming redundant in warfare, in face of cannon that were increasingly effective. Meanwhile, the number of licences to *crenellate reached a peak in the second quarter of the 14th century as magnates throughout the country topped their curtain walls and residential buildings with *battlements. By the early 14th century the keep had been abandoned. Smaller baronial castles used high walls and massive square corner towers to enclose a courtyard.

In the more settled times under the Tudors castles fell out of fashion. Those which were refortified by Royalists in the Civil War of the 1640s were dismantled after the Parliamentarian victory. Others were allowed to decay gradually until serious interest in their preservation began in the 19th century.

Catholic Emancipation Act (1829). Roman Catholics were prohibited from membership of the House of Commons, even after the inclusion of Ireland in the *United Kingdom in 1801. The election of Daniel O'Connell for Clare, in 1828, dramatized the situation and led to the cancelling of this disqualification.

Catholic Record Society. A society housed at 114 Mount Street, London WC2Y 6AH, which was founded in 1905 to publish historical records concerning Roman Catholicism in Britain, including registers of baptisms, burials, and marriages from the later 18th century, Recusant Rolls (1592–1691) kept at the *Public Record Office, monographs, etc. *Recusant History* (from 1951) is the historical journal of the society.

causey, causeway. A series of flagstones laid down on wet or soft terrain to prevent the formation of holloways. Individual causeys cannot be dated on stylistic grounds, but most surviving examples are probably from the 17th, 18th, and 19th centuries.

caveat. A legal process to suspend proceedings.

cell. A small dwelling used by a hermit, or an apartment in a monastery.

cellars were an essential feature of the medieval town houses of *merchants and craftsmen. They were not normally a feature of rural *vernacular architecture before the 18th century. In the 19th century cellar accommodation became a notorious method of housing the poorest sections of society in the largest industrial towns.

Celtic fields. The name given to prehistoric fields whose outline is preserved on the ground or can be seen from aerial photographs.

cemeteries and crematoria. The idea of landscaped public cemeteries came from Italy, France, and Sweden. The Clifton Graveyard, Belfast, dates from 1774, and Calton Hill, Edinburgh, from the late 18th century, but England did not follow the fashion until the severe overcrowding of churchyards made them a health risk. Before the middle of the 19th century such cemeteries were generally established and run as commercial ventures, but after the passing of legislation in the 1850s and 1860s enforcing the closure of urban churchyards, municipal cemeteries became the rule.

Cemetery records have sometimes been deposited at local *record offices, but others are still kept at the office on the site. They usually give the name, address, age, and occupation of the deceased, the date of death and of burial, and the position of the grave. These records are arranged chronologically, and are not indexed alphabetically.

census returns. The first census for the whole of Britain, except Ireland, was taken in 1801, but no central archival material survives from that exercise or from the following censuses of 1811, 1821, and 1831.

From 1841 the census has been collected by the office of the *Registrar-General. A number of enumerators were appointed for each sub-district, to issue forms and collect them the day after census night, and to copy the information into books. The transcriptions, or 'enumerators' returns', for 1841–91 survive. Those for England and Wales are available for consultation in microfilm form at the *Public Record Office Census

Rooms, Chancery Lane, London, WC2. Microfilm copies of the returns for particular districts are often available at public *libraries and local record offices or at *Mormon branch libraries. The Scottish system of enumeration differed in minor ways. The records are kept in the New Register House of the *Scottish Record Office, Edinburgh.

The enumerators' districts of 1841 were retained, as far as possible, up to at least 1891, so that comparisons with previous data could be made. The information provided by the 1841 census enumerators' returns is not as full as that given in later years. The arrangement is by *households (or by institutions, e.g. *workhouse or *prison), but the relationship of each member to the head of the household is not recorded. The ages of people over 15 were rounded down to the nearest five, so that the population could be classified in age-bands. The occupation of each person is then noted; this is necessarily a succinct description that takes no account of dual occupations or *by-employments. The final column does not record the birthplace, but merely notes whether the person was born in the same county as his or her present residence, or whether the place of birth was in Scotland, Ireland, or 'foreign parts'. From 1851 onwards the enumerators' returns provide fuller information. Nightworkers who were not at home on census night but who returned the following morning were now listed with other members of their household. The relationship of each person with the head of household was noted. The returns purport to record the exact age and place of birth, but this information needs to be handled cautiously.

Despite the inclusion of Ireland within the *United Kingdom in 1801, the procedure for making a census of the Irish population was quite different. The first official census was taken in 1821. It gave names, ages, occupations, and relationships to heads of household, also the acreages of land and the number of storeys in the house. The Irish census returns for 1861, 1871, 1881, and 1891 were destroyed by government order; those for 1821, 1831, 1841, and 1851 were destroyed in an explosion and fire in Dublin (1922). The 1901 and 1911 census returns were stored locally and were thus preserved from destruction in 1922. They are now available for inspection at the National Archives, Dublin. Although the enumerators' returns do not survive, published reports from 1841 to 1911 give the acreage, population, number of houses, and valuation of each individual townland.

Identifying a particular family can be a time-consuming task in a city, particularly in London. The boundaries of the enumerators' districts sometimes ran down the middle of a street, and even in the large towns houses were rarely numbered before the 1850s, and often much later.

censuses, local. For most places in England, Scotland, and Wales the national census of 1801 is the first count of the population; for Ireland it is

1821. However, individual places sometimes held a local census for a particular reason. The records of local censuses appear in miscellaneous collections in local *record offices.

centuriation. The laying out of roads and fields in a regular pattern by the Romans.

ceorl. The lowest class of *Old English freeman.

chain. A linear measure of 22 yards used in surveying, which remains in use as the length of a cricket pitch.

champion land. A term used in the early modern period to denote land given over to cereals in *open-fields as distinct from *wood pasture, fens, moors, etc. The term conjures up a picture of a certain kind of landscape with large fields, few hedges, and little timber. It also implies the settlement of people in *villages rather than hamlets or scattered farms.

chancel. The eastern part of a church (now known as the sanctuary) containing the high *altar and reserved for the clergy and choir. The maintenance of the chancel was the responsibility of the *tithe owner.

Chancellor. An official secretary, e.g. of the *chapter of a cathedral. The Chancellor of England (Lord Chancellor or Lord High Chancellor) became the highest officer in medieval England; he presides over the House of Lords and remains a member of the Cabinet and the highest judicial officer. The Chancellor of the Exchequer became the highest finance minister.

Chancery, Court of. In the early Middle Ages the decisions of the king's council were put into effect through the Chancery, under the direction of the *Chancellor. The records of the Chancery date from 1199. Chancery became a court of law about 1348. It acted as a court of *equity to deal with cases for which there was no provision under Common Law, and later with cases where the plaintiff might have been at a disadvantage. In 1873 equity jurisdiction passed to the Chancery Division of the Supreme Court of Judicature.

The Court of Chancery has extensive records, which are housed at the *Public Record Office. All records before 1873 begin with the letter C, afterwards with the letter J. See the Public Record Office Records Information leaflet, no. 30, 'Chancery Proceedings (Equity Suits)'. The records of cases include pleadings (statements made by parties to a case; known collectively as Chancery Proceedings), evidence in the form of affidavits (statements on oath) and depositions (examinations of witnesses), and court decisions and opinions, though these last are the most difficult documents to locate in the archive. Cases were mostly in English. Families of middling means often used the court, and the witnesses were drawn from all sections of local society. Most of the records are indexed only by the name of the plaintiff.

chantry chapel. A private chapel, normally attached to a parish church or a *chapel-of-ease, with an *altar for the celebration of mass for the souls of the founder and his or her nominees, or for the souls of the members of *guilds and fraternities who had erected such a chapel. The system began in the 13th century, but became fashionable in the later Middle Ages, particularly after the *Black Death. Chantry chapels were built at the end of the aisles of the *nave, extending along the side walls of the *chancel, or within the transepts of cruciform churches. They were dedicated to the saints nominated by the founders. The endowment of a chantry chapel allowed for the employment of a priest who received either a money payment or land to farm or rent. These properties were confiscated when Edward VI dissolved all chantries in 1547.

chapbook. Cheap popular books, published in London from the 16th to the 18th centuries and sold by *book sellers, *chapmen, or *pedlars throughout the land. The texts consisted of traditional stories and *ballads, histories, and moral and religious tales.

chapel-of-ease. A term used to indicate a building used for religious worship that was created for the ease of the inhabitants of an outlying part of a *parish. These included the places of worship in many of the medieval new towns. The *tithes of the inhabitants of a *chapelry went to the *rector of the parish; the chapels were served by curates. Many chapels-of-ease obtained rights of baptism, marriage, and burial. Most were made into parish churches during the 19th century.

chapelry. The area served by a *chapel-of-ease.

chaplain. A priest serving a private individual or family, a private body, e.g. a *hospital, or a public institution, e.g. the army.

chapman. A middleman.

chapter. 1. The governing body of a cathedral or a *collegiate church.
2. The daily assembly of the members of a religious house. The name is derived from the practice of reading a chapter from the rule of the order of that assembly.

chapter house. The building used for the meetings of a *chapter.

charcoal was obtained from the underwood of *coppices, which was charred in hearths that did not admit air, so preventing rapid combustion. The process lasted for several days in order to get rid of moisture in the wood. Charcoal burners were referred to as colliers and are thus often confused with coal miners. Leases allowed the 'coaling' of coppiced wood. Whilst the job was under way, the charcoal burners lived in temporary huts constructed of poles and turf sods.

charity boards. Lists of the charitable endowments within a parish, painted on boards which normally hang inside the tower or porch of the parish church. They usually date from the 18th and 19th centuries.

Charity Commissioners. The Charity Commission for England and Wales was established in 1853 to oversee the accounts and activities of registered charities. The Charitable Trusts Act (1860) empowered the commission to appoint or remove trustees and to change the purpose of a trust if the original purpose was outdated. The Charities Act (1960) provides the basis for the work of the present Charity Commission, which maintains a central register of charities at 14 Ryder Street, London SW1 (for national charities and those in southern England) and Graeme House, Derby Square, Liverpool (for northern England and Wales). Documents over 30 years old are open to public inspection.

charnel house. Before the practice arose in the 17th century of marking graves with permanent *gravestones, churchyard graves were often reused. The bones from previous burials were collected together in a charnel house next to the church or at the edge of the churchyard. *Crypts were sometimes used for the same purpose.

charter. A document granting rights or privileges. Thus, a *lord of a manor who wished to create a *market or to hunt in a *park or *chase had to obtain a royal charter. Anglo-Saxon charters are a major source for the study of ancient *estates and boundaries.

Charter rolls. Records from the Court of *Chancery, dating from 1199 to 1517, of royal grants of land or rights, and confirmations of such grants. They are housed at the *Public Record Office under C 53 and have all been published. Those for the reign of King John (1199–1216) were printed by the Record Commissioners in 1837, the rest in six volumes in the PRO's *Calendar of Charter Rolls* (1903–27). They are particularly important for the study of the history of *boroughs.

chartered company. A company of *merchants, e.g. the Merchant Adventurers', the *East India Company, and the *Hudson's Bay Company, which were incorporated by royal or parliamentary *charter, and received certain monopoly privileges.

Chartism. The Chartist movement acquired its name from the six points of the charter published in 1838 by the London Working Men's Association. The Charter demanded universal male suffrage, equal electoral districts, annual Parliaments, payment of members, secret ballots, and no property qualifications for MPs. All this was eventually achieved, except for annual Parliaments, but at the time it was considered revolutionary.

The Chartist movement grew from earlier agitation, going back to the constitutional societies of the 1790s, but is regarded as the first genuinely working-class mass political movement. Their support was greatest in the manufacturing districts, where they were able to get many of their members elected to local councils. Their activities are well recorded in local *newspapers. But their failure in 1848 heralded their decline in a subsequent period of prosperity.

chase. A hunting area allowed by royal *charter, the private equivalent of a royal *forest. Chases were larger than *deer parks and were not enclosed by ditches and palings.

chattel. Personal property that is not real estate or *freehold.

cheap. Old English *chepe*, meaning market, has given rise to street names in many parts of England.

cheese trade. In the 17th century, particularly after 1660, certain areas began to acquire a national reputation for the quality of their cheese. By 1750 all the cheese-producing areas that were of national importance in Victorian times were already sending their cheese to market in London.

Chelsea Hospital. A retirement home in south-west London for army pensioners, founded by Charles II in a building designed by Wren, and completed in 1692. Its registers of baptisms (1691–1812), marriages (1691–1765), and burials (1692–1856) can be consulted at the *General Register Office, St Catherine's House, London.

chevage. A payment made to a lord by a *villein who wished to move from one *manor to another.

chief rent. Formerly, rent paid by a *tenant-in-chief; now *quit rent.

chimney. The term was originally applied to a fireplace, hence the alternative name for the *hearth tax was the chimney tax.

Chinese immigrants. The Chinese population in Britain has grown from less than 5,000 in 1946 to about 250,000 in 1993, mostly as a result of immigration from Hong Kong. About 70,000 live in the Greater London area. In earlier times the Chinese population was largely concentrated in London, though small colonies were also found in some other ports.

chirurgeon. Surgeon; often a barber-surgeon.

Chivalry, High Court of. The court within the College of *Arms which has jurisdiction over armorial matters in England, Wales, and Northern Ireland.

choir. That part of a medieval cathedral, monastery, or *collegiate church, between the high *altar and the pulpitum, which was occupied by the stalls of the monks, minor clerics, and boys, who sang the music of divine services. Victorian clergy began the practice of introducing choir stalls for lay singers in the *chancels of parish churches.

cholera. A water-borne disease endemic in India, which struck Britain in 1831–2 and again in 1848.

chrisom. 1. The images of dead infants on tombs and memorial *brasses, showing children wrapped in the white chrisom cloths that were commonly worn for a month after baptism, and used as a shroud if they died within the month.
    2. (or chrism). The mixture of olive oil and balsam used in baptism, confirmation, and consecration services.

Christmas. The modern forms of celebration at Christmas are largely Victorian. In the Middle Ages and beyond Christmas was followed by 12 days of celebration during which activities which at other times of the year would have been suppressed were tolerated. Church services at Christmas were simple affairs before the 19th century.

chronicles. The keeping of chronicles of important events was an ancient monastic tradition, going back to the *Anglo-Saxon Chronicle*. Chronicles written by laymen were published in the 16th century. A number of towns kept chronicles of important local events.

church ales. A common form of fund-raising for the maintenance of parish churches and the poor in the Middle Ages. On special occasions home-brewed ales were sold either in the *nave of the church or in an adjacent church-house. Some 16th-century examples of church-houses survive. After their suppression at the *Reformation some became secular *alehouses.

Church in Wales. In 1920 the four dioceses of Bangor, Llandaff, St Asaph, and St David's were formed into a disestablished and separate province of the Anglican communion, with its own archbishop. The Department of Manuscripts and Records in the National Library of *Wales, Aberystwyth, is the approved repository for non-parochial records; parish records may be deposited locally or at the Library.

Church of England. The Church of England was created by a series of Acts of Parliament between 1529 and 1559. Most of the clergy who had been parish priests before the Reformation remained in office and the medieval buildings which had long served as parish churches were simply adapted to the new liturgical requirements. Moreover, the

Church of England was governed on similar lines to its Catholic predecessor, with two archbishops and 24 bishops.

Church of Ireland. The Anglican Church in Ireland since the 16th century. It was disestablished in 1869. Some *parish registers exist from the middle of the 17th century onwards; they are housed in the *National Archives in Dublin.

Church of Scotland. At the *Reformation the Catholic Church was replaced by *Presbyterianism as the official state religion of Scotland. A new hierarchical structure was created, headed by an annual General Assembly in Edinburgh, and descending through synods, presbyteries, and kirk sessions, all of which were courts as well as administrative bodies. Nearly all the records of the Church of Scotland are kept at the *Scottish Record Office.

The Church of Scotland has experienced many schisms since the 18th century. The main division occurred in 1843, when a long-standing dispute over patronage came to a head with the withdrawal of 474 ministers, a third of the total, to form the Free Church of Scotland. A third Presbyterian body, the United Presbyterian Church, was formed in 1847.

church rates. Until 1868 churchwardens were allowed to levy a rate on all householders in a *parish in England and Wales (regardless of whether or not they attended the services of the *Church of England) in order to help maintain the parish church and *churchyard.

church seating plans. During the 17th century churches became filled with pews. It became the custom in most places, particularly in the countryside, for the right to sit in a pew to be regarded as part of the property of a farm or *cottage; in this way, the social structure of a parish was formalized during a church service. The owners or tenants of the largest farms sat at the front, the smallholders were seated in the middle, and the cottagers occupied the seats to the rear. In towns, the most prominent pews were set aside for the mayor and *aldermen. Few seating plans survive from the 17th century, but a number of later ones are displayed in churches or are occasionally found in the records of *ecclesiastical courts. The present seating arrangements commonly date from the period 1840–90.

church sites. Most parish churches were sited near the *castle or manor house of the *lord of the manor. Some now appear isolated because the lord's residence, and even the village that lay alongside it, have decayed and disappeared. Other churches occupy what seem to be strange sites because they were deliberately sited to convert adherents from pagan forms of religion.

churchwardens' accounts. A few accounts survive from the 14th century; others become much more plentiful in later years. Churchwardens' accounts note expenditure on the maintenance, cleaning, and decoration of the parish church and provision for the services. Those that survive from the 15th and 16th centuries are an important source of information about changes associated with the *Reformation, e.g. the removal of *rood screens and gilded images.

In addition to their responsibilities for the parish church, the churchwardens often paid for the shooting of birds and vermin, gave relief to the itinerant poor, and paid the ringers for celebrating national events.

churchyards are normally larger on the south side than on the north, though 19th- and 20th-century enlargements may have obscured this arrangement. This was because well into the 18th century (and sometimes beyond) the north side was regarded as the Devil's side, where excommunicants, the unbaptized, suicides, etc. were buried. The present appearance of most churchyards dates from the Victorian period.

Cinque ports. The south-eastern ports of Dover, Hastings, Hythe, Romney, and Sandwich (and, later, Rye and Winchelsea) which in the Middle Ages enjoyed trading privileges in return for their contributions to naval defence. These privileges were mostly abolished in the 19th century.

Cistercians. Monastic order founded at Cîteaux in Burgundy in 1098 in an attempt to return to the original simplicity of the *Benedictines, from whom they were immediately distinguished by their white habit.

The first Cistercian house in Britain was established at Waverley (Surrey) in 1128; by the end of the century over 100 Cistercian houses had been settled in England and Wales. The early Cistercians sought remote sites and renounced the lavish buildings and ritual of the *Cluniacs. The Cistercian ideal was the frugal, devotional, and meditative life, but the monks relied on the manual labour of large numbers of *lay brothers. The wealth of their monasteries came from the farming and industrial activities of the lay brothers, many of whom worked at outlying *granges.

civil registration. From 1 July 1837 the state took responsibility for the registration of all births, marriages, and deaths in England and Wales. Civil registration began in Scotland on 1 January 1855 and in Ireland on 1 January 1864. The system continues to this day. The indexes of the events registered in England and Wales are kept at the *General Register Office, St Catherine's House, 10 Kingsway, London WC2B 6JP. Those for Scotland are kept at the General Register Office, New Register House, Edinburgh EH1 3YT. Irish records are kept at the Office of the Registrar General, Joyce House, 8–11 Lombard Street, Dublin 2, and the General

Register Office, Oxford House, 49–55 Chichester Street, Belfast BT1 4HL. Microfiche copies of indexes are also available at major public *libraries and some *record offices, the Society of *Genealogists, the research centres of the *Mormon Church, and various family history societies.

The indexes are kept in bound volumes on open shelves, in sections arranged according to births, marriages, and deaths. Each of the three sections is arranged chronologically, with the years divided into quarters labelled March, June, September, and December. The indexes for each quarter are arranged alphabetically by surname, and then under each surname by first name. The next column notes the name of the Superintendent Registrar's District where the event was registered. The final column contains a reference giving a volume and page number. All this information (including the year and quarter on the spine of the index) should be entered on an application form for a certificate and presented at the counter with the fee.

The registration districts were based on the *Poor Law Unions that were created in 1834, but some changes were made from 1 January 1852. Local Register Offices do not have the staff or facilities to deal with general enquiries, and indexes are not available there for public consultation, but specific requests can be dealt with if the information about name, place, and date of event is already known.

Birth certificates give the precise date of the event, followed by the place of birth. The next columns give the name and sex of the child, the father's forename and surname (or a blank space for an illegitimate child), and the mother's forename, surname, and maiden name. The final columns contain the date of registration and the signature of the registrar.

The indexes of marriages are arranged in the same way as those of births. From March 1912 onwards the name of the spouse was entered in the index alongside that of the bride or groom. Marriage certificates give the date of the event and the name of the church, chapel, or register office where the ceremony was performed. They then record the names of both partners, their ages, and their 'condition' as bachelor, spinster, widower, or widow. The next columns note the 'rank or profession' of each partner, their places of residence at the time of marriage, and the full names and ranks or professions of their fathers.

From 1866 the indexes of death give an extra piece of information, namely the age at death. The death certificates record the date and place of death, the forename(s) and surname of the deceased, and his or her sex, age, and occupation. The next columns note the cause of death and give the signature, description, and residence of the informant, followed by the date of registration and the signature of the registrar.

The Irish certificates of births, marriages, and deaths from 1864 are similar in form to those for England and Wales. As in England and

Wales, the 163 Poor Law unions formed the registration districts. Records for each superintendent's district are held locally as well as centrally. Scottish certificates give more information than the English, Welsh, and Irish ones. The birth certificates note the date of marriage of the parents; marriage certificates record the names of both parents of each partner; and death certificates note the names of both parents. From 1929 onwards birth certificates also note the mother's maiden surname.

clandestine marriage. Until Lord Hardwicke's *Marriage Act came into force in 1754 it was possible to be married without the calling of *banns or the obtaining of a marriage licence. Certain clergymen got the reputation of being willing to perform such ceremonies. Prison chapels, most notoriously the Fleet, where 217 marriages were performed on the day before Hardwicke's Act came into operation, were commonly used. The *Public Record Office holds about 300 registers of clandestine marriages.

clans, Scottish. The popular concept of Highland clans is largely the invention of Sir Walter Scott. Clans were not distinguished by their own tartans before the 1745 rebellion. The tradition of wearing a distinctive tartan grew up with the Highland regiments that were formed in the second half of the 18th century. The occasion of George IV's celebrated visit to Edinburgh in 1822 was responsible for many clans first adopting their own tartan.

The chiefs of clans were mostly known by the name of their estates. It is debatable whether Highland surnames were distinguished by clan or whether a variety of names could be found within a clan. A clan was a unit which contained families of different lineages; common descent is often assumed but it cannot be demonstrated.

clapper bridges consisting of long slabs of stone, or sometimes just a single slab, are found in south-western England and the Pennines. Their age is often greatly exaggerated, for despite their primitive appearance many are 18th-century.

Clarenceux King of Arms. The second ranking King of Arms in England.

class, social. The term was not widely used until the 19th century, though examples of its usage can be found from the 17th century onwards. In the early modern period commentators spoke of orders of society rather than classes. Class is a basic tool of Marxist historians.

classical orders. The five types are the Doric, Ionic, Corinthian, Tuscan, and Composite. The term 'order' refers to the base, shaft, capital, and entablature of a column.

Clearances, Highland. After the defeat of Bonnie Prince Charlie's rebellion at Culloden in 1746, the Highland chiefs lost many of their former powers. Many of them left the Highlands and Islands to live in Edinburgh or London and ceased to speak the Gaelic language. Their commitment to the former semi-feudal society based on the *clan system was weakened. It became obvious that their estates could be run more profitably by the grazing of sheep and cattle than by farming the land in small crofts. Their agents pursued a policy of clearing the cottages of the *crofters, by raising rents and sometimes by violent methods. Between 1763 and 1775 about 20,000 inhabitants of the Highlands and Islands emigrated to America and Canada. The numbers of emigrants grew enormously during the 19th century.

clerestorey. The upper part of a wall (particularly of a church), characterized by a range of windows.

clerical subsidy. In the Middle Ages religious bodies paid taxes separately from lay people. The records are kept in the *Public Record Office under E 179. Names of priests appear only in the *poll tax returns of 1377–81 and in the early 16th century; names of chaplains only in 1450 and 1468.

clerk, parish. Originally, a man who was appointed to assist the parish priest and who held his office for life. He was paid from church funds. His duties included making arrangements for services and leading the responses. The civil parishes which were created in 1894 have a parish clerk as their administrative officer.

clerk of the peace. The principal officer who kept the records of the *quarter sessions and the lieutenancy.

clipping. 1. A church ceremony, often held on *Shrove Tuesday, whereby parishioners held hands to form a chain around the parish church to ward off evil spirits.
   2. The clipping of coins was a capital offence tried at the *assizes during the 16th, 17th, and 18th centuries.

cloister. A covered way in a monastery, for walking and recreation, enclosing a usually quadrangular area, and with a number of cubicles for private study or meditation leading off. They were usually placed on the south side of the church.

close 1. (cathedral). The enclosed area around a cathedral, which contains the houses and offices of the principal officers: dean, treasurer, chancellor, and precentor, and the bishop's palace, forming a separate jurisdiction.

2. (field). A small, hedged or walled field, either at the edge of cultivation or taken in ('enclosed') from the *open-fields, and so not subject to rights on the *commons and wastes.

Close rolls. Records of the Court of *Chancery, housed in the *Public Record Office under C 54, so called because registered copies of private letters and documents were closed with a seal. The rolls record large numbers of *bargains and sales of land, including sales of confiscated land during the *Interregnum.

close studding. The method of arranging vertical timbers close together in the walls of a *timber-framed building.

clothiers. The term covered a wide range of activities in the cloth trade. The wealthiest merchants of medieval and early modern England were often described as clothiers. The term continued in use to mean those engaged in selling cloth, but it was also used from the 16th to the 19th century to describe those men whose families manufactured pieces of cloth.

clover was introduced from the Low Countries into East Anglia in the early 17th century, but it was not until the 1650s that agricultural writers began to speak of its merits in the *meadow and the grass *ley. Imported seed was expensive and some early experiments failed. By the 18th century it had become recognized that the value of clover lay not so much in improving traditional meadows, but in its use in an arable rotation on otherwise bare *fallows, on suitable soils in a dry climate.

club men. In the Civil War farmers armed with clubs tried to protect their crops and livestock against plundering armies. They were active in Dorset, Hampshire, Gloucestershire, Wiltshire, and Somerset in 1645–6 and 1648.

Cluniacs. Monastic order founded at Cluny in Burgundy in 910 and much favoured by the Norman kings and barons. The first Cluniac priory in England was founded at Lewes (Sussex) in 1077. Only three Cluniac houses were built in Scotland and none at all in Wales and Ireland.

coaches. According to John *Stow, 'In the yeare 1564 Guilliam Boonen, a Dutchman, became the Queene's Coachman, and was the first that brought the use of coaches into England . . . within twenty years began a great trade of coach making.' At first the use of coaches was confined to the London area, but by the end of the century noblemen were using them in other parts of the country and by the 1630s public stage-coaches provided links with London within a 30-mile radius of the capital. A more comfortable ride was made possible by the use of steel springs in coaches from 1754. Many more stage-coach routes were opened once the principal highways were *turnpiked in the 18th century. Provincial *directories from the late 18th and early 19th centuries are a major source of information about routes and coach proprietors. *Newspapers often contain advertisements of the services that were available, and private letters and journals give other details.

coal. Those coalfields which had seams near the surface have documentary evidence of small-scale mining since the 13th century. The first coalfield to be developed in a major way was that in Durham and Northumberland, which had the inestimable advantage of being near the sea and therefore able to export its products at prices that could not be matched by its landlocked competitors. The term 'sea-coal' was widely used, even in places far distant from the sea, as a generic word for coal, to distinguish it from *charcoal and the white-coal of the *lead smelters.

The *canals and, especially, the *railways enabled the landlocked coalfields to compete on a national scale. It has been estimated that there were about 50,000 coalminers in Britain by 1800; by 1914 the number had risen to well over 1 million. What has come to be regarded as the 'traditional' pit village rarely lasted for more than 100–120 years and often had a much shorter life-span of two or three generations.

coastal erosion. The relative level of the sea to the land has varied over the centuries. It rose in the late Roman period, receded in the Anglo-Saxon period, rose again from about 1250 onwards, and continued well into the 15th century.

coat of arms. Distinctive heraldic bearings. The name is derived from the 13th-century fashion of applying armorial bearings to a surcoat.

cob. A traditional building material, especially in Devon, Dorset, and Cornwall, consisting mostly of mud, with pebbles, straw, or horse hair for binding.

Cobbett, William (1763–1835). Writer and politician. A lover of the country who was concerned about the changes that were occurring, he is best remembered for his *Rural Rides* (1830).

cock fighting was originally an outdoor 'sport' held in circular pits dug into the ground. Throwing stones at cocks was a traditional pastime of *apprentices on *Shrove Tuesday. During the 17th and 18th centuries smaller cockpits were constructed indoors.

codicil. An addition to a *will that seeks to explain or alter previous provision.

coffee house. The first coffee house in England was reputedly established in London in 1650 at the Angel. They became popular after the *Restoration and remained so during the 18th century. The fashion spread quickly to provincial towns.

cognate. Related on the mother's side.

collar beam. A short horizontal beam connecting the principal rafters at a higher level than a *tie-beam.

college. The colleges that were founded in the Middle Ages were intended as residences and places of prayer and study for priests. Many colleges were dissolved in 1547, for they were regarded in the same light as *chantry chapels, but those whose purpose was principally educational survived. The word 'college' thus became applied to institutions of higher education.

collegiate church. Some of the largest parish churches in the Middle Ages were endowed by rich benefactors who made provision for them to be served by a college of priests who were not bound to any specific monastic rule. They normally had endowments for a provost or master and up to 12 priests, but a few were much larger. Collegiate churches can often be recognized by their grand *chancels, which retain stalls with *misericords. The constitutions of priestly colleges varied considerably, but from the middle of the 14th century the great majority, including almost all those associated with parish churches, were *chantry foundations, and as such were dissolved in 1547.

collier. The term has come to be used exclusively for a coal miner, particularly one who works at the coal face, but before the 19th century it included wood-colliers or charcoal burners.

Combination Acts. The Acts of 1799 and 1800 prohibited combinations of workers in *trade unions. They were passed during the *Napoleonic wars, when fear of revolution after the French example was at its height. They were repealed in 1824.

comes. A Latin word which was Anglicized as count.

Commissary Court. An *ecclesiastical court presided over by a commissary acting on behalf of a bishop where the area served by the court lay well away from the bishop's residence.

Common Pleas, Court of. A royal court of justice sitting at Westminster, whose origins go back to the reign of Henry II (1154–89). From the reign of Edward I (1272–1307) its work became restricted to common law actions between private subjects. It became a division of the High Court in 1873. The records are kept at the *Public Record Office under CP. The archives of most use to local and family historians are the *final concords which end fictitious suits, whose real purpose was to transfer property.

commons and wastes. In *open-field villages the manorial tenants had the right to graze livestock not only on the common at the edge of the settlement, but on the *fallow field, and on the other open-fields after harvest. Settlements on the edges of the moors, *woods, or fens often had rights over extensive commons and wastes. Some of these areas were inter-commoned by neighbouring manors. Common rights were vital to the ability to survive on a small farm; in *deeds they are referred to as the '*appurtenances' of a property. Common rights were basically those of pasture (for cattle, sheep, and horses), pannage (for pigs), turbary (peat), estovers (wood), piscary (fish), and common in the soil (sand, stone, gravel, etc.), but they varied from manor to manor. Occasionally, the jury of a manor court noted the customs of the manor and the rights which could be claimed by the tenants.

Manorial *courts insisted that only those tenants of 'ancient enclosures' had rights over the common and that these rights were in direct proportion to the size of the holding. This was crucial to the question of compensation for the loss of rights at the time of *enclosure. Common rights did not imply common ownership; they are best regarded in the same way as the right to use a footpath over somebody else's land. Manorial juries often found it was necessary to limit common rights so as to prevent overstocking of the commons. The rights were therefore 'stinted' to so many 'cow gates', etc., according to the size of the holding. The poor inhabitants of a manor had a different view of the common from that expressed by the manorial courts and they felt dispossessed by enclosure.

Thousands of acres of commons and wastes survived the period of parliamentary enclosure and continue to be administered by local authorities. Under the Commons Registration Act (1965) a national register has been made of these commons, whose main use is now for recreational activities.

Commonwealth, the (historical). The period of republican government following the execution of Charles I in 1649 until the *Restoration of Charles II in 1660. In 1653 the Rump Parliament was dissolved by the army and Oliver Cromwell became Lord Protector. He was succeeded upon his death in 1658 by his son Richard.

Commonwealth immigrants. Immigration on a large scale began on 8 June 1948 when 492 passengers sailed from Kingston, Jamaica, to settle in Britain. Many more West Indians, predominantly Jamaicans, followed during the 1950s and 1960s. Another large group of immigrants came from the Indian sub-continent; in the 1950s Sikhs came from eastern Punjab, and smaller numbers of Hindus, Muslims, and Parsees came from other parts of India. The newcomers settled mainly in the large conurbations which were losing population and where there was prospect of work.

The Commonwealth Immigrants Act (1962) restricted entry to dependants and skilled workers. The variety of New Commonwealth immigrants increased during the 1960s and 1970s with the arrival of refugees from Kenya (1967) and Uganda (1972), who were mainly business and professional people with family roots in India. Other refugees arrived later, e.g. Malawis in the mid-1970s and Somalis in the 1980s. A series of Acts passed between 1968 and 1981 imposed further restrictions on entry.

communion tables. The medieval church used stone *altars, inscribed with small crosses at each corner and in the middle. In 1550 wooden communion tables replaced stone altars. During the 1630s Archbishop Laud tried to introduce more ritual into church services, including the installation of permanently placed east altars beyond the communion rail, at which communicants could kneel. In 1643 Parliament abolished all east altars and communion rails.

commutation. The change from paying *tithes in kind to a fixed money payment. The Tithe Commutation Act (1836) made this change compulsory.

comperta. 'Things discovered' at an *ecclesiastical visitation of a parish by a bishop or archdeacon.

Compotus rolls. Accounts of royal and seigneurial estates. The records of royal *escheators are kept in the *Public Record Office under E 136 and 357. The compoti of manorial lords are mostly housed in local *record offices.

Compton ecclesiastical census. An *ecclesiastical census, taken in 1676 for the Provinces of Canterbury and York. The returns have been published as Anne Whiteman (ed.), *The Compton Census of 1676: A Critical Edition* (1986). The answers given by the incumbents of parishes were recorded in three columns, which gave the total number of Conformists, Papists, and Nonconformists.

compurgation. The process whereby an accused person could call upon 12 people to swear to his innocence or the truth of his statement. It was abolished in 1833.

coney, or cony. The original English name for *rabbit.

Conference of Regional and Local Historians. Founded in 1978 to promote regional and local history among teachers in higher and further education.

confirmation rolls. Records of the renewal of privileges by the Crown from 1483 to 1625, housed at the *Public Record Office under C 56.

Congregationalists. The Congregationalists originated as a *Puritan sect led by Robert Browne in the 1580s. They were known at first as Brownists and, until well into the 18th century, also as *Independents. Their distinguishing feature was their insistence on the independence of each congregation. The Congregational Union of England and Wales was formed in 1831. In 1972 the Congregationalists and English Presbyterians joined together to form the United Reformed Church.

consanguinity. Blood-relationship; descent from a common ancestor.

consecration cross. When a bishop consecrated a new church he anointed each of the 24 crosses marked high on the walls, half of which were on the outside. Each cross was painted red and enclosed in a small circle.

Conservative Party. Sir Robert Peel, *Prime Minister 1834–5 and 1841–6, is recognized as the first leader of the Conservative Party, which grew out of the *Tory Party of the late 17th and 18th centuries.

consistory court. See ECCLESIASTICAL COURTS.

constable. The office was manorial in origin; the constable was the link between the lord and his tenants, the keeper of law and order. He was appointed by the jury of the *court leet. Where manors decayed during the 17th and 18th centuries, the appointment was made by the parish *vestry meeting. The constable served for one year and was usually elected on a rotation basis from the farmers and craftsmen, the better-off members of the community. The office was unpaid and no expenses were given for loss of earnings. The constable raised taxes, kept accounts, and presented these for approval at the end of his year of office. He was also responsible to the Head Constable of the *hundred or *wapentake for certain duties and to the *Justices of the Peace for others.

In dealing with petty law and order the constable was responsible for the *stocks, *pillory, and village lock-up. He raised the *hue and cry, saw to the *whipping of vagrants, and secured prisoners and escorted them to the *quarter sessions or *assizes. His other duties included the collection of county rates which paid for the *house of correction, *roads, and *bridges, lame soldiers, travellers with passes, and the assizes, etc., and of national taxes such as the *poll tax, *hearth tax, and *land tax. His military duties included the raising of the local *militia, the provision of accommodation and transport for armed forces, and the lighting of *beacons. He was responsible also for weights and measures and the supervision of *alehouses, including the provision of lists of alehouses for licensing at the *brewster sessions. Surviving constables' accounts in local *record offices and the records of quarter sessions reveal the variety of tasks that fell to the constable during his year of office. The office was replaced by the establishment of a national police force in the mid-19th century.

contumacy. Refusal to appear before an *ecclesiastical court or to accept its authority.

conventicle. The term used in the late 17th century for a meeting of religious Dissenters. *Quarter sessions licensed conventicles during periods when they were tolerated and prosecuted those who attended conventicles when they were not.

conventionary tenure. A system of tenure peculiar to Cornwall and parts of Devon, by which tenants obtained a seven-year lease at a negotiated rent, with no automatic right of renewal.

convertible husbandry. Also known as alternate, or up-and-down husbandry, this method of farming allowed the temporary conversion of arable strips in the *open-fields into grass *leys. Some leys remained under grass for up to 10 years; others became permanent grass.

coppice and coppicing. The art of coppicing has been practised since prehistoric times. Most surviving broad-leaved woods were coppiced for centuries up to about the First World War. The cycle of years varied according to the product that was required; on average, it was seven years in the Middle Ages, but by the 19th century the average length had doubled. Some underwood was cut in the first year of growth, but for pit props the cycle was over 30 years.

copyhold tenure. A form of customary tenure by which a tenant held a copy of the entry in the rolls of the manorial *court baron which recorded his or her possession of a holding on agreed terms. In the early Middle Ages the tenant performed services to the lord, but by the 16th century services had generally been converted into money payments, involving large entry *fines and nominal annual rents. During the same century copyhold began to be replaced by *leasehold agreements. Copyhold was abolished in 1922.

corbel table. A series of projecting supports under a roof. In Norman churches these were carved with animal heads, etc.

cordwainer. A boot-and-shoe maker.

corn exchange. During the second and third quarters of the 19th century the corporations of the more substantial market towns built large, imposing corn exchanges for trading in samples.

corn laws. From at least the 12th century, the English government attempted to regulate the export and import of grain. The laws became controversial at the end of the *Napoleonic wars. The supply of imported grain from Continental Europe had been severely affected by the long war with France, so British farmers had been encouraged by government bounties to increase their production. The onset of peace made farmers fearful of bankruptcy. The government therefore agreed to a policy of protection which prohibited imported corn under a certain price. Sliding scales of prices were introduced in 1828 and adjusted in 1842, but the corn laws were not repealed until 1846 after much public pressure from the Anti-Corn Law League.

cornet. The lowest commissioned rank in a cavalry regiment; the man who carried the colours, traditionally the youngest in the regiment.

Cornwall, Duchy of. The oldest duchy, founded in 1337. The estates of the Duchy are chiefly, but not exclusively, in Cornwall, Devon, and Somerset. A few records are kept at the *Public Record Office, but most are available for consultation at the Duchy's own estate office in Buckingham Gate, London.

coroner. The office was created in 1194, when coroners were appointed to enquire into cases of sudden or unexplained death. They gradually acquired other functions, including confiscating property from *outlaws. Records survive from the 14th century under 'Justices Itinerant' at the *Public Record Office. The Coroners Act (1887) and the Coroners Amendment Act (1926) created the modern office. Coroners' inquests are usually reported in local *newspapers, but the official records are closed to public inspection for 75 years.

Corpse Way. In large parishes coffins sometimes had to be carried several miles for burial in the *churchyard. Burial parties followed traditional routes, fearing that if they deviated from the 'corpse way' the ghost of the deceased would rise to haunt them.

Corpus Christi. The Body of Christ, or the Feast of the Blessed Sacrament, on the Thursday after Trinity Sunday. Corpus Christi is a movable feast that depends on the day of Easter; it falls between 21 May and 24 June. Established in England in 1318, until the *Reformation this was the day on which the *guilds of the major cities performed their *mystery plays, telling the Biblical story from the Creation to the Day of Judgement.

corviser. A boot-and-shoe maker.

cote. A cottage or animal shed.

cottages / cottagers. The term 'cottage' has come to be widely applied to any small or medium-sized domestic building, but most of the older structures that are now referred to as cottages were originally the houses of *yeomen, *husbandmen, and craftsmen. Cottages were smaller, inferior buildings inhabited by the poorest sections of society.

Cottages appear in manorial records, often as *encroachments upon the *commons and wastes. The fines that were levied were a roundabout way of charging rent. Manorial surveys sometimes describe cottages, e.g. as 'one-bay thatched'. An Act of 1589 insisted that new cottages should have at least four acres of land attached, but this legislation was not enforced consistently. Increasing numbers of poor cottagers led to decisions being taken at some manor courts and parish *vestries to restrict further building and sometimes to demolish recently constructed cottages. Disputed cases ended up at the *quarter sessions. Encroachments for cottages are normally identified in *enclosure awards, for the cottagers' rights on the commons were often disputed.

cottar. The term used in the *Domesday Book and other medieval records for *cottagers.

cotton. Raw cotton originally came to Britain from the Levant into London, then during the second quarter of the 17th century it came from the East and West Indies. By the early 18th century American and West Indian cotton was being imported through Bristol, Lancaster, and Liverpool; after 1750 Liverpool became the leading port for this trade and Manchester became the chief market.

By the end of the 18th century all the processes for making cotton goods had been brought into *factories. The *spinning process was the first to be mechanized. The early industry was concentrated in Derbyshire, but it soon moved to Lancashire. The earliest cotton mills were water-powered and therefore sited in remote valleys. These mills depended largely on the labour of children and made much use of pauper *apprentices; from the 1770s until the passing of the Factory Act (1833) several thousand children grew up in apprentice houses. By 1803 cotton had overtaken *wool as Britain's leading export, a position which it kept until 1938.

council housing. The Housing of the Working Classes Act (1890) authorized the building of 'council houses'. The new powers were taken up mainly by urban authorities in order to clear slums and rehouse families that were living in insanitary conditions. The Housing, Town Planning, Etc. Act (1909) gave local authorities planning powers over land for development. The first major Scottish programme followed the report of the Royal Commission on the Housing of the Industrial Population of Scotland (1917). A succession of Housing Acts after the First World War, beginning in 1919, led to the creation of large council estates on the edges of towns and the building of smaller estates alongside villages in many parts of Britain. The minutes of the relevant housing committees, which are kept at local *record offices, are the major source of information, though local *newspapers are also informative.

Council in the Marches of Wales. 'The Lord President and Council of the Dominion and Principality of Wales and the Marches of the Same' was created in the late 15th century but acquired much greater powers upon the Union of Wales and England (1536–43), with a headquarters eventually settled at Ludlow Castle. Its civil and criminal jurisdiction extended over the whole of Wales and the English border shires. It was abolished during the Civil War but revived at the *Restoration until 1689.

Council in the North. 'The King's Council in the Northern Parts' was established at York in 1537 in order to counter the threat of rebellion. The Lord President was seated at the King's Manor. The Council was abolished in 1641. Surviving records are fragmentary.

council schools. The Education Act (1902) empowered county and county borough councils as local education authorities. They took over responsibility for *board schools and built many new schools. The Education Act (1944) set up the tertiary system of elementary, secondary modern, and grammar schools.

counties, origins of. Some shires were based on ancient tribal divisions. Kent, Cornwall, and Devon are named after Celtic tribes, and Berkshire and Dorset have names with Celtic roots. Norfolk and Suffolk were the districts populated by the north folk and the south folk of the kingdom of *East Anglia; the east, middle, and south Saxons settled in Essex, Middlesex, and Sussex; and Dorset and Somerset are early folk names. The other Anglo-Saxon shires were not necessarily based on tribal divisions but were created for military reasons around a town or royal estate. The earliest shires were Berkshire, Dorset, Hampshire, Somerset, and Wiltshire, which were formed in 8th- and 9th-century *Wessex. The east midland shires were created under the *Danelaw during the 10th century and were named after the military centres that became their county towns: Derby, Nottingham, Leicester, Northampton, Huntingdon, Bedford, and Cambridge; Lincolnshire united the two Danish armies based on Lincoln and Stamford. Rutland was the only county south of the Humber that had not come into existence by the time of the Norman Conquest.

North of the Humber the only county that was in existence before the Norman Conquest was Yorkshire, the area occupied by the Danish army at Jorvik (York). After the Conquest, Lancashire was created from territories which had previously formed part of Cheshire and Yorkshire, but which by the 12th century were grouped together as the Honour of Lancaster. Cumberland and Westmorland were also created in the late 12th century, though they were based on older territories. County Durham was that area which formed the central part of the lands of the prince bishops of Durham. Northumberland was the shrunken remnant of the ancient kingdom of *Northumbria.

The Scottish Lowland counties were created by Malcolm II in the 11th century on similar lines to those south of the border. Those in the Highlands date from the 16th and 17th centuries. The Welsh counties were created after the Act of Union with England (1536), on the English model. During the second half of the 16th century Ireland's four provinces of Ulster, Connacht, Leinster, and Munster were divided into 32 counties, which were based on older *lordships.

country. The word 'country' was used not only for describing the whole of England, Scotland, Ireland, and Wales, etc., but more imprecisely to convey a sense of a district much wider than that of a town or rural parish, but smaller than that of a county. The identity of a 'country' was determined largely by topography and the nature of the work, but also by the residential persistence of a group of core families.

county councils. Elected county councils, together with county borough councils for towns with a population of over 50,000, were created in 1888 and abolished in 1974. They took over the administrative responsibilities of the county *quarter sessions and were empowered to appoint medical officers. County councils acquired housing and planning powers from 1890 onwards. In 1902 county councils took over responsibility for elementary and secondary education from the school boards. The minutes and other records of the council and its committees, the letter books and files of the clerk, and the treasurer's accounts are deposited in local *record offices.

court, manorial. Although *custumals and *surveys survive in a written form from c.1180 to c.1240, records of manorial courts do not start until the mid-13th century. In the second half of the 13th century, especially in the 1270s and 1280s, the practice of keeping manorial records became widespread as landlords copied the example of the king's courts. The courts were presided over by the lord's steward. Manorial juries, consisting of 12 *homagers, were sworn in. Their first duty was to deal with the lord's financial interests in his manor. They then appointed officers, e.g. the *constable, judged pleas brought by individuals, and laid *pains or fixed penalties on categories of petty offences.

By the early modern period many manorial courts had declined and some had disappeared. Nevertheless, some others continued to thrive. Some manors have long runs of records from the 13th to the 19th or 20th centuries, but the records of many smaller manors have been lost or destroyed. Surviving manor court rolls are normally housed at local *record offices or in national collections at the *Public Record Office, *British Library, etc. Except for the period of the *Commonwealth, records were normally written in Latin until 1733.

court baron. The manorial *court which dealt with the transfer of *copyhold land, upon inheritance or sale, which determined the customs of the manor, and which enforced payment of services which were due to the lord. It was normally held every three weeks.

court leet. The manorial *court which dealt with petty law and order and the administration of communal agriculture. By the late Middle Ages the court leet and the view of *frankpledge came to be treated as alternative names for the same jurisdiction. Rolls were often headed: 'The Court Leet with View of Frankpledge'. It was normally held every six months.

courtyard house. A distinctive type of late medieval manor house, arranged around a rectangular open space which was entered by a broad arch.

credit was widely available in the early modern period. Probate *inventories regularly note the debts that were due to the deceased, and sometimes the debts that he himself had incurred. These included bills and *bonds on which interest was paid.

creek. Small harbours which came under the jurisdiction of neighbouring ports.

crenellate, licence to. A royal licence was necessary before a house could be fortified. The records of such licences, dating from the 12th to the 16th century, are kept mostly in the *Patent rolls at the *Public Record Office.

crime, associations for the prevention of. In the late 18th and early 19th centuries, before the establishment of a local police force, property owners commonly formed a local organization that was pledged to bring offenders before the courts. These bodies had names such as Association for the Prosecution of Felons.

Crimean war. Fought by British, French, and Turkish troops against the Russians, 1854–6.

croft. 1. An enclosed piece of land by a dwelling.

2. In the Scottish Highlands and Islands, a smallholding centred on a *cottage.

crofter. The Scottish crofters held a small area of arable land and grazing rights on the *commons and wastes. They supplemented their income by *weaving, fishing, and the burning of seaweed (*kelp). Many were driven out of their holdings by the landowners of great estates during the 18th and 19th centuries, whereupon thousands emigrated to Canada and the United States of America. Security of tenure was achieved by the Crofters Act of 1886.

crop marks. On intensively cultivated land, where ancient sites have been obliterated by the plough, crop marks seen from aeroplanes can give remarkably accurate indications of the ground plans of former structures.

crop returns. The Home Office files at the *Public Record Office (H.O. 67) contain the returns of a national survey of 1801, arranged by *diocese and *parish. The ministers of each parish in England and Wales were asked to complete printed forms by noting the acreages devoted to wheat, barley, oats, potatoes, peas and beans, and turnips and rape. Some correspondents also noted rye, lentils, and flax. The returns were not concerned with pasture or meadow and therefore vary in importance from one farming region to another. Space was left for comments, many of which are revealing about local farming practices. Returns do not survive for all parishes and the minister was not always well informed.

In 1854 Parliament ordered the gathering of information from 11 representative counties—Berkshire, Breconshire, Denbighshire, Hampshire, Leicestershire, Norfolk, Shropshire, Suffolk, Wiltshire, Worcestershire, and the West Riding of Yorkshire—on crops, livestock, grassland, and waste.

From 1866 agricultural returns have been collected each March for livestock and each June for crops (except for certain years). These returns are housed at the Public Record Office under M.A.F. 68. See the Public Record Office Records Information leaflet, no. 14, 'Agricultural Statistics: Parish Summaries'.

cropper. A skilled craftsman who cropped the imperfections in a piece of finished cloth with a large pair of shears.

crosses. Intricately carved crosses, standing several feet high, in *churchyards or in isolation, survive in many parts of the British Isles, but mainly in northern England and Ireland from the era of the Celtic church or from the *Anglo-Saxon and *Viking periods. Their purpose has never been explained convincingly. Some may have marked preaching sites, but others were personal memorials.

The tradition of erecting wayside crosses ceased in England, Scotland, and Wales upon the *Reformation. Some survive in mutilated form. Crosses of a simple form which survive in churchyards usually served as markers in churchyard processions; they are similar in form to crosses which marked the boundaries of *parishes, *townships, *manors, or monastic estates.

crown (coin). Gold crowns and half-crowns were first issued in 1526. After 1551 they were minted in silver and a crown was worth 5 *shillings.

crown estates. Administratively, the crown estate fell into distinct parts. The first were those rents collected by *sheriffs. The main estates were, for much of Henry VII's and Henry VIII's reigns, in the hands of bodies collectively called General Surveyors. The former monastic lands (and the other lands which came to the crown in the 1530s) were administered by the Court of *Augmentations established for that purpose. In 1547 General Surveyors and Augmentations were merged; and in 1554 the 'second court of Augmentations' became part of a reconstructed Exchequer. The Duchy of *Lancaster was (and remains) a separate element, with its own legal status, management, and tradition of record-keeping. The Duchy of *Cornwall was administered by the Exchequer when there was no duke, but this practice was not restored when Charles I became king in 1625, since when the Duchy has had a continuous existence.

crucks. A distinctive method of supporting the roof of a *vernacular building was the cruck frame. A pair of curving timbers, known as cruck blades, were hoisted on to stone footings by means of poles inserted into holes near the bases of the blades, so as to provide a secure foundation, prevent rising damp, and sometimes to acquire extra height. At mid-level the two blades were joined by a tie-beam and at the top by a collar-beam and by a variety of techniques. Sometimes, the two cruck blades were split from the same tree. Pairs of crucks were then connected by ridge-poles, purlins, and wall-plates in order to form a bay. Cruck buildings could be several bays long, but were commonly of only two or three bays. *Dendrochronology dates show that surviving examples date mostly from the 13th to the 17th centuries, and that some are later.

Crusades. Western Christendom organized several Crusades between 1095 and 1269 to capture the Holy Land from the Muslims. During the 13th century Muslim armies recaptured all their lost territories.

crypt. A vaulted chamber below the *chancel of a medieval parish church, or beneath the *choir of a cathedral or *abbey, containing the tomb or relics of a saint or martyr, and sometimes an *altar. Some of these shrines attracted pilgrims.

cucking stool. A wooden contraption whereby a woman was ducked in a pool or a river as a punishment for *scolding, etc., during the early modern period.

cupola. A dome, e.g. on a church or *town hall. The term was also used for a reverberatory *furnace, particularly for coke-smelted blast furnaces in the *iron industry.

Curia Regis. The king's council, established by William I, out of which in the 13th century grew the courts of *Exchequer, *Common Pleas, and *King's Bench. Records dating from the late 12th and the 13th centuries are kept in the *Public Record Office under KB 26.

curtilage. A legal term for the land on which a dwelling and outbuildings are situated.

customs and excise. From the reign of King John (1199–1216) duties have been payable on certain imported goods, and customs men have been employed by the government to collect the duties and prevent *smuggling. In 1643 excise duties were introduced on certain home-produced goods and a Board of Excise set up for their collection. It was not until the creation of the Board of Customs and Excise in 1909 that the two collecting bodies were amalgamated. See the *Public Record Office Records Information leaflet, no. 106, 'Customs and Excise Records as Sources for Biography and Family History'.

Custos rotulorum. The principal *Justice of the Peace who was responsible for the safeguarding of the records of the *quarter sessions.

custumal. A record of the customs of a *manor, drawn up by the manorial jury.

cypher. A personal monogram, popular in the 18th and 19th centuries.

Dame. The form of address for a woman of rank or position.

dame schools. Elementary schools run by women before the setting up of *board schools.

Danegeld. A payment made to the Danes by the *Anglo-Saxon kingdoms to prevent invasion in the 10th and 11th centuries. The money was raised by a tax on land. Similar taxes were raised later by Cnut and the early Norman kings to pay for national defence. Danegeld was abolished in 1162.

Danelaw, the. A collective term for those shires which were ruled by the Danes from the 9th to the 11th centuries. The Danelaw comprised four areas: *Northumbria; the territory of the *Five Boroughs; *East Anglia; and the south-eastern midlands. Its southern boundary was Watling Street, the Roman road whose line is largely followed by the present A5 road from London to Chester.

Dark Ages. An old-fashioned term for the period beginning with the withdrawal of the *Romans in the 5th century to the later *Anglo-Saxon period of the 8th century onwards, for which there is relatively little evidence.

datestones. A fashion which began in the second half of the 16th century for gentlemen and *yeomen farmers to carve a date on the stone of their door lintel, or perhaps on the chimney breast. The date was often combined with the initials of the forenames of husband and wife and of their surname placed centrally above.

daughter. The term could include a daughter-in-law.

day labourer. A labourer paid by the day, and not living in the farmer's household.

deacon. 1. A clerk in holy orders who assists a priest.
2. An officer of the Presbyterian and *Congregational churches.

dean. The head of a *chapter of a cathedral or of a body of *canons in a *collegiate church. A rural dean heads a *deanery.

deanery, rural. A group of *parishes that form a subdivision of an *archdeaconry. Although deaneries are Anglo-Scandinavian in origin, they often did not achieve their final form until after the Norman Conquest.

death duty. The Legacy Duty Act (1796) imposed a tax on certain types of bequests and residues of the personal estate of deceased persons. These duties were extended by further Acts in 1805 and 1815. A duty on succession has been payable since 1853. Registers from 1796 to 1903 record bequests chargeable with these duties. They list the name of the deceased, the date of the *will, the place and date of probate, the names and addresses of executors, and details of estates, legacies, trustees, legatees and their degree of *consanguinity, *annuities, and the amount of duty paid. They are kept in the *Public Record Office under IR 26 and 27 and are indexed in the *List and Index Society's volume 177. See the Public Record Office Records Information leaflet no. 66, 'The Death Duty Registers'.

death rates. The number of deaths in a year expressed as a rate per thousand of the total population. As the number of burials in *parish registers is under-recorded, a correction factor is used to produce estimated death rates.

Debrett, John, Peerage and Baronetage. John Debrett (d. 1822) published the first edition of his *Peerage* in 1802 and that of his *Baronetage* in 1808. The *Peerage* went through 15 editions in his lifetime and was continued by others after his death. It was eventually combined with the *Baronetage* in an annual volume.

Decorated architecture. A style introduced in major religious and secular buildings in the late 13th century and characteristic of parish churches in the first half of the 14th century. The Decorated style involved the use of flowing window tracery and ogee-arches, and a delight in decorative sculpture.

decoy. A trap for ducks and other wildfowl in *forests, *chases, *parks, and especially in fens. The birds were enticed into funnel-shaped arms of pools or rivers and caught in nets. The word is of Dutch origin and the use of decoys seems to have originated in the early 17th century. Duck-decoys became increasingly complex during the late 17th and 18th centuries. Tame ducks and dogs assisted in the trapping.

decree. A judgement of a court; a judicial decision; an edict.

deed, title. A legal document which transfers property or rights from one person (or institution) to another. The Law of Property Act (1925) reduced the need to prove title back to 30 years.

deed poll. A deed involving only one person or body, e.g. for changing a *surname.

deer park. It has been estimated that at least 1,900 deer parks were created in England alone during the Middle Ages. A few were recorded in the *Domesday Book, but most were created during the 12th and 13th centuries. The fashion declined during the 15th and 16th centuries, but enjoyed a brief revival during the reign of Charles II. As deer were the property of the Crown, a lord was supposed to obtain a royal *charter to empark. However, there are many well-documented parks for which no royal licence exists.

The main types of deer which were kept in parks in the Middle Ages were the native red and roe deer, and fallow deer, which are thought to have been introduced by the Normans.

defaulter. In the Middle Ages, an absentee who was fined for not attending a manorial *court.

Defoe, Daniel (1660–1731). For local historians his most important work is *A Tour through the Whole Island of Great Britain* (1724–6), a record of journeys undertaken over many years which provides a vivid and informed account of Britain in the first quarter of the 18th century.

deforciant. A defendant.

Delft ware. Blue-and-white pottery, originally from Delft (Holland). The first Delft ware factory in England was established in Norwich in 1567 by two Dutchmen. Delft ware was popular throughout the country in the 17th and early 18th centuries and was often recorded in probate *inventories.

demesne. Land on a *manor that was reserved for the lord's own use, as distinct from land held by tenants. The demesne was effectively the same as the so-called 'home farm' of 18th-, 19th-, and 20th-century estates. The term 'ancient demesne' was used to describe manors held by the king at the time of the Norman Conquest. Lords no longer found it profitable to farm their demesne after the *Black Death, but were content to lease their lands to others. There was a revival of interest from the late 15th century onwards.

demise. To convey property by *will or *lease for a term of years or for life.

dendrochronology. The technique of dating timbers by their annual growth rings. Large databases of computerized information have been compiled and some remarkably accurate results have been achieved.

denization. A grant by letters patent by which an *alien was allowed some of the privileges of naturalization, e.g. the buying and devising of land. The records, from c.1400 to 1844, are kept in the *Public Record Office under C 66 and 67. They are useful in naming an immigrant's place of origin. See also the Parliament Rolls for the same period (C 65), and the *Close Rolls (C 54), which have enrolments of Naturalization Certificates, 1844–73.

deodand. A legal term for the instrument which caused a person's death.

deponent. One who makes an oral or written statement (deposition) on oath in a court of law. It was usual in civil cases in the 16th and 17th centuries for both sides to present supporting statements of this sort, often in the form of answers to leading questions. The records of quasi-judicial enquiries under special commissions initiated by the Exchequer are kept at the *Public Record Office under E 133, 134, and 178.

deserted medieval villages. Over 3,000 deserted villages in England alone have now been identified. It has become recognized that desertion was a long-drawn-out process, stretching from the 11th to the 18th centuries.

detached pasture. In areas of *intercommoning of a moor, marsh, *wood, etc., the inhabitants of some *manors had common rights on pastures that were physically detached from the rest of the fields and commons. These detached pastures could be several miles away from the homes of the farmers.

detached portion. Many *parishes were not compact entities, but had detached portions that were surrounded by the lands of neighbouring parishes. Such arrangements reflect ancient tenurial history, often from before the Norman Conquest.

devise. To convey or bequeathe land, as distinct from personal property.

dew pond. A familiar sight on chalklands and limestone since the 17th century, such ponds were used to collect rain-water for cattle.

diaries. The keeping of diaries as a record of personal experience and development began in the 17th century and in most cases was inspired by piety. In the 19th and 20th centuries working-class people began to keep diaries and to record their memories in the form of an autobiography.

Dictionary of National Biography. The *DNB* was launched in 1882. It included short biographies of notable British people from earliest times up to 1900. Supplements have been published every 10 years. A *New Dictionary of National Biography* was started in 1994.

dioceses. A diocese is an ecclesiastical administrative territory under the jurisdiction of a bishop.

The medieval English dioceses were created as follows: Canterbury (AD 597), London (604), Rochester (604), York (625), Winchester (662),

Lichfield (669), Hereford (676), Worcester (c.680), Bath and Wells (909), Durham (995), Exeter (1050), Lincoln (1072), Chichester (1075), Salisbury (1078), Norwich (1091), Ely (1109), and Carlisle (1133). Six new dioceses were created by Henry VIII in the 1540s, following the *dissolution of the monasteries: Chester, Peterborough, Gloucester, Bristol, Oxford, and Westminster (which lasted only a decade). No further *Church of England dioceses were created until 1836, since when 20 have been founded in response to population changes; the cathedrals of these new dioceses are often enlarged versions of medieval parish churches.

The Welsh dioceses of Bangor, St Asaph, St David's, and Llandaff were created in the mid-6th century, and that of Sodor and Man in the 11th century. The Irish dioceses were mostly created in the *Viking period, e.g. the diocese of Cork was essentially the territory of the Mac Carthaigs. However, these territories were based on even older units. By the early 14th century Ireland was divided into four provinces and 35 dioceses: Armagh (11), Dublin (6), Tuam (8), and Cashel (10). The 13 medieval dioceses of Scotland were swept away at the *Reformation.

For administrative purposes dioceses are divided into *archdeaconries, rural *deaneries, and *parishes. The records of the diocese are available for public consultation at the various diocesan *record offices, some of which are amalgamated with county or city record offices.

diphtheria was a winter disease which mainly attacked children under the age of five.

directories. The first London directory was Samuel Lee's list of the City merchants in 1677. The industrial towns took the lead in the provinces. These early publications contain far less information than the directories of the Victorian era, but they arrange the names of people in each trade in alphabetical order and give their addresses, together with details of postal, coach, and carrying services.

In the late 18th century a number of directories covering much wider areas than single towns were published. The first national series was that of James Pigot, published between 1814 and 1853, after which the firm was taken over by Francis Kelly. Kelly's became the most famous series of directories up to the middle of the 20th century, though there were other well-known names, such as William White. In contrast, many other publishers of directories did not remain in the business very long.

The general trade directories began each entry with brief notes on the history and topography of the settlement, with some account of recent economic developments, and with notes on land-ownership, tenures, and the administrative details of *townships, *parishes, and *manors. They then listed the 'principal inhabitants' and arranged the names of professionals, businessmen, and tradesmen in alphabetical order under different occupations. Even the best directories are not comprehensive in their listings, nor did they record labourers, *domestic servants, and other employees. They do, however, give a good indication of the commercial life of a town and the names of farmers and craftsmen in a village.

disafforestation. The process by which some of the royal *forests were sold and converted to other agricultural purposes, particularly during the reigns of James I (1603–25) and Charles I (1625–49), when the Crown was attempting to rule without revenue authorized by Parliament.

dispensaries. A charitable provision in many 18th- and 19th-century towns, whereby poor people nominated by the subscribers were able to get free medical treatment.

disseisin. Forcible or involuntary eviction.

dissenting academies. In the later 17th century various *Nonconformist preachers started to provide education for those who wished to enter the ministry and for the sons of members of their congregations. These academies became leading educational institutions after the Toleration Act of 1689, but gradually declined in the middle and later years of the 18th century.

dissolution of the monasteries. In the five years between 1536 and 1540 all 650 monasteries in England and Wales were dissolved. A new ministry, known as the Court of *Augmentations, had been established at the beginning of dissolution in March 1536 in order to deal with the newly acquired spoils. Only about 2.5 per cent of the plunder was given away, and sales started almost immediately.

distraint. Originally the seizure of livestock or other possessions for a breach of *feudal dues, the term came to be used for the seizure of goods to compensate for unpaid rent.

divorce. Before the *Reformation marriages could not be dissolved by formal procedures. By the end of the 16th century all the *Protestant countries except England had divorce laws. In Scotland, by the mid-16th century, divorce was permitted on the grounds of adultery or desertion and the innocent party was allowed to remarry. In England and Wales no changes in the law of divorce were made before the *Matrimonial Causes Act (1857). This Act was never extended to Ireland. In practice, however, the ending of unsatisfactory marriages was possible through the common law and the *ecclesiastical courts and by Act of Parliament. See the *Public Record Office Records Information leaflet no. 127, 'Divorce Records in the Public Record Office', which also outlines the further legislation of 1873–1969. For the poorer classes from the 16th to the 19th century there was the option of *wife-selling, which followed customary rules in a public place.

The Matrimonial Causes Act (1937; extended to Northern Ireland, 1939) broadened the grounds of divorce in England and Wales to include desertion and cruelty, unsoundness of mind, rape, sodomy, and bestiality. The Divorce Reform Act (1969) made the irretrievable breakdown of marriage the sole ground of divorce in Britain; this was taken to have occurred if there was adultery, unreasonable behaviour, desertion for at least two years, or if the parties had been living apart for five years. In the Republic of Ireland, however, an Act of 1937 forbade the dissolution of marriage.

docks, dockyards. Maps, prospects, and *travellers' accounts, notably those of *Defoe, are useful sources for the 18th century. The construction of a dock sometimes required a private Act of Parliament; maps and plans deposited prior to an application, together with records of naval dockyards, are found in the *Public Record Office under WORK 41 to 44. Other records are kept under MT 19 (1848–63, arranged by harbour), and MT 10 (from 1864, arranged chronologically). See also MT 21, 22, and 26 for individual ports.

doctors. Early medical practioners included *apothecaries, barber-surgeons, and physicians. In the 18th century medical training was still largely by apprenticeship, except for those who graduated at Edinburgh University or who had studied at Leiden. From the late 18th century onwards a number of provincial medical schools were established. In 1858 medical education came under the authority of the General Medical Council.

Dodsworth, Roger. Early 17th-century Yorkshire antiquary whose manuscripts are kept in the *Bodleian Library.

dole. 1. A donation to charity. These are often recorded on charity-boards in the towers or porches of parish churches. Some churches retain their dole-cupboards in which bread was kept for distribution to the poor. This sense is preserved in the expression 'on the dole'.

2. A division of the common *meadows, shared out annually by rotation or by lot. The name is sometimes preserved in minor place-names and in the expression 'to dole out'.

Domesday Book. William the Conqueror decided on a survey of all his new lands in England to determine who owned what both before and after the Norman Conquest and what each of their holdings was worth. The whole of England, except Cumberland and northern Westmorland, was surveyed during 1086. The survey was organized by county, under the headings of the *tenants-in-chief of each county.

The returns from each county were gathered at Winchester, where they were recorded (in abbreviated Latin) in two volumes, now housed at the *Public Record Office. The volume that contains the unabridged returns for Essex, Norfolk, and Suffolk is the most detailed; the other volume has clearly lost much of the original material through editing. The greatest loss is that the surveys of County Durham and Northumberland and of major towns, including London and Winchester, were not transcribed. Some surviving contemporary surveys, notably the *Exon Domesday, may have been preliminary work for the compilation of the Domesday Book.

In many cases, the Domesday Book reference is the earliest documentary source of information about a place and the first recorded spelling of its name. The only people to be named in the Domesday Book are the tenants-in-chief and their *sub-tenants, both before and after the Conquest. The *villeins, *cottars, *bordars, freemen, *sokemen, and slaves are simply numbered. Some social groups are significantly under-recorded. The Domesday Book is not an accurate guide to the early Norman landscape. The only buildings mentioned are churches and *mills, and even those figures are minimal. Historians are divided on the accuracy of the figures for woodland. The importance of livestock in the economy is largely ignored, for the compilers were chiefly concerned with arable land. Nor were they usually concerned with crafts and industries. The information about towns was unsystematic and incomplete.

The Domesday Book is a description of rights, charges, customs, duties, and titles.

Domesday of Inclosures. Most of the findings of a Commission of Inquiry, which was set up by Wolsey in 1517 to investigate the *enclosure of arable land and its conversion to pasture, were published under this title, in two volumes, by I. S. Leadham in 1897.

domestic economy. The term is used to describe the system of manufacture which was in widespread use before the *factory system was developed in the late 18th and 19th centuries. The place of work was the home, and much manufacture was combined with farming. Each member of the family had particular tasks.

domestic servant. Entering domestic service as a young teenager and continuing in such employment until marriage was the normal expectation of girls from farming, craft, and labouring families in the early modern period. Most girls did not travel far, but some ventured to London or the nearest provincial city. In the later 19th and the first half of the 20th century domestic servants sometimes moved much further away, though most stayed near to home. The 1851 census return recorded 1 million female domestic servants; by 1901 there were 1.4 million.

doom painting. The public part of a medieval church (the *nave) was separated from the priest's part (the *chancel) by a stone arch and a wooden *rood screen which supported an image of Christ on the cross. A painting of the Last Judgement (a 'doom') often occupied the space above the arch. This depicted Christ in majesty and the weighing of the souls of the dead. Good Christians are shown ascending to heaven, sinners as descending into hell. These dooms were painted over at the *Reformation, but over 60 have been restored.

doomsman. A juryman of a manorial *court.

dorse. The reverse side of a sheet of paper or parchment. Any writing on that side 'endorsed' a document.

dorter. The monks' dormitory, usually on the first floor of the building on the south side of the *cloister and connected by a stair to the church.

dovecotes. Surviving dovecotes date from the 12th to the 18th century. They are built of stone, brick, or timber and are difficult to date. They were originally confined to the *demesne lands of manorial lords and monasteries, but ordinary farmers broke down this monopoly in the 17th and early 18th centuries.

dowager. A widow whose title is derived from her late husband.

dower. The widow's third; that part of an estate which by common law passed to a widow on the death of her husband for the duration of her lifetime or until she remarried.

dowry. Property that a wife gave to her husband on the day of their marriage; also known as 'a marriage portion'.

dozener. A name derived from the head of the dozen or jury, applied to the *constable or other officer in some *boroughs.

dreng. A Scandinavian word for a well-to-do farmer.

drovers. The droving trade grew considerably during the early modern period and was at its peak from the 17th century to the railway era. Cattle were brought from Scotland and Wales to the lowland pastures of midland, southern, and eastern England.

The documentation for the history of droving is meagre. From 1552 to 1772 drovers and *badgers were expected to be licensed at *quarter sessions (except in the six northern counties of England). A drover had to be a married householder of at least 30 years of age.

drystone walls. Most are a product of the period of parliamentary *enclosure of the *commons and wastes in the 18th and 19th centuries, though walls close to villages and farmsteads may be earlier. The oldest walls use upright boulders—'orthostats'—but they are difficult to date.

dual economy. A term used to describe the combination of farming a smallholding (or sometimes a larger property) with another employment.

Dugdale, William, Sir (1605–86). Warwickshire country gentleman, antiquary, and distinguished member of the College of *Arms. His *The Antiquities of Warwickshire* (1656) is one of the finest of the old county histories.

duke. A title created in England by Edward III in 1337 as the most senior rank of the peerage.

Durham Ox. A famously huge Shorthorn bred by Charles Colling in 1796, which was exhibited at numerous *fairs.

Dutch immigrants. The term 'Dutch' was used in England not only for the people of Holland, but also those of Flanders, Brabant, and sometimes Germany ('Deutsch'). Large numbers of immigrants from the Low Countries settled in London, Norwich, Colchester, Sandwich, and other south-eastern towns during the second half of the 16th century. Together with French *Huguenot immigrants they introduced the *New Draperies. They were also largely responsible for the development of *market gardening around the capital city. As well as this, they were noted potters, glass-makers, brick-makers, tailors, haberdashers, and craftsmen in leather, printing, brewing, goldsmithing, and the making of clocks and spectacles. They established a centre of tapestry-making at Mortlake in 1619.

dyeing. Concern over the high prices of imported dyes in the 1570s and 1580s led to the Elizabethan government actively encouraging the cultivation of *woad, *madder, *saffron, and *weld for use in the textile industries. Manchester and the Merseyside towns became the leading centres of the production of coal-based dyes in the mid-19th century. The German contribution to the development of this industry was crucial.

dykes. Linear earthworks dating from the *Bronze Age to the *Anglo-Saxon period, constructed as boundaries.

dysentery. A disease which inflames the mucous membrane and glands of the large intestine, thus causing severe pain and loss of blood. It was transmitted by impure drinking water.

ealdorman. The chief royal official of a county in Anglo-Scandinavian England; cf. the post-Conquest *sheriff.

earl. Derived from Scandinavian *jarl*, earl is the oldest English title and rank. Later in the Middle Ages it was placed below the new ranks of *duke and *marquess. An earl's wife is a countess.

Earl Marshall. The officer responsible for state ceremonies. This has long been a hereditary role of the Duke of Norfolk.

Early English architecture. The earliest of the *Gothic styles, introduced into England from France in the third quarter of the 12th century. Windows designed as single lancets or as Y-tracery are the most readily identified feature of this style.

East Anglia, kingdom of. The *Anglo-Saxon kingdom of East Anglia comprised most of present Norfolk and Suffolk. It was conquered by the Danes in 869 and became part of the *Danelaw.

East India Company. Incorporated on 31 December 1600, this joint-stock company established trading stations in India and the East Indies and served as the agent of British administration there. After the Indian Mutiny of 1857 the company was taken over by the Crown.

The Company's archives can be consulted at the India Office Library, Orbit House, Blackfriars Bridge Road, London SE1. The records of baptism, marriage, and burial in India date from the late 17th century. From 1803 annual printed lists name all the Company's work-force.

Easter book. A list of householders in a parish, compiled as a record of those liable to pay personal *tithes on the profits of trade, crafts, wages, and other dues to the incumbent at Easter. Such books date from the second half of the 16th century until the Tithe Commutation Act (1836).

ecclesiastical censuses. On two occasions in 1563 and 1603 the *Privy Council required bishops to make returns of the number of people in the *parishes and *chapelries of their *dioceses. These are found in the Harleian manuscripts 280, 594, 595, and 618 at the *British Library. Returns survive for 12 dioceses in England and Wales. The returns of 1603 survive for only seven dioceses. They record numbers of communicants, Protestant dissenters, and Roman Catholics.

The only census of attendance at religious worship ever taken by the state was that for England and Wales on Sunday, 30 March 1851. The returns provide detailed information, parish by parish, on the places of worship of each denomination, on the number of sittings available, and the numbers attending the morning, afternoon, and evening services that were held by different denominations during that day. These returns are kept at the *Public Record Office under HO 129. The returns also note the number of children who attended Sunday School in the morning or afternoon. The foundation date of a particular meeting or of the place of worship was often recorded.

ecclesiastical courts. During the Middle Ages the Church exercised jurisdiction over matters which were dealt with by ecclesiastical law rather than by common law. At the *Reformation ecclesiastical authorities tackled administration with a new zeal. The highest ecclesiastical court in the land was the High Court of Delegates, beneath which sat the Court of *Arches and its northern equivalent and the *prerogative courts of Canterbury and York. Below these were the bishops' and archidiaconal courts. During the 19th century ecclesiastical courts withered as the state took over many of their powers (notably, in 1858, their jurisdiction over probate) and as the *Church of England no longer tried to enforce public morality or to suppress dissent in this manner.

The records of the consistory courts of bishops and archdeacons are notoriously difficult to read and interpret, because of their use of technical terms and scribbled abbreviations. The more legible ones include cause papers, which contain details of arguments and evidence in particular cases, and *Act books which summarize the procedure of a case. The number of surviving records increases from the late 16th century onwards. A particularly fruitful source for local and family historians are the depositions of witnesses in such cases. These begin with a note of the witness's name, occupation, age ('or thereabouts'), residence, etc. and sometimes an account of previous jobs and places of residence. Many cases deal with church matters such as the conduct of the minister, *plurality, the state of the church fabric and furniture, *Roman Catholicism or Protestant *Nonconformity, non-attendance at services and sacraments, the payment of dues, etc. Disputes over the non-payment of *tithes were frequently contested. The officers of the consistory courts also saw themselves as the guardians of public morality. They became known in some places as 'bawdy courts' because they dealt with sexual misconduct and defamation.

ecclesiastical visitations. Bishops were supposed to visit all parts of their diocese every three years and archdeacons to visit their archdeaconries annually. Ministers and churchwardens would travel to a nearby town to answer questions about attendances at services, the state of the church as a building, the conduct of their parishioners, the names of Recusants and Nonconformists, etc. These records are available at diocesan *record offices.

Ecclesiologist, The. Published by the *Camden Society between 1841 and 1868, this journal greatly influenced the course of church building and restoration in the Victorian period. Its pages are now an important source of information about Victorian church architecture.

Eden, Sir Frederick Morton (1766–1809). Eden's enquiry into *The State of the Poor* (3 vols., 1797) is a major source of information about the *workhouses that were set up under the Old Poor Law before the *Poor Law Amendment Act (1834). The abridged (single-volume) version of his report contains descriptions of a selection of workhouses throughout England.

Eleanor crosses. Memorial crosses erected at resting places along the route by which the body of Queen Eleanor, wife of Edward I, was brought from Nottinghamshire for burial at Westminster in 1290.

electoral register. The Parliamentary Reform Act of 1832 required the publication on a *parish basis of lists of persons eligible to vote. As the franchise has been gradually extended, so the lists have become more comprehensive. Since 1928 (when the age that women were allowed to vote was lowered to 21) they list the names and addresses of all adults who have registered. Copies may be seen at county and borough *record offices and public libraries.

electricity. Michael Faraday's publications led to the use of electrical lighting in lighthouses and street lamps in the 1860s and 1870s. In 1880 Sir William Armstrong, the Tyneside armaments manufacturer, made his home at Cragside (Northumberland) the first house in the world to be lit by hydro-electric power.

enclosure, parliamentary. Parliamentary enclosure occurred where an agreement to enclose by all the owners of land in a *parish or *township could not be obtained; a hostile minority could be overruled by a private or public Act of Parliament. The first Act was that for Radipole (Dorset) in 1604, but it was well into the 18th century before this method became common and not until after 1750 that it became dominant. Over 85 per cent of parliamentary enclosure was completed or on the statute book by 1830. In all, 5,341 awards were made for England and 229 for Wales. These were of two types: those which dealt with both *open-fields and common pastures, and those which were concerned only with *commons and wastes. In Scotland, most enclosure was enacted under legislation that predated the Union with England in 1707 (even though the timing of enclosure was much later).

The sponsors of individual Acts of parliamentary enclosure are named in the petition and bill, and in the subsequent Act and award. The progress of the bill through Parliament can be followed in the journals of the *House of Commons and *House of Lords. The size of any opposition was noted at the Report Stage in both Houses.

In England and Wales 38 per cent of all Acts were passed in the first main period of activity between 1755 and 1780. These early Acts were concerned mainly with the heavy soils of the midland clay belts. A second wave of activity from the 1790s to the mid-1830s was at its height during the French Revolutionary and *Napoleonic wars, when grain prices were high and farming prosperous. Indeed, the war years accounted for 43 per cent of all parliamentary enclosures. The Welsh uplands were enclosed a little later, half of them after 1840. A 525,880 acres were enclosed in Wales by the 229 acts of Parliament.

The area of open-field arable that was enclosed by Acts of Parliament measured almost double the area covered by commons and wastes. Much of the heavier soils were converted to pasture.

enclosure, private and piecemeal. 'Enclosure' was a general term which differed in its impact according to time and place. The enclosure of land in the *open-fields in the midlands aroused strong opposition, culminating in the Midland Revolt of 1607, but elsewhere enclosure could be carried out amicably and by agreement. When *commons and open-fields were enclosed by a hedge, fence, or wall, common rights over them were extinguished. A typical prelude to enclosure was the amalgamation of a holding by the exchange or purchase of *strips. The agreements that were drawn up often do not survive, but some can be found amongst parish records, *estate papers, and solicitors' collections in local *record offices. An alternative method was to contest a fictitious suit in the Court of *Chancery.

enclosure awards and maps. The parliamentary *enclosure of *open-fields and *commons and wastes in England and Wales was achieved through thousands of private Acts of Parliament.

The new *allotments were set out in an award which contained a schedule and an accompanying map. The copy of the award that was deposited in the parish chest is now normally kept at the appropriate county *record office, though a large number are housed at the *Public Record Office. The map is often the earliest one available for a particular *township or *parish.

Awards describe the position and acreage of the new allotments and list their owners and tenants. The awards also set out public roads, bridleways and footpaths, watercourses and drains, and other conveniences such as public wells. The maps mark (with a letter T on the inside boundary) which owners were responsible for the maintenance of walls.

enclosure roads. The commissioners responsible for individual Acts of parliamentary enclosure had, as one of their tasks, to define public rights of way, including roads, bridleways, and footpaths. These were described in their *enclosure award and set out on the accompanying map. Some of the roads followed the lines of ancient highways, but others were new routes across former *open-fields, *commons, and wastes. They were given standard widths, e.g. of 30 or 40 feet, and were enclosed with hedges or walls. They are characteristically long and straight.

encroachment. The extension of a piece of private property so as to enclose part of a *green or *common or someone else's land.

end. A part of a *village, sometimes detached from the rest of the settlement, or a hamlet.

endogamy. The practice of marrying within a *clan or local society. The term is used by social historians when discussing the geographical origins of marriage partners.

enfeoffment. The surrender of property to a group of trustees.

enfranchisement. The conferring of freedom, e.g. making land *freehold.

English Place-Name Society. Founded in 1923, the society has published surveys of place-names for many English counties and its work continues.

engrossing. The amalgamation of two or more farms into one.

ensign. The lowest commissioned rank in an infantry regiment; the man who carried the flag.

entail. To bequeath an estate in a named sequence of succession. The practice was common from medieval times. The *Scottish Record Office has a Register of Entails or Tailzies from 1685. In 1914 the creation of new entails was prohibited.

ephemera. Handwritten or printed papers which were not meant for posterity but which are now often valuable historical sources.

epitaphs. Inscriptions on monuments or *gravestones commemorating the deceased. The Elizabethans started the fashion for lengthy epitaphs, often in verse, which described a man's family background and his achievements and extolled his virtues. The style degenerated into ridiculous flattery and bad verse during the 18th century.

equity. 1. (legal) General principles of justice used to correct or supplement common and statute law.

2. (commercial) Stocks and shares which do not have a fixed interest.

escheat. Escheated property reverted to a lord when a tenant was guilty of a *felony or when he died without adult heirs. The term will often be found in manorial records.

espousal. A betrothal, which until the 17th century was considered almost as valid as marriage. This practice sometimes explains why a child was baptized less than nine months after a marriage.

esquire. Originally the shield-bearer to a *knight, by the 16th century an officer of the Crown, and in the following two centuries a man with a *coat of arms who was a superior gentleman. In the 19th century 'esquire' became more widely used as a style when addressing letters to a gentleman, and later to all men.

essoin. An acceptable excuse for absence from a manorial *court.

estate, early or multiple. Territorial estates in medieval England and Wales which demonstrate remarkable continuity from Roman, and possibly even earlier, times.

estate records. In the post-medieval period archivists often catalogue records that were previously described as manorial accounts and rolls as 'estate papers'. These include correspondence, accounts of the management of the estate, maps, *surveys, *leases, and *rentals. Most of these records have now been deposited at county *record offices.

estover, right of. The right to take timber, brushwood, bracken, etc. from *commons for use in building, repairing fences, or as fuel etc.

estreat. An extract from a list of *fines, returned to the *Exchequer.

evangelical revival. A Protestant movement in the late 18th and 19th centuries, which included 'Low Church' members of the *Church of England and most of the *Nonconformist sects, and which emphasized salvation by faith alone.

eviction. Families living in *tied houses or *cottages could be summarily evicted by the owner. *Newspapers sometimes reported evictions, but often the only information about such events is through *oral history. The threat of eviction was often sufficient to enforce the wishes of an owner.

Exchequer, Court of. The administrative body that collected royal revenue and the court which originally dealt with fiscal matters, but which became an ordinary court of justice. The records are kept at the *Public Record Office under class E; many have been printed. The court was merged with the High Court of Justice in 1880. In Scotland, after the Act of Union (1707), a remodelled Exchequer was responsible for forfeited estates, particularly after the failure of the rebellions of 1715 and 1745. The records are kept at the *Scottish Record Office, which has published extracts and summaries.

excommunication. The exclusion of a person from the communion of the Church, imposed by an *ecclesiastical court for offences ranging from non-attendance at church to heresy. Christian burial was denied to ex-communicants.

execution, public. Capital punishment was normally performed in public throughout the Middle Ages and the early modern period. Successive Tudor governments turned it into street theatre, with set-piece executions for high-born traitors and later for common felons.

The number of capital offences increased greatly during the second half of the 17th century and the first part of the 18th century. The most infamous gallows was at *Tyburn, which was approached on a 'hanging day' by a long procession through the streets of London. The last hanging at Tyburn was in 1783; later hangings in London took place instead within the confines of Newgate Prison, but many sentences were commuted to *transportation. Public executions were abolished in 1868. Capital punishment within prisons was abolished in 1965.

Exon Domesday. A survey of the south-western counties, preserved in Exeter Cathedral and printed in volume iv of the Record Commission edition of the *Domesday Book. It includes a count of farm stock, which is not given in the final version of the Domesday Book.

expectation of life. The average expectation of life before the 20th century was lowered considerably by the high rate of *infant mortality. In the Elizabethan period, for instance, if a person survived childhood he or she could expect to live into what is now called middle age (though sudden death at all ages was a common experience) and some lived as long as the oldest people of today. The great difference between the present age and the past is that a high proportion of the population are now elderly. Society was formerly much more youthful in its composition.

extent. A detailed *survey and valuation of an estate, especially a manorial one. It records the names of tenants, the size and nature of their holdings, and the form of their tenure.

extra-parochial. An area outside the jurisdiction of an ecclesiastical or civil *parish. In 1894 all such areas were incorporated into parishes or made into new ones.

eyre, in. A system of justice introduced in 1166 by which the king's justices travelled on circuits to county sessions. General eyres were replaced by *assizes in the late 13th century.

factor. An agent, dealer, or middleman.

factory. The original meaning was trading station, the place of work of a company's *factors. The change took place in the 19th century when *cotton 'manufactories' became known by the shortened form.

Factory Acts. The Factory Act (1819) prohibited children under 9 from working in *cotton mills and restricted older children to a 12-hour day. The Factory Act (1833) reduced the daily hours of children under 12 working in textile mills to nine, with a maximum of 48 hours a week, and those aged 13–18 to 12 hours a day, with a maximum of 69 hours a week; children at these mills were obliged to have two hours' schooling a day; and factory inspectors were appointed to enforce these regulations. The Factory Act (1844) ordered that women were not to work more than 12 hours a day in textile mills and that children were to spend half their day at school. Further reforms were passed by the Factory Acts of 1853, 1867, 1874, 1891, 1901, and 1937.

faculty. A licence from a bishop to alter or add to church buildings or a *churchyard.

fairs. From the late 12th century onwards the right to hold a fair was granted by a royal *charter. Fairs already in existence were claimed by prescriptive right. The greatest period of creation, as with *markets, was between the Norman Conquest and the *Black Death. The rapid methods of communication in modern times have destroyed the great majority of fairs. In a report of 1889 on market tolls and rights, the Government published a list of markets and fair charters down to 1483.

The staple commodity of most fairs was cattle, followed by sheep, then horses. The major fairs catered for a variety of commerce, including *pedlars' goods, but those held at remote country sites were limited to one speciality. The most famous fair in Britain was that held in a field at Stourbridge on the outskirts of Cambridge.

falling sickness. Epilepsy.

fallow. Arable land which is left unploughed for a year in order to recuperate. In *open-field systems an entire field was left fallow in rotation. The jurors of the manorial *court determined when and how the fallow could be grazed in common.

families, core. The population of medieval and early modern Britain was far more mobile than was once realized. Movement beyond the *parish boundary was commonplace. Nevertheless, most movement was restricted to a radius of between 20 and 25 miles, within an area bounded by the nearest market towns.

Much of the movement in and out of parishes was by young *farm and *domestic servants and *apprentices. Young people often returned upon inheriting the family farm or *cottage. Studies of communities and local societies in many different parts of the country have emphasized the contrast between this mobility and the stability of core groups of families over the generations.

The members of core families feature large in the lists of local officials, e.g. *churchwardens, *constables, overseers of the *poor and of the *highways, witnesses to wills, and appraisers of probate *inventories. The core families which remained in a particular locality for at least a century or two were largely drawn from the middle ranks of society.

Family Division, Principal, Registry of. Since 1858 all *wills in England and Wales have been proved at the registry in Somerset House, Strand, London. The annual indexes, which name the testator and (until 1967) executor(s), can be consulted free of charge. A fee is payable to see the will. The indexes to letters of *administration may also be consulted; before 1870 these are indexed in separate volumes.

family reconstitution. The technique of compiling family trees for as many people as possible in a chosen area of study, e.g. a *parish, so as to obtain detailed demographic data on matters such as age at *marriage, or *expectation of life.

famine. The great dearth of 1258 was the worst in the 13th century, but it was far surpassed in severity by the succession of harvest failures and livestock epidemics between 1315 and 1322. In some parts of Britain famine conditions persisted until the *Black Death of 1348–50.

Early modern England did not suffer from famines on a major scale. After 1623 famine conditions seem to have disappeared in England, though it has been argued that dearth was partly responsible for the high mortalities of 1723–30. In the 1840s Ireland experienced a disaster comparable in its effects to the Black Death.

famuli. Workers on medieval estates who were paid, as distinct from those tenants who provided *boon labour.

farm, model. In the late 18th and early 19th centuries great landowners employed architects to design farm buildings that were aesthetically pleasing as well as being an efficient use of space.

farm servants. The distinction between a farm servant and a farm labourer was that a servant was an adolescent boy or an unmarried man who was hired for a year and who lived on the farm, whereas an *agricultural labourer was usually a married man who lived elsewhere (often in a *tied cottage) and who was paid a daily or weekly wage for the job that he performed. Farm service was the normal career expectation of teenage boys from about the age of 14 during the medieval and early modern period, and in some parts of Britain during much of the modern era.

farmer. 1. A collector of taxes, who paid the Crown an agreed sum and made a profit on the collection.·

2. In its modern sense, conveying no idea of acreage farmed or social status, the word began to replace *yeoman and *husbandman during the 18th century.

farthing. A quarter-penny. Until 1279 it was formed by cutting a penny into four quarters. The farthing ceased to be legal tender in 1956.

father-in-law. The term was often used to mean stepfather, i.e. a mother's second husband. A father-in-law in the modern sense was often termed 'father'.

fealty. An oath of allegiance to the king, given when a new tenant paid homage to the lord who was his immediate superior, thus recognizing his obligations.

Federation of Family History Societies. Founded in 1974 to co-ordinate the activities of the growing number of family history societies, the federation publishes *Family History News and Digest* twice a year and a series of booklet guides to the availability and use of records. Conferences are held twice a year under the auspices of member societies. The federation represents the points of view of family historians to official bodies.

fee simple. *Freehold land which is unlimited in duration and extent of ownership and which can be disposed of according to the wishes of the owner.

fee-farm. An annual rent paid by chartered *boroughs to the Crown in the Middle Ages.

feet of fines. From the late 12th century until 1834 a record of title (usually made after a purchase) was written out three times on a single sheet of parchment. The three copies were then cut apart along wavy lines to prevent forgery. Two parts were given to the parties involved, and the copy at the foot of the fine was filed among the rolls of the Court of *Common Pleas, now kept at the *Public Record Office under the references CP 25 and 27. Until 1688 the rolls were arranged under counties; this has enabled several county record societies to publish editions.

felony. Crimes such as murder, rape, arson, robbery, burglary, etc. were regarded (except in Scottish courts) as being more serious than *misdemeanours. The penalties included forfeiture of land and goods. Forfeiture was abolished in 1870.

female descent. Any line of descent through a woman.

feodary. A survey of the obligations of tenants of the Crown; the officer who enforced such obligations.

feoffee. One of a group of trustees appointed to manage a private tenant or an endowed institution, e.g. a charity school.

feoffment. The original form of conveyance by a symbolic handover known as livery of *seisin. It guaranteed a *fee simple.

fertility rates. These are measured in various ways, so the precise method in use needs to be stated. Fertility rates refer to the number of births per female of reproductive age in the population under scrutiny, normally expressed as so many per thousand. Sometimes age-specific rates are used.

feudal aids were originally gifts from a free tenant to his lord, but the system was abused. *Magna Carta (1215) insisted that a lord might exact an aid on only three occasions: to pay a ransom for the lord, upon the lord's eldest son becoming a *knight, and upon the marriage of the lord's eldest daughter.

feudalism. A term used to describe the political and economic system in European countries during the Middle Ages, by which land was held on condition of homage and service to a superior lord. The nobility held their estates in return for military service to the Crown; the peasantry farmed their holdings under the protection of a *lord of the manor in return for *boon work, customary payments, and military service when required. In England the system broke down during the 13th and 14th centuries as services and obligations were commuted to money payments. Historians use the term 'bastard feudalism' to describe conditions in the later Middle Ages, when the system was breaking down. Feudal tenure was abolished in 1660, long after it had ceased to operate in practice.

fief. A hereditary estate held under a superior lord on condition of homage and service.

field books. The notebooks used 'in the field' by surveyors.

Fiennes, Celia (1662–1741). Her account of journeys undertaken at various times in the later 17th and early 18th centuries is a marvellously rich source of observations on society and the developing economy of late Stuart England.

Fifth Monarchy men. A millenarian *Puritan group that emerged during the Civil War. Their name was taken from the Book of Daniel, which foretold the rise and fall of four successive monarchies, to be followed by a fifth monarchy which would last for ever. This fifth monarchy was identified as the rule of Jesus Christ and his saints. The group was influential in the Barebones Parliament of 1653. After the *Restoration they attempted a rising in London, in January 1661, which failed. They quickly declined as a creditable movement thereafter.

final concord. An agreement drawn up at the conclusion of a fictitious suit, whose true purpose was to convey real estate.

Fine Rolls. Records of payments to the Crown for writs, grants, privileges, and pardons, of appointments of royal officials, and of orders sent to sheriffs, etc. The rolls are kept at the *Public Record Office. A published *calendar covers the period 1272–1509.

fines and rents. In the late medieval and early modern period tenants who held their property by *copyhold or *leasehold paid an entry fine upon acquiring a holding through *inheritance or purchase. This fine was a lump sum, which might be either 'certain', that is, fixed by custom, or 'arbitrary', that is, open to negotiation.

Copyholders and leaseholders also paid low annual rents, which were known variously as rents of assize, quit rents, reserved rents, or by some other local name.

During the second half of the 17th and the 18th centuries the system of levying fines on the grant or renewal of leases was gradually abandoned in favour of *rack rents. The fine system declined slowly, but survived on ecclesiastical property well into the 19th century.

fire insurance. The *Guildhall Library, London, has a collection of fire insurance records. These start with the Sun Fire Office and the Hand in Hand in 1710, the London Assurance from 1720, and the Royal Exchange Assurance (whose earlier records are lost) from 1773. The registers note the address of the insured property, the owner's name and occupation, and any transfer of ownership, and give a brief description of the structure, including its building materials.

firebote. The right to remove wood from the *commons for fuel.

First Fruits and Tenths, Court of. The profits of a *benefice during the first year after the death or resignation of an incumbent, originally made to the see of Rome, were confiscated by Henry VIII in 1523, together with a payment equal to one-tenth of the value of each benefice. A new court to administer this revenue was set up in 1541, but was abolished in 1553 upon the accession of Mary Tudor. The records of the court are kept at the *Public Record Office under E 331–47.

fish. In the Middle Ages fish formed a major part of everyone's *diet, especially during Lent and other religious festivals. The mid-16th-century household accounts of Sir George Vernon of Haddon Hall (Derbyshire) show that even in the most land-locked parts of Britain it was possible to obtain a regular supply of both salted and fresh fish from local *fairs and markets. The 18th and 19th centuries saw a great development of deep-sea fishing and the rise of large fishing-ports.

fish ponds. In the Middle Ages fish ponds were a normal feature of both lay and ecclesiastical estates, for the consumption of red-blooded meat was forbidden during Lent and at other times.

Fitz-. From the French *fils*, meaning 'son of'. It was not associated with illegitimacy until Charles II named his bastards in this manner.

Fitzherbert, Master. The author of the earliest English book of advice on farming, published as Revd W. W. Skeat (ed.), *The Book of Husbandry, by Master Fitzherbert, 1534* (1882).

Five Boroughs. The Five Boroughs of the *Danelaw were Nottingham, Derby, Leicester, Lincoln, and Stamford.

Five Mile Act. An Act of 1665 which forbade clergymen who had been ejected from their livings for refusing to subscribe to the Act of Uniformity (1662) from dwelling within five miles of a corporate town.

flail. A hand-tool for threshing corn, consisting of two wooden rods tied together by leather thongs.

flatt. A term used in the north of England for a *furlong, a block of *strips in an *open-field.

flax. In the 17th to 19th centuries flax was grown as a specialist crop in certain areas. A parliamentary bounty had encouraged its growth during the *Napoleonic wars.

fleet. An Old English word for a channel or stream, especially along the south-eastern and southern coast.

Flemish immigrants came from Flanders and Brabant and spoke a Dutch dialect. Flemish weavers were encouraged to settle in England by Edward III (1327–77). A second wave came to escape the Spanish occupation of the Low Countries in Elizabeth I's reign.

florin. A gold coin issued by Edward III (1327–77), worth 6 shillings or 6s. 8d.; the name given to various continental gold coins; a silver coin, first minted in 1849, worth two shillings.

foldcourse. The practice of grazing sheep in a restricted area so that manure could be collected to improve arable land.

folio. A leaf of parchment or paper, either loose or in a book, numbered only at the front.

folly. A general term for the romantic structures built in Classical, *Gothick, or Chinese styles in landscaped *parks during the 18th and 19th centuries. Some were eye-catchers, others memorials or imitations of famous structures elsewhere. Few served any practical purpose other than that of a summerhouse.

fonts. The earliest surviving fonts are late-Saxon and Norman. From 1236 covers were compulsory; some later covers were very elaborate canopies.

football. Although it was an ancient pastime, the game had few rules before the Victorian period.

foreign church. A church established in a town by a group of foreign immigrants in the 16th and 17th centuries.

foreshore. That part of a beach that stretches between the medium low-tide mark and the medium high tide mark and which belongs to the Crown or its grantee.

forest. The popular sense of the word is of a dense wood, but medieval forests were never more than partly wooded and often covered moors, heaths, and fens rather than woodland. The term 'forest' had a legal meaning; it referred to an area that was under forest law (with its own courts and officials, known as verderers), in which deer and other game could be killed only by the forest owner, usually the king. Many forests were 'disafforested' in the first half of the 17th century. The Forestry Commission was established in 1919 to restore the losses to native woodlands which occurred during the First World War.

forestalling. The practice of trading before the ringing of the market bell in order to avoid tolls.

forfeiture. The Crown received the possessions of those who were convicted of high treason. The possessions of other offenders who were sentenced to death or banishment went to the Crown for one year and then to the *lord of the manor.

forge. The term includes a variety of structures from a blacksmith's shop to a large ironworks.

forks were introduced from Italy early in the 17th century, but remained rare until Charles II popularized their use.

forts, coastal. In 1539 Henry VIII began a programme of coastal defences involving the construction of artillery forts and the strengthening of urban fortifications from the Thames estuary to Cornwall. Fear of Scottish attacks led to similar defensive work at Hull and Tynemouth. Similar considerations in Elizabeth's reign led to further strengthening of south-coast forts and to major defences at Portsmouth and Berwick.

foss(e). From the Latin *fossa*, meaning a ditch or trench. The word is usually found in connection with *castles or other fortifications.

foundlings. Abandoned infants, mostly illegitimate, upon being found became the responsibility of the parish overseers of the *poor. In 1741 Thomas Coram opened his Foundling Hospital in Guildford Street, London. The records are kept at the Greater London *Record Office.

fox hunting. The first reference to fox hunting is from 1539; hare coursing dates from about the same time. Fox hunting did not become a popular organized sport until the 17th and 18th centuries.

Foxe's Book of Martyrs. The popular title of John Foxe's *History of the Acts and Monuments of the Church*, first published in Latin in 1554, and translated into English in 1563.

framework knitting. Stockings, socks, shirts, gloves, handkerchiefs, underwear, and other fabrics were knitted by men, women, and children in their own home, or in a small workshop, in the towns and villages of Nottinghamshire, Leicestershire, and south Derbyshire from the second half of the 17th century to the beginning of the 20th century. *Parish registers (which often used the abbreviation FWK) show that in many midland villages for much of the 19th century the majority of the inhabitants were working at this trade.

franchise court. A *liberty exempt from normal jurisdiction.

frankalmoign. Land granted to an ecclesiastical body by a lay person in return for prayers for the souls of the donor, his family, and his descendants.

franklin. A medieval term for a substantial *freeholder below the rank of gentleman.

frankpledge. A system of suretyship and mutual responsibility for bringing criminals to justice. In much of medieval England every householder formed part of a group of 10 or 12 known as a *tithing, who were responsible for the good behaviour of one another and for bringing members to a manorial *court leet to face charges. From time to time a manorial court would hold a view of frankpledge to make sure that every man and boy was included. By the end of the Middle Ages the term 'frankpledge' was synonymous with court leet.

free miner. A miner born in the *hundred of St Briavels in the *Forest of Dean, who upon reaching the age of 21 has worked for a year and a day in a coal or iron-ore mine in the hundred and who is thus entitled to own up to three mines.

free warren. The sole right (granted by royal *charter to a *lord of the manor) to hunt certain beasts and fowls—the pheasant, partridge, hare, and rabbit—within a given area, such as a *chase. Many charters were granted between the late 12th and the early 14th centuries.

freebench. The custom on some manors whereby the widow of a *copyholder retained between a third and all (usually, in practice, a half or more) of her late husband's land until her death or until she remarried.

freehold. A tenurial status for property which was not subject to manorial customs, as were *copyhold or *leasehold. A freehold was originally held either in *knight service or in *socage.

freehold land societies were formed by the lower-middle and working classes in the 19th century to acquire plots of land on which to build good-quality houses.

freeman rolls. Admission to the freedom of a corporate city allowed a man to practise his trade and to vote at elections. Freedom was achieved either upon the completion of an *apprenticeship or through following a father's trade to adulthood. The names of freemen were registered annually on a series of rolls. These are now kept at local *record offices, and some have been published.

At their best, the registers note the date of admission, the name of the freeman, the name and occupation of his father, and (where the freedom has been obtained through the completion of an apprenticeship) the name and occupation of the master.

freemason. Originally, a mason who worked the best-quality freestone. A system of lodges was developed to suit the itinerant nature of the job. By the 17th century these lodges had ceased to have any connection with the craft, but had become fellowships acknowledging God as the Great Architect of the Universe. The United Grand Lodge of England (founded in 1717) has records of members' names, their lodge, and the date of entry.

French origin, families of. In the Middle Ages and early modern period France provided more immigrants to Britain than any other country. The chief landowners after the Norman Conquest were from Normandy and Brittany.

During the early 16th century French *iron-workers and *glass-makers introduced new technology into southern England. They were followed by Protestant (*Huguenot) refugees, who were persecuted in their home country from the 1560s onwards, culminating in the treacherous massacre on the eve of the feast of St Bartholomew in 1572. They were welcomed by the government for their craft skills. Most settled in towns, with about half going to London. Other Huguenots fled to England in the 17th century, particularly in the troubled times of the 1680s. A much smaller group of refugees were the landed families who fled the French Revolution, some of whom never returned.

friary. The various mendicant orders of friars were founded in the early 13th century. The men who joined the Dominicans (black friars), Franciscans (grey friars), or the Friars Minors (the 'little brothers' of Francis) were not originally attached to any particular house, but were free to move around preaching and evangelizing. Great emphasis was placed on sermons. About 100 friaries were founded by the early 14th century. Numbers had declined long before 1538, when all orders were dissolved in a single operation.

friendly societies. A few friendly societies were formed in the early 18th century, but most date from the late 18th or 19th centuries. Their heyday was during the Victorian and Edwardian era.

The main purpose of a friendly society was to act as a benefit club in times of sickness and death, but some societies built halls to provide social and educational facilities, and some lent money for *mortgages.

fruit. Fresh fruit was not grown on a commercial scale in Britain before the 16th century.

Fuller, Thomas (1608–61). Clergyman and antiquarian, best known as the author of *The History of the Worthies of England* (1662).

fulling mills. After a piece of cloth had been woven it was taken to a water-powered fulling mill, where wooden hammers would pound it with fuller's earth in order to scour and cleanse it. Fulling mills were known in northern England as walk mills and in the south-west as tuck mills.

funerary monuments. Stone or wooden figures representing a dead person were first placed in churches during the 12th century. From the 13th century onwards local lords were depicted in a reclining position clad in armour, often with their feet resting on some mythical animal.

A lord or knight is sometimes shown lying next to his wife with representations of his children (including dead ones) on the sides or at the base of the tomb.

From the 16th century these figures are often portraits. The design of tombs containing effigies in the Elizabethan and Stuart era was influenced by the Italian Renaissance. From the later 17th century full figures in an upright position or busts in a classical style were favoured. The Victorian fashion was for large monuments in a variety of styles.

funfairs. The towns led the way to converting the ancient annual livestock *fairs into pleasure fairs. By the 1820s and 1830s Easter and Whitsuntide funfairs were being held in, or close to, major centres of population. By the last quarter of the 19th century steam roundabouts and steam organs were an essential part of the attraction.

furlong. Originally, the length of a furrow in an *open-field, 220 yards. The term was also used for a block of *strips within an open-field. Such blocks were often sown with different crops from the rest of the field and were subject to piecemeal *enclosure.

furnaces. The charcoal blast-furnace was introduced into south-eastern England by French ironworkers. The first furnace was built at Newbridge, in Ashdown Forest, in 1496. The main expansion outside the Weald began in the 1580s. The earliest successful use of coke was at Coalbrookdale in 1709.

Galilee. A vestibule at the western end of a cathedral or monastic church, used as a chapel for penitents.

gallery. 1. Elizabethan *prodigy-houses started the fashion for a long gallery on the top storey.
2. In the 17th and 18th centuries churches and chapels provided extra seats in upper galleries. In most Anglican churches these were removed in the *High Church movement of the 19th century.

galleting. From the French *galet*, meaning a pebble. The practice of placing pebbles in the mortar of *vernacular buildings was common in parts of south-eastern England and East Anglia.

game laws. The strict preservation of game was a concern of land-owners from Norman times, but reached new peaks from the second half of the 17th century. In 1671 the property qualification for taking game was set at £100 a year for *freeholders and £150 for *leaseholders; this was enforced by a £5 fine or three months' imprisonment. After 1707 the possessors of illegally acquired game or of 'engines' to kill game faced the same penalty. An Act of 1770 threatened with a year's imprisonment those who took game at night. The laws became increasingly severe in the first half of the 19th century. In 1800 a single JP was empowered to punish poachers with imprisonment and hard labour; in 1803 armed resistance to arrest was punishable by death; and in 1817 armed poachers caught at night were transported for seven years. In the years after the *Napoleonic wars committals for poaching increased substantially. At the same time, the use of spring-guns to catch poachers was at its peak. The ferocity of the game laws was to some extent counter-productive, however, for some judges and juries preferred to dismiss charges rather than impose harsh penalties.

gangs, labour. A system in the eastern counties of England whereby gangs of people, especially women and children, under the direction of a gang master, moved from farm to farm to meet seasonal demands for labour. About half the work-force consisted of children aged 7–13. The *Report on the Employment of Women and Children in Agriculture* (1843) provides a great deal of information on the hardships endured under this system.

gaol delivery. A Commission of Gaol Delivery ordered *sheriffs to bring prisoners awaiting trial before specially appointed justices. The records are kept at the *Public Record Office under JUST.ITIN. 3 and PL. 25.

gardens. By the Middle Ages both kitchen and flower gardens were prominent features of towns and villages, monasteries, *castles, and manor houses. The Italian Renaissance inspired the design of gardens as an art form and introduced the idea of botanic gardens. The Elizabethans favoured formal gardens with symmetrical and knot patterns.

After the *Restoration French and Dutch garden designs were widely used for country and town houses. They made much use of water in the form of fountains, canals, and ornamental pools and of classical statuary, and introduced the idea of segregated garden areas. Most of these gardens were swept away in the landscape gardening movement of the 18th century.

Eighteenth-century gardens were also influenced by Chinese designs and by a delight in the *Gothick and the Picturesque. The 19th century saw a huge influx of new trees and shrubs from all over the world. The great walled gardens were brought to a high state of cultivation and all styles of garden layout were attempted, including the reintroduced formal Italianate garden and gardens to show off plants.

garderobe. A latrine in a medieval *castle or house, placed within the thickness of a wall, with a shaft descending to a cesspool or *moat.

Garter King of Arms. The principal King of Arms at the College of *Arms.

garth. From an Old Norse word meaning an enclosure. In northern England garth is still used as a field name, but its derivative 'yard' has a more general meaning of a small, enclosed space, as in *churchyard, courtyard, farmyard. 'Garden' is also derived from the same word.

gas. Gas extracted from coal was first used in Britain in 1792.

gate / yat. In areas of Scandinavian settlement in northern and eastern England 'gate' meant a road.

gatehouses. The gatehouses of medieval *castles were strong defensive structures. As the need for defence receded, gatehouses became increasingly decorative.

gavelkind. A system of *inheritance, particularly in Kent, and anciently in Wales, whereby estates were equally divided amongst sons, and in the absence of male heirs equally amongst daughters. The system was abolished in Wales by Henry VIII, elsewhere not until 1925.

geld. A tax calculated upon the holding of land.

Genealogists, Society of. Founded in 1911, the Society is based at 14 Charterhouse Buildings, London EC1M 7BA, where it has the largest specialized library of books, journals, manuscripts, indexes, and micro- fiche and computer databases on genealogy. The Society holds regular lecture meetings and publishes guides to records, as well as the quarterly *Genealogists' Magazine*, and a quarterly newsletter *Computers in Genealogy*.

General Register Office. Currently at *St Catherine's House, London, where indexes of birth, marriage, and death certificates from 1 July 1837 to the present day may be consulted.

General Views of Agriculture. The series of county reports published by the *Board of Agriculture from the 1790s to the early 19th century.

generation. An imprecise reckoning, roughly 30–40 years.

Gentleman's Magazine. Published from 1731 until 1868, this monthly magazine is a mine of miscellaneous information. Particularly valuable are the topographical descriptions of provincial towns and villages sent in by readers. These describe local antiquities and give a contemporary account that is now of historical interest. G. L. Gomme edited this material for a series of county volumes published about the turn of the 20th century. Two general indexes covering the period 1731–1810, an index of marriages 1731–68, and indexes of obituaries and biographies 1731–80, have also been published.

gentry. Although the word 'gentil' originally meant 'noble', by the 15th century a gentleman was one who was superior to a *yeoman but inferior in status to a *baron. Between 1530 and 1688 the heralds attempted to restrict the use of the term gentleman to those who could prove a legal claim to a coat of *arms, but they were unable to enforce their decisions, for in popular usage the term was applied loosely to one who did not work with his hands.

geological surface maps. The Institute of Geological Sciences has pub- lished a series of maps of drift geology, based on the *Ordnance Survey 1:63,360 (one inch to one mile) maps for practically the whole of Great Britain, but many of the early ones are no longer in print. This series is being replaced by a new one using the scale of 1:50,000. Sheets are also available on larger scales for much of Great Britain. Other series show the solid geology of Britain.

German immigrants. London was the destination of 16th- and 17th- century German immigrants who were *Protestant refugees. With the accession of the Hanoverian kings more German merchants and crafts- men were attracted to London. In the 19th century German business- men were also attracted to the industrial towns.

gibbet. The post from which the corpse of an executed criminal was hung in chains at prominent crossroads to deter others.

Gilbertines. The only religious order to originate in England. Founded in 1131 by Gilbert, the parish priest of Sempringham (Lincolnshire), 12 monasteries were soon established in his native and neighbouring counties. Ten of these monasteries were double houses for *canons and *nuns. The order had a reputation for high standards and for its charity, but its membership declined rapidly in the 14th century. It was extinguished at the *dissolution of the monasteries.

Gilbert's Act (1782). A reform of the *Poor Law which restricted indoor relief to the impotent poor and allowed the able-bodied to obtain employment outside the *workhouse. Children under seven years were not separated from their parents, orphans were boarded out, the use of the pauper's badge was abandoned, and paupers were sent to workhouses no more than 10 miles away. Inspectors were appointed to enforce these laws and the building of workhouses by unions of parishes was encouraged.

gin. 1. A spirit distilled from malted grain and originally flavoured by juniper berries. The name is contracted from 'geneva' (from the Dutch for juniper).
    2. A short form for 'engine', used for example in horse-gin.

glass. Glass was used sparingly in most domestic buildings in the Middle Ages because of the cost, but it was used on a lavish scale in major secular and ecclesiastical buildings. Until the second half of the 16th century better quality glass was imported from the Continent.
    After 1610 *coal rapidly replaced wood as the fuel in the manufacturing process, and so the industry was re-sited in the coalfields. The great conical furnaces which became typical of the industry were introduced around 1700. By the mid-19th century bottle, plate, crown, and flint glass were being produced on a large scale in Lancashire.

gleaning. The practice of collecting stray ears of corn and straw from a field after reaping was an ancient custom. It was popularly supposed that a landowner had no right to prevent the practice. In numerous court cases in the 19th century farmers tried to restrict gleaners, or at least to enforce regulations.

glebe. Land farmed (or leased out) by a *parish priest. Over the centuries parishioners bequeathed small portions of land, e.g. a *strip or two in an *open-field, to their minister, though the major part of his income came from the *tithes. The amount of glebe land varied considerably from parish to parish.

An *ecclesiastical visitation commonly produced a glebe terrier which gave an account of the *parsonage and the land that belonged to the incumbent. These terriers are preserved amongst diocesan records or in parish records deposited at county *record offices.

Glorious Revolution. The name given to the events of 1688, whereby James II, the Roman Catholic king, was deposed and William of Orange, the Protestant ruler of the Netherlands, became joint ruler of England, Scotland, Ireland, and Wales with his wife Mary, the daughter of the deposed king. The revolution brought constitutional government and toleration for *Nonconformists.

gloss. A marginal commentary on a text.

godparent. A family friend who sponsors a child at baptism. The ancient practice was for a child to have two godparents of his or her own sex and one of the other. Godparents had an important influence on choosing the name of their godchild.

Goodwife. A form of address in the Middle Ages and early modern period for the mistress of a house, below the status of a gentlewoman. The term is sometimes found in records as a prefix to a *surname.

gore. A triangular piece of land.

gorse was collected from the *commons and wastes for fuel.

Gospel Oak / Gospel Thorn. A place-name on a parish boundary where a passage from the Gospels was read at the annual *Rogationtide *perambulation or 'beating of the bounds'.

Gothic. Originally a term of abuse coined in the 17th century by admirers of classical architecture, who compared the replacement of the *Romanesque style from the late 12th century onwards with the destruction of ancient Rome by the Goths. The Gothic style was introduced from France for monasteries and cathedrals and was used subsequently for parish churches and secular buildings. Thomas Rickman divided the Gothic ecclesiastical styles into *Early English, *Decorated, and *Perpendicular. The term 'Tudor Court Gothic' is used to describe Hampton Court and other royal palaces and the Elizabethan *prodigy-houses which were influenced by them. The Gothic style never completely disappeared, though historians speak of 'Gothic survivals' in the 18th century and the 'Gothic revival' of the 19th century.

Gothick. The term is used for architectural features in buildings erected in the 18th and early 19th centuries which were loosely based on medieval *Gothic designs. Such buildings were often romanticized or given a fake air of antiquity. In literature the term is used to describe novels with improbable dramatic plots set in ruined *abbeys, decayed manor houses, etc.

Gough, Richard. 1. (1735–1809). Antiquarian and collector. His vast collection of antiquarian material—maps, plans, prints, drawings, notes, coins, and medals—is kept in the *Bodleian Library and other repositories. He is best known as the author of *British Topography*, 2 vols. (1768, 2nd edn. 1780), and of *Sepulchral Monuments of Great Britain* (1768), and as the editor of *Camden's *Britannia* (1789 and 1806).

2. of Myddle (1635–1723). The author of *Antiquityes and Memoyres of the Parish of Myddle* (1700), and *Observations concerning the Seates in Myddle and the Familyes to which They Belong* (1701–2), a remarkable account of all the families of this Shropshire parish.

grange. Monasteries were often given land which was situated too far away to be worked from the monastery itself. The *Cistercians therefore developed a system of granges, which were outlying farms worked by *lay brothers and hired labourers. Many farmhouses are built on the sites of former granges, but 'grange' became a popular choice of name for a Victorian house with no monastic connections.

grave, greave. A person chosen by the tenants of a *manor to act as their representative in dealings with the lord.

gravestones. The earliest inscribed gravestones are those placed within a church by the wealthier inhabitants during the 16th century. Graves in parish *churchyards were originally unmarked, or were perhaps marked by an impermanent wooden cross. During the 17th century the *yeomen and better-off *husbandmen and craftsmen began to erect tombstones in churchyards.

great chambers were a feature of the *prodigy-houses and other substantial halls and *manor houses of the Elizabethan and Jacobean period. They acted as upper-floor retiring or withdrawing rooms for the owner and his family and guests away from the communal life of the open hall below.

Great Exhibition. Held in 1851 at the Crystal Palace, London to display the manufactured goods of industrial Britain.

Great Rebuilding. In a pioneering aricle, 'The Rebuilding of Rural England, 1570–1640', *Past and Present*, 4 (1953), W. G. Hoskins argued that agricultural prices increased so much during the Elizabethan and early Stuart period that 'no yeoman with his wits about him could fail to accumulate money savings on a scale hitherto unknown' and that this led to much rebuilding of houses and a great increase in the standards of domestic comfort. The essay remains a useful starting-point in the study of *vernacular architecture, but the ideas have now been considerably refined.

Great Seal. A seal depicting the sovereign on horseback on one side and enthroned on the other, which was used to authenticate important documents issued by the Crown.

green. A large number of medieval villages had a small green, often in a central position, perhaps with a duck pond. These greens were used for recreation and some rough grazing. Many disappeared through *encroachments or at the time of parliamentary *enclosure. In some villages the central green is a larger, planned space of regular shape; they originated in the Anglo-Scandinavian or Norman periods, occasionally later. Greens are also the focal points of hamlets in areas of scattered settlement. Many place-names in different parts of England incorporate the 'green' element.

green lane. A popular term for unmetalled tracks in the countryside.

green men. The carved figures known as green men are of two types. Some are doleful or grimacing faces peering through foliage, others have leaves sprouting from their mouths and ears, or even from their nostrils or eyes. They are often discovered in the stonework or woodwork of medieval churches throughout Europe, especially as roof bosses. They may have been demons or pagan symbols of spring that have been adapted to Christian usage as representations of the festival of Easter, or various other fancies that had a remarkably tenacious hold on popular consciousness.

Greenwood, Charles and James. Publishers of a beautifully engraved *Atlas of the Counties of England* (1834), mostly from their own surveys. They also published large-scale maps of 33 English counties.

Gregorian calendar. Introduced in Catholic Europe in 1582 by Pope Gregory XIII to replace the old *Julian calendar. Britain did not change until 1752, when 11 days between 3 and 14 September were lost to bring the country into line. At the same time the start of the official year was changed from 25 March to 1 January.

gressom. A fine paid to a *feudal lord upon entering a property.

Grim. One of the names of the Anglo-Saxon god Woden.

grisaille. Silvery-grey *stained glass used from the 12th to the 14th centuries.

groat. A coin in circulation between 1351 and 1662, worth four pence.

grottoes. Architectural features at the edges of lakes in 18th-century landscaped *parks, imitating water-filled limestone caves and including nymphs, dryads, and often the figure of Neptune.

grouse. Although grouse and other game birds had been shot on the wing in earlier times it was only after parliamentary *enclosure divided the *commons and wastes in the late 18th and early 19th centuries that large tracts of moorland came under private ownership. Aristocratic and other owners often preferred to use these moors for shooting rather than for growing timber.

guardians. The *Poor Law Amendment Act (1834) took away parish responsibility for the poor and created instead Boards of Guardians for the management of poor relief through unions of parishes. These guardians were elected by local landowners and rate-payers. Their records are kept at local *record offices and include *workhouse admission registers, accounts, day books, minute books, general ledgers, and correspondence. The Local Government Board Act (1871) created a central government department with responsibility for poor relief and public health. In 1919 its functions were taken over by the newly created Ministry of Health.

guide stoops. Inscribed waymarkers erected by order of *Justices of the Peace under the terms of an Act of 1697.

guild. The term 'guild' or 'gild' was used loosely in the Middle Ages to mean any kind of urban religious fraternity or craft organization. Guilds originated in the 12th century as supportive religious societies, offering mutual charitable help and composed of men and women working at a common craft, and living at close quarters in a single parish. They came to be hierarchical trade organizations, with power to control entry into a trade through *apprenticeship and the enrolling of freemen, and power to insist on common standards for goods through the appointment of searchers. They were also mutual protection societies which provided for the poor, sick, and needy, and social organizations devoted to feasting and ornate processions, especially at *Corpus Christi. They obtained their authority through the grant of a royal charter. In small towns the guild fulfilled the role of the *borough until a charter of incorporation was obtained, often in the post-*Reformation period.

Guildhall Library and Record Office. Located in central London by the Guildhall, and open to the public since 1873, the Library is a major source of printed historical and genealogical material. It is particularly strong in all aspects of the history of London. The Record Office houses the archives of the City of London, including parochial records, ward *rate books, the records of the City's *livery companies, and the archives of various *fire insurance companies, individual families, estates, businesses, societies, schools, and other institutions, including the Diocese of London and St Paul's Cathedral. The records range in date from the 11th century to the present day. The Print Room has an unrivalled collection of prints and drawings relating to London and south-east England.

guinea. A coin introduced in 1663 and named after the Guinea Coast of Africa, from where gold was obtained for minting. Initially valued at 20 shillings, from 1717 it was valued at 21 shillings. The last guineas were struck in 1813, but the fashion for charging fees in guineas continued until the introduction of decimal coinage.

gunpowder was first used in England during the late 13th or 14th centuries. Mills worked by water power were in use by the 16th century.

Guppy, H. B. Author of a pioneering work, *Homes of Family Names in Great Britain* (1890), which drew attention to the striking geographical distributions of British *surnames.

gypsies. The name originates from the mistaken belief that the first groups to arrive in England in the 16th century came from Egypt. The Romany language shares some characteristics with Sanskrit and later Indian languages and contains some loan words that suggest a migration via the Middle East into south-eastern Europe. References to their being moved on can be found in *parish and *quarter sessions records.

ha-ha. A landscape feature introduced in the early 18th century, which remained popular until Victorian times. The desire to have an uninterrupted view from a house was balanced by the need to keep livestock out. This was achieved by a sunken ditch supported by a wall that did not rise above ground level. The origin of the term is uncertain.

habeas corpus. A writ requiring the bringing of a person under arrest before a court to ensure a legal hearing. This ancient right, which predates *Magna Carta, was sometimes abused before it was guaranteed by the Act of 1679.

hafod. A Welsh upland pasture, grazed in summer.

hair powder duty. A duty payable between 1795 and 1798.

half-baptized. Term describing someone baptized at a private christening, as distinct from a service in a church.

hall. In the Middle Ages and later the largest room in both great and small houses was the *open hall. In large houses this served as the communal dining room and fulfilled many other purposes. It was gradually replaced in the later 17th and 18th centuries by a large reception hall. In smaller houses during the later Middle Ages and the early modern period the hall was chambered over and a *parlour and service rooms were provided at either side, to form a characteristic three-unit plan. The central room in such buildings retained the name hall, but was known in the north of England as the house, fire-house, or house-body. As the internal designs of houses have changed since the 18th century, the term 'hall' has been relegated to mean the small entrance space.

hallmark. A mark used at Goldsmiths Hall, London, and by provincial assay offices to approve the standard of the gold and silver articles on which it is engraved.

hammer pond. The mill pond of an iron *forge, particularly in the Weald, where they flourished during the 16th and 17th centuries.

Hansard. The official record of the proceedings of the two houses of Parliament since 1803.

harden cloth. Coarse, hard cloth, often of *hemp, recorded in probate *inventories for use on beds and tables.

hardwareman. A term used in the early modern period for an iron-monger or a *chapman specializing in iron wares.

Harleian Society. Founded in 1869 to publish records relating to *her-aldry and genealogy, notably the pedigrees approved at the Heralds' Visitations of various English counties, and many of the *parish regis-ters of London.

Harrison, William (1534–93). Clergyman and antiquarian. His *Descrip-tion of England* (1577) was one of the earliest topographical descriptions of the country.

harrow. A heavy frame with iron teeth for breaking down the clods of freshly ploughed land and for removing weeds.

hatchment. Derived from the heraldic term 'achievement', a display of the arms and other heraldic insignia upon a person's death. The dia-mond-shaped hatchments, painted on wood or canvas, which can be found in churches, date from the mid-17th to the mid-19th centuries.

haybote. The right to collect wood from the *commons in order to erect and maintain fences.

hayward. The manorial officer responsible for hedges and fences and for preventing cattle from straying.

headborough. Originally, the man at the head of a *tithing or *frank-pledge. The term came to be applied in some places to the *constable or his deputy.

headland. The untilled land at the end of a block of *strips in an *open-field, which allowed access and room for the plough-team to turn.

hearth penny. A payment made by the owners of a house with a fireplace to the minister of a parish on *Maundy Thursday; also known as a smoke penny.

hearth tax. The tax was levied twice a year—at *Lady Day and *Michaelmas—between 1662 and 1688. The tax returns are kept at the *Public Record Office under E 179; some counties have copies of indi-vidual returns in local *record offices.

Each hearth was taxed at the rate of 2 shillings a year, payable in two instalments. Those people who were too poor to be rated to church and poor rates, or who occupied premises worth less than 20 shillings a year, or who possessed property worth not above £10 were exempt, as were charitable institutions such as *hospitals and minor *almshouses. Some lists simply note 'Poor' in the margins, others list the poor at the end. In other cases, however, the poor are not recorded or the lists are incomplete. The returns for each county are arranged by *hundreds or *wapentakes, which in turn are divided into townships. The name of each householder was recorded, together with the number of hearths that he or she possessed. The hearth tax returns usually provide the best base for assessing population levels before the first *census of England and Wales in 1801. The returns are of great interest to students of vernacular architecture as they indicate the complete range of houses at a fixed point in time. They also provide information about individual houses. In Scotland a hearth tax was levied on several occasions between 1691 and 1695. The surviving returns are kept at the *Scottish Record Office under E 69. They list householders and are arranged by counties and parishes. In Ireland the hearth tax was introduced in 1662 and continued to be levied until the Act of Union (1800). The original rolls were destroyed by fire in 1922, but copies exist for some areas.

hedges. A method of dating hedges was suggested by Max Hooper. The number of species of trees and shrubs in a sample 30-yard length of hedgerow was said to increase with the age of the hedge, at the rate of one new shrub every 100 years. This dating method has been much criticized; general opinion now holds that a large number of shrubs does indeed indicate an ancient hedge (except where there has been a conscious effort to plant several species) but that the date cannot be estimated with any degree of accuracy.

heir. One who has inherited a title or property. An *heir apparent* is one whose right to succeed is inalienable; an *heir presumptive* is one who does not have inalienable rights.

hemp. An industrial crop. It requires a rich alluvial soil, so it was grown particularly in the fens and along rivers.

henge. A modern term for circular monuments of the *Neolithic period and early *Bronze Age.

Heptarchy. The seven separate kingdoms of *Anglo-Saxon England: *Wessex, Sussex, Kent, Essex, *East Anglia, *Mercia, and *Northumbria.

heraldry. The origins of heraldry are obscure but can be dated to the second quarter of the 12th century. The rules and terminology of heraldry were laid down during the 13th century. The Heralds were incorporated as a College of *Arms by Richard III in 1484. Their county surveys—known as Heralds' Visitations—began in 1530 and continued until the *Glorious Revolution of 1688. Many of the records of county visitations have been published by the *Harleian Society or by county record societies.

hereditament. Anything that can be inherited. The term is commonly used in *deeds to include anything not specifically mentioned.

heriot. A payment (often the best beast) from an incoming tenant to the *lord of the manor.

heritor. A Scottish term for the landowners in each *parish, who until 1845 were responsible for the local poor and until 1925 for the maintenance of the church, *manse, and school. Valuations made of parishes (mainly in the 19th century), known as heritors' records, are kept at the *Scottish Record Office.

herringbone. A distinctive pattern of courses of *rubble stone, used by masons in the late Saxon and early Norman period in the erection of churches and *castles.

hide. An area of land, varying according to the quality of the soil and the nature of the terrain, which a team of eight oxen could plough in a year, sufficient to support a family. It normally covered about 120 *acres. The hide became a unit of tax assessment in southern England and was used as such in the *Domesday Book. Its equivalent in the *Danelaw was the *carucate.

High Church movement. A section of the *Church of England emphasizing the importance of sacraments, the apostolic succession, and use of ritual. Its prominence in early Victorian times led to profound and lasting changes to the physical appearance of churches and the arrangements for worship.

High Commission, Court of. The highest *ecclesiastical court in England from 1570 to 1641 and from 1686 to 1689. The records of the Province of Canterbury are kept at the *Public Record Office under SP, those for the Province of York at the *Borthwick Institute of Historical Research, York.

High Court of Justiciary. The supreme criminal court in Scotland.

High Farming. A phrase coined in the 1840s described the epoch of prosperity between 1837 and 1873 as the Age of High Farming. 'High' was used in the sense of 'excellent' or 'superior', but it was a complex expression meaning different things to different users. It included 'high feeding' as well as increased cereal production.

High Sheriff. By the 17th century the ceremonial duties of the *sheriff's office were performed by a high sheriff, while the administrative tasks were undertaken by an under-sheriff.

Highland zone. Sir Cyril Fox applied the concept of a Highland zone and *Lowland zone, long used by geographers, to the study of prehistory. The concept was used to good effect by W. G. Hoskins in his studies of the English landscape. The frontier of the two zones in England is drawn from the mouth of the Tees in the north-east to the mouth of the Exe in the south-west.

highways, overseers of. An Act of 1555 required the annual appointment at Easter of a 'Surveyor of the Highways' for each *parish or *township. Like the overseer of the *poor, this officer was empowered to raise local rates; his accounts had to be approved at the end of his term of office, and he was answerable to the *Justices of the Peace. A particular responsibility was the supervision of *statute labour, whereby local people were called upon to maintain their roads. The office of overseer was unpaid and was usually filled by rotation. Accounts of the overseers of the highways do not survive in the same bulk as do the accounts of the overseers of the poor; most date from the late 18th and early 19th centuries. In 1835 a new system was introduced whereby JPs appointed paid surveyors for groups of parishes.

hiring fairs. Martinmas hiring fairs were known as 'statute' or 'stattis' fairs because an Act of Parliament of 1677 endorsed the yearly bonds that were made at that time. Contracts between farmers and their servants expired on Old Martinmas Day (23 November), the end of the farming year. The practice of holding such fairs survived in market towns until Edwardian times, but rarely beyond the First World War.

Historical Association. The association which promotes the teaching of history in schools and universities, through conferences, lectures, its quarterly journal, *Teaching History*, and its Short Guides to Records series. Its headquarters is at 59A Kensington Park Road, London SE11 4JH.

Historical Manuscripts, Royal Commission on. This permanent body was first appointed in 1869 to locate and make accessible records in private ownership. In the following year it began to publish reports on the most important collections in the British Isles. In 1945 it set up the *National Register of Archives to collate information about historical manuscripts and to make this available to researchers. In 1959 a new Royal Warrant revised and enlarged the Commission's powers and made it the United Kingdom's central advisory body on all matters concerning the location, preservation, and use of historical manuscripts and archives outside the public records.

Historical Monuments, Royal Commission on. The Commission has been surveying ancient and historical monuments since the beginning of the 20th century. Separate branches deal with England, Wales, Scotland, and Northern Ireland. In 1994 the RCHM (England) completed a move to the converted premises of the Great Western Railway's General Office in Kemble Drive, Swindon SN2 2GZ. These premises house the National Monuments Record Centre (NMR), which combines the National Archaeological Record, the National Buildings Record, and the National Library of Air Photographs.

The Commission has a number of regional offices, which are responsible for surveying and for publishing complete inventories of earthworks and monuments from prehistoric times up to the year 1850, county by county.

History Workshop. Based at Ruskin College, Oxford, the History Workshop are a group of historians whose principal concern is the history of working-class men and women from the 18th century onwards.

Hocktide. The second Monday and Tuesday after Easter, when church fund-raising activities took the form of binding people with ropes until they had paid a ransom for their release. The custom originated in the 15th century and soon became widespread before its demise at the *Reformation.

holding. A term for a farmer's landed property, as in smallholding.

Holinshed, Raphael (d. *c.*1580). Author of *The Chronicles of England, Scotland, and Ireland* (2 vols., 1577).

Hollar, Wenceslaus (1607–77). Bohemian engraver who is best known for his panoramic view of London from Bankside (1647).

holograph. A deed, letter, or document wholly written by the person under whose name it appears.

homagers. The twelve jurors of a manor *court.

homilies. Official sermons of the second half of the 16th century.

honour. A term used by the Normans for the large *lordships that were centred on *castles.

hops. The fruits of a climbing plant, used for flavouring beer. They were first grown in England for this purpose in the mid-16th century.

horse racing. The early Stuart kings made Newmarket famous by their patronage. The 18th century saw the laying out of courses and the building of grandstands in or near towns and the holding of small meetings in the countryside.

hospice (historical). A lodging for travellers, maintained by a religious order.

Hospitaller, Knights. The Knights of the Hospital of St John of Jerusalem were a military-religious order founded after the capture of Jerusalem from the Turks in the *Crusade of 1099. They provided accommodation and care for the sick, the poor, and pilgrims, and built and garrisoned castles against the Turks. They attracted substantial endowments of land which they administered from their headquarters at St John's Priory, Clerkenwell, London, and from about 50 'preceptories' in various parts of Britain.

hospitals and infirmaries. Medieval hospitals were charitable institutions founded by religious bodies, *guilds, *livery companies, and private individuals.

Most medieval hospitals were dissolved at the *Reformation. The numerous *almshouses and small hospitals of the early modern period were founded privately, often by a bequest made in a will. The 18th century saw a great growth in the provision of hospitals. By 1800 or shortly afterwards most large provincial towns had opened infirmaries and *dispensaries as a result of voluntary contributions. A striking development of the second half of the 19th century was the creation of infirmaries from the sick wards of *workhouses.

hotel. The first hotel in England was built in Exeter in 1768.

House of Commons Journals. Records of the proceedings of the House of Commons, including the receiving of petitions and the passage of bills. The journals do not summarize debates. The passage of bills through the House of Commons can be followed from the formal procedure and the presentation of petitions.

house of correction. In the early modern period *Justices of the Peace established houses of correction for those found guilty of offences at the *quarter sessions.

House of Lords Journals. Records of the proceedings of the House of Lords, including the receiving of petitions and the passage of bills. They give no clue to the tenor of debates. The Journals have been published from 1510. The passage of public and private bills can be followed from the indexes.

House of Lords Record Office. The collections in this office which are of most use to local and family historians are the original texts of public and private bills and Acts of Parliament and their associated petitions and papers. They cover such topics as *railways, *canals, *turnpike roads, *enclosure, *reservoirs, etc.

house platform. A feature of *deserted and shrunken villages, marking the slightly raised foundations of former houses.

housebote. The right to take wood from the *commons to repair houses.

household. Demographic historians have shown that the nuclear household of parents and children (including *apprentices and *domestic or *farm servants) was the norm from the Middle Ages to the 20th century. The majority of households contained fewer than five persons.

hoy. A small, rigged ship for conveying passengers and goods along a coast.

huckster. A hawker.

Hudson's Bay Company. Founded by English royal charter in 1670 with a grant of all the land within Hudson's Bay not already belonging to others and a monopoly of the fur trade there. In 1869 the Company ceded its lands to the Canadian government. Microfilm copies of its records are kept at the *Public Record Office, but permission to see them must be obtained from Hudson's Bay & Annings Ltd, 77 Main Street, Winnipeg, Manitoba R3C 2RI, Canada.

hue and cry. A parish responsibility, whereby victims of, or witnesses to, a *felony had to shout an alarm and all who heard this were obliged to pursue the felon.

Huguenot immigrants. The term Huguenot, denoting a French *Protestant of Calvinistic persuasion, is of disputed origin, but it was in use in France by 1560. After the Massacre of St Bartholomew in 1572 many Huguenots fled to Protestant countries such as England. English people tended to use the word Huguenot also to describe Walloon refugees who emigrated from the Low Countries to avoid Spanish control. French Protestants were granted religious freedom by the Edict of Nantes (1598), but this was revoked in 1685, provoking further emigration.

The Huguenots and Walloons settled principally in London and the towns of eastern and south-eastern England, notably Norwich, Canterbury, Sandwich, Maidstone, and Southampton. They made a significant contribution to the introduction of new craft skills. On arriving in England, a Huguenot refugee had to apply for *naturalization or *denization. The records of this process, and many other records, have been published by the Huguenot Society.

hundred. Hundreds were subdivisions of counties, from the 10th century onwards, in those parts of England that lay south of the *Danelaw. They had military, judicial, and administrative functions, some of which they retained well into the modern period.

Hundred Rolls (1279). The operation of local government through *hundreds was investigated at Edward I's command in 1274–5. As a result, in 1278 all holders of franchises, such as the right to hold courts or markets, or the right to hunt, were made to justify their claims at *Quo Warranto enquiries. The surviving records are not comprehensive; they were published in two volumes as *Rotuli Hundredorum* in 1812 and 1818.

Huntingdon Connexion, Countess of. Selina Hastings, Countess of Huntingdon (1707–91), financed the Calvinist branch of the *Methodist movement, led by George Whitefield, whom she appointed her chaplain in 1751. At the time of the *ecclesiastical census of 1851 the Connexion had over 100 chapels. Their registers are kept at the *Public Record Office.

husbandman. The old word for a farmer below the rank of *yeoman. A husbandman usually held his land by *copyhold or *leasehold tenure and may be regarded as the 'average farmer in his locality'. The words 'yeoman' and 'husbandman' were gradually replaced in the later 18th and 19th centuries by 'farmer'.

hydropath. Hydropathy was the name given to the treatment of illness by hot and cold water used both outwardly and inwardly.

ice houses. Introduced from France in the 17th century and much used on country estates until the invention of refrigerators, ice houses had a domed roof and were approached via a short tunnel. Ice was packed with straw in winter, kept as airtight as possible, and used for summer drinks and for preserving meat and vegetables.

illegitimacy. Illegitimate births are recorded in *parish registers by such comments as 'base', 'bastard', 'spurious', or a capital letter B, or by some Latin equivalent. Illegitimacy rates were not high during the early modern period: for most of the time illegitimate children accounted for no more than 1 or 2 per cent of baptisms. Illegitimacy rates were at their highest in the second quarter of the 19th century, when national population growth reached unprecedented levels. From 1837 the information provided by parish registers can be supplemented by that from the *civil registration of births. Illegitimacy rates reached a high point of 7 per cent, but then gradually declined to 4 per cent by the 1890s.

Imperial Gazetteer The six volumes of J. M. Wilson's *The Imperial Gazetteer of England and Wales* (1870) are a reliable source of statistical and other information for towns, *parishes, and rural *townships. They are noted for signalling, in parishes, whether land was 'much subdivided' or 'divided among a few'.

impropriation of parishes. The annexation of a *benefice, and thus of the great *tithes of a *parish, especially by a monastery or a *college, which would then appoint a *vicar to serve the parish. If the minister of a church is known as a vicar rather than a *rector, then it means that impropriation will have taken place during the Middle Ages.

improvement commissioners. In the 18th and early 19th centuries private Acts of Parliament established 'improvement' or 'street' commissioners in towns. These bodies used their powers of administration to perform many of the tasks of local government. Their records, which include minute books, *rate books, and building plans, should be sought in local *record offices.

incised slabs. Medieval slabs shaped like coffins and incised with crosses, and occasionally with human figures, laid into church floors as personal memorials.

inclined plane. A method of raising boats from one level of water to another on the smaller *canals of western England, either hydraulically or by *steam power or water wheels.

income tax. Introduced during the *Napoleonic wars. Returns for 1799–1816, giving the names of individual taxpayers on a parish basis, are kept in the *Public Record Office under E 182.

indenture. A formal agreement, so-called from the practice of separating two identical texts by cutting along an irregular line, to prevent forgery. Indentures were used for title *deeds and for contracts, e.g. with *domestic servants or *apprentices.

Independent Labour Party. Founded in 1893 in Bradford under the leadership of Keir Hardie.

Independents. The 17th-century *Nonconformists who rejected national organization in favour of loose affiliations of independent congregations. From the 18th century they were generally known by their alternative name of *Congregationalists.

India Office Library and records. The archives of the *East India Company and the India Office, from 1600 to 1947, are kept at Orbit House, Blackfriars Road, London SE1.

indictment books. The record of charges brought before the *Justices of the Peace at *quarter sessions. These are kept with the order books from the same sessions at county *record offices.

indulgence. A system begun at the time of the first *Crusade whereby repentant sinners who prayed for forgiveness and made a personal commitment were offered relief from suffering in purgatory.

infangentheof. The right of a manorial or borough *court to try and punish a thief arrested within its jurisdiction.

infant mortality. More than one-fifth of all children born in England during the reign of Elizabeth I, and about one-quarter of those born during the 17th century, died before the age of ten. Well over half of these deaths, and almost two-thirds of those in Elizabeth's reign, occurred during the child's first year.

Infant mortality remained high in Victorian England, at 150 per thousand live births, which is more than ten times the rate in the late 20th century. These crude national figures mask the differences between social groups and different countries. The Irish rate of infant mortality was about 40 per cent below that of the English, and the Scottish rate was 20 per cent below.

infield / outfield system. The infield (which was referred to variously as 'croftland', 'inbyland', and 'mucked land') was the inner circle of land around a settlement, which was farmed in common (in *strips) on a rotation that included a *fallow every third year. The infield received all the manure. The outfield lay in irregular patches beyond the settlement. It varied in size, according to local conditions, but was generally about three times as large as the infield. It was poorer in fertility and drainage. The outfield was also farmed in common, but less intensively. Parts would revert to natural grass and weeds for several years at a time to allow recovery.

inflation. The three greatest periods of inflation have been those of 1180–1220, when food prices doubled or trebled, the late 15th to the mid-17th centuries, when prices rose four- or fivefold, and that of the later 20th century, when prices rose tenfold between 1960 and 1990.

influenza. Virulent forms of influenza have been amongst the greatest killers in the past. The worst international outbreak of influenza ever recorded was that which killed millions of people immediately after the First World War.

Inghamites. A *Nonconformist sect founded in 1754 by Benjamin Ingham, after a break with the *Moravians.

ingle-nook. A seat built into the wall by the fireplace.

ings. Low-lying meadows and pastures, liable to floods.

inheritance customs. The inheritance customs of the British Isles have varied considerably from region to region and over time. The basic distinction between *primogeniture and *partible inheritance was blurred by customs which ensured that younger children obtained a share of the patrimony and which enabled women to protect their own property and the interests of children by a previous marriage through formal or informal marriage settlements.

inland revenue records. Housed at the *Public Record Office under IR.

inns. During the 17th century facilities were greatly increased. (See the *Carriers' Cosmographie* (1637) and the account of guest beds and stabling in towns and villages throughout England and Wales in 1686 (*Public Record Office, WO 3/48) and the lists of innkeepers and alehouse keepers licenced at the '*brewster sessions' by *Justices of the Peace.)

Inns of Court. Gray's Inn, Lincoln's Inn, and the Inner and Middle Temple are the surviving Inns of Court in London at which barristers-at-law have been trained since the Middle Ages. The admission books record the name and date of entry of a student, together with the name, status, and residence of his father.

inoculation against *smallpox was practised in the eastern Mediterranean and parts of Asia during the 17th century and was first reported in England in 1701.

Inquisition of the Ninths (1341). An assessment of the agricultural value of each parish in most of the area covered by 27 English counties, published by the Record Commission as *Nonarum Inquisitiones in Curia Saccarii* (1807).

inquisition post mortem. An inquest held by the king's *escheator or his deputy after the death of a *tenant-in-chief of the Crown to establish the extent of the estate and to confirm the rightful heir. A jury of 12 local men of high repute gave information under oath. Records from the 13th century onwards are kept at the *Public Record Office, under C 133–142 and E 149–150. *Calendars and indexes are available for many reigns, and some county record societies have published detailed calendars. Such records survive in large numbers, especially for the period 1270–1350.

Institute of Heraldic and Genealogical Studies. Housed at Northgate, Canterbury, the institute was founded in 1961 to provide study, research, and training facilities in family history. It has a large library, and publishes aids to study and the journal *Family History*.

intakes. Irregular-shaped fields enclosed from the edges of *commons.

intercommoning. A system whereby several settlements around a marsh, *wood, or moor had rights on the *commons within that area.

International Genealogical Index. This microfiche and CD-ROM index of births / baptisms and marriages covering most of the world has been compiled by amateur researchers who are members of the Church of Jesus Christ of the Latter Day Saints (the *Mormon Church). The entries from Britain comprise baptism and marriage entries in *parish and *Nonconformist registers (including those kept at the *Public Record Office) and miscellaneous other sources up to 1885. The IGI has been made widely available for public consultation in *record offices and public libraries, and in the record-searching facilities created by the Mormons in various parts of the country. The entries are arranged under (pre-1974) counties, in alphabetical order of surnames, and then of forenames (in chronological order).

Interregnum. The period between the execution of Charles I in 1649 and the restoration of his son, Charles II, in 1660.

intestate. A person who died without making a *will.

inventories, probate. From the early 16th century to the mid-18th century (and in some districts until much later) it was the custom of the *ecclesiastical courts that proved *wills in England and Wales to insist that the executors should appoint three or four local men to make 'a true and perfect inventory' of the personal estate of the deceased. The inventory was filed with the will, or where a person died intestate with the letters of *administration. The appraisers, or valuers, swore a solemn oath that they would carry out their duty truthfully. They proceeded to list every item of furniture and utensils in the house, then they noted the livestock, crops, and equipment or the tools and finished goods in workshops, and whatever else was movable and therefore constituted personal estate, as distinct from real estate, i.e. the value of the house, land, etc.

Tens of thousands of probate inventories survive for most parts of England and Wales. They are mostly kept with wills at the *record offices of the ancient dioceses, except for the period 1653–60, when all wills and inventories for England and Wales were proved at the *Prerogative Court of Canterbury; these are now kept at the *Public Record Office under PROB 3.

Many of the words used by the appraisers are archaic terms, often of a technical kind, and frequently employing dialect forms. Little work has yet been done on their value as a source for the study of regional speech. The study of farming history in the early modern period has been transformed by the use made of inventories. Inventories have also been used with profit for the study of *vernacular architecture. Probate inventories are an unrivalled source for the study of furnishings and for demonstrating the rise in standards of domestic comfort. The full potential of craftsmen's inventories has not yet been realized.

There are many problems to be faced in interpreting individual inventories and in the statistical analysis of inventories in bulk. The major omission is that of real estate, whether *freehold or *copyhold property. The other major item which is often omitted is that of the debts which were owed by the deceased.

Irish emigration. The population of Ireland rose from over 4 million in 1781 to over 8 million in 1841. Long before the *famine years of the late 1840s Irish men and women emigrated to England and south Wales, and to a lesser extent to Scotland, in search of work.

The famine years from 1846 onwards saw massive emigration from Ireland to the rest of the United Kingdom and to the United States of America. By the end of the 19th century the population of Ireland had dropped to half the size it had attained by 1851. The favourite destinations for those who crossed the Irish Sea were London, Liverpool and other Lancashire towns, and parts of Lowland Scotland.

The Irish continued to arrive in considerable numbers during the later decades of the 19th century, particularly in the late 1870s and 1880s when farming was particularly depressed. The creation of an independent southern Ireland in 1922 and the long depression in Great Britain during the inter-war years reduced the flow of Irish immigrants, but after the Second World War and the revival of the British economy in the 1950s and 1960s large numbers of new Irish settlers arrived in search of work.

iron. The quality and quantity of wrought iron improved during the Middle Ages. Water-powered bloomeries were in use in England from the 14th century and remained important in some regions until the middle of the 17th century. The iron industry grew considerably in the 16th and 17th centuries after blast furnaces were introduced into England by French ironworkers in Ashdown Forest in 1496. The Wealden industry grew quickly in the next 50 years, and the new technology arrived in the midlands and the north of England in the 1560s. The era of the charcoal blast furnace lasted until the mid-18th century.

In 1709 Abraham Darby's works at Coalbrookdale was the first to use coke successfully. In the later 18th century the design of coke-fuelled furnaces changed rapidly and Henry Cort's puddling process was widely adopted. The 19th-century iron industry was far more complex and varied than its 18th-century predecessor. The furnaces had a far greater capacity and *steam power was now in common use.

Iron Age. The last of the prehistoric periods, from c.800 BC to the Roman invasion of AD 43, characterized by the use of iron tools and weapons, hill forts, and farmhouses of roughly circular plan whose outlines are often revealed by aerial archaeology.

Irvingites. The followers of Edward Irving (1792–1834), the founder of the Holy Catholic Apostolic Church, which was based in London.

Issue Rolls. Records of payments made from Crown revenues, from 1240 to 1480 and from 1567 to 1700, kept at the *Public Record Office.

Italian immigrants. Although individual Italians had settled in Britain since the Middle Ages, it was only in the 19th century that a community was established in London, especially in Clerkenwell and Soho. Many more Italians left their home country in the late 19th century. In London, numbers trebled from 3,500 in 1881 to 11,000 in 1901. Another wave of immigrants came in the 1950s and 1960s.

Jacobites. Supporters of the deposed King James II and his descendants after the *'Glorious Revolution' of 1688, which placed William of Orange and his wife Mary on the throne. Armed conflict occurred in 1689–90 (culminating in James's defeat at the Battle of the Boyne, in northern Ireland, on 1 July 1690), in 1715 ('The Jacobite Rebellion'), and in 1745–6, ending in the battle of Culloden and the suppression of the Highland *clans.

jagger. A north country term for a man in charge of a team of *pack-horses carrying *lead, *coal, etc.

Jesse window. A depiction in *stained glass of the Tree of Jesse, often in the east window of a church, showing Christ's descent from Jesse, the father of King David.

Jesuit. A member of the Society of Jesus, which was formed in Paris in 1534 by Ignatius Loyola as a body of scholars and missionaries dedicated to the aims of the Counter-*Reformation.

Jewish immigrants. A small Jewish community settled in London after the Norman Conquest. By the middle of the 12th century other English cities, e.g. King's Lynn and Norwich, had attracted Jewish money-lenders. Anti-semitism broke out during the heightened emotions of the first *Crusade.

These early settlers were *Sephardic Jews, whose name is derived from a Hebrew word meaning Spaniards. A small group resettled in London from 1541 onwards; by 1734 the number of English Jews had risen to about 6,000. Most of these were Sephardic Jews who had come from Portugal as traders; many were wealthy. They were followed by other Sephardic Jews from different parts of the Mediterranean.

The other Jews who had settled in England by 1734 were from a different tradition. They were known as *Ashkenazic Jews from a Hebrew word meaning German, for they had once been concentrated in the Rhine valley before moving east into Poland, the Baltic States, and Russia. Their native language was Yiddish, a type of German written in Hebrew characters. Their numbers increased steadily after 1800, especially after the persecutions in Central and Eastern Europe of 1848–50 and 1863; then in the last two decades of the 19th century thousands of families from Russia, Poland, Lithuania, and other parts of the Russian

Empire sought refuge. The favourite destination was the East End of London, especially Stepney, followed by Leeds and Manchester.

jointure. A fixed annual sum paid to a widow out of her husband's *freehold estate until she remarried or died.

journeyman. A *day labourer, often one who worked away from home; a man who had completed an *apprenticeship but had not set up as a master himself.

Julian calendar. The calendar in use since the time of Julius Caesar until the *Gregorian calendar was introduced into Catholic Europe in 1582 and into Britain in 1752. By the time that it was abandoned in Britain, the Julian calendar was 11 days out of line with the Gregorian.

jury. A body of 12 people sworn to give a verdict in a court of justice, manorial *court, coroner's court, etc. Jury service was dependent upon a property qualification defined in 1285 and extended in 1664 and 1692. From 1696 lists of eligible jurors (men aged 21–70 who possessed *freehold, *copyhold, or life-tenure property worth at least £10 a year) were presented by each *parish to meetings of the *quarter sessions and may now be consulted in county *record offices. From 1730 long-term *leaseholders of property valued at or above £20 were also eligible to serve. In 1825 jury service was restricted to those aged 21–60 and the property qualification was revised.

The Grand Jury was drawn from the ranks of the minor *gentry and substantial *yeomen who decided which cases should proceed to trial at the quarter sessions. Records of such proceedings are not well preserved.

jury of presentment. By ancient custom, confirmed in 1166, 12 men from each *hundred and four men from each *vill were liable for bringing suspects before the justices of the hundred court. These courts withered under the Tudors.

Justices of the Peace developed from the 'Keepers of the Peace' who were appointed by a commission under the *Great Seal in 1277 and 1287. They had acquired their name by 1361. JPs were appointed by the Crown from the ranks of the major landowners of a county.

The duties of the JPs were greatly extended under the Tudors. The commission of peace by which justices were appointed was revised in 1590 to authorize them to hold regular sessions, to enquire by jury into a variety of offences, and to try cases upon indictment. The JPs had to try offenders and consign some of the guilty to gaols and *houses of correction, to oversee the operation of the *Poor Law and the laws concerning vagrancy, to attend to the regulation of *fairs and markets, wages and *prices, and *weights and measures, to see to the upkeep of *roads and *bridges, to license *Nonconformist meeting houses, *ale-houses, playhouses, *badgers, *drovers, and *pedlars, and to levy rates. Justices were also appointed to perform similar duties in some *boroughs.

They began to lose their powers in 1888 when their administrative functions were transferred to elected councils in each county and large town.

juxta. A Latin word, meaning 'near', used in some place-names to mean 'by'.

keep. The tower of a *castle, which contained the living quarters of the noble family and which acted as the ultimate place of defence. During the 1240s keeps went out of fashion.

kelp. Seaweed, used as a manure and as an alkali in the chemical industry.

Kennett, White (1660–1728). Clergyman and author of *Parochial Antiquities Attempted in the History of Ambrosden, Burcester and Other Adjacent Parts in the Counties of Oxford and Bucks* (1695), the first *parish history.

kerseys. Cheap, coarse cloths manufactured in many parts of medieval and early modern England.

kidder. Alternate term for a *badger.

Kilvert, Francis (1840–79). Clergyman and author of a diary (1870–9), kept while he was a curate, most famously at Clyro (Radnorshire).

King, Gregory (1648–1712). Pioneer statistician and demographer. In his *Natural and Political Observations and Conclusions upon the State and Condition of England* (1696) he used taxation returns to analyse English society and to estimate the numbers in each social group, starting with 'Ranks, Degrees, Titles and Qualifications' and descending a social ladder via the merchants and professionals down to the humblest paupers. His table has been frequently reprinted.

king post. A post which rests on a *tie-beam and extends upwards to a ridge-pole. This method of supporting a roof-truss was common in the northern half of England.

King's Bench, Court of. One of the three courts that had become separate from the *Curia Regis by the reign of Edward I (1272–1307). At first, it dealt with cases involving the king, but in time it tried both criminal and civil cases as the highest court of the realm other than Parliament. It was abolished in 1875 and merged into the High Court as the King's Bench Division. Records from the late 12th century onwards are kept at the *Public Record Office under KB. A number of early rolls have been published by the Record Commission, *Pipe Roll Society, and *Selden Society.

King's Evil. It was once popularly supposed that scrofula, a disease of the lymphatic glands, could be cured by a touch from the king or a reigning queen. The last monarch to attempt this cure was Queen Anne.

King's highway. Any public road, described in medieval and early modern records as *via regis*, or the king's highway.

knight. Originally the fighting men who accompanied William the Conqueror to England. William I rewarded them by grants of land (a *knight's fee) which they held in return for *knight service. This was gradually commuted to a money payment. Knighthood therefore became a personal rather than a hereditary honour. A register of knights has been kept at the College of *Arms since 1662.

knight bachelor. The lowest degree of knighthood. A knight bachelor commanded a small unit of personal retainers.

knight of the shire. A Member of Parliament who was elected to represent a county.

knight service. The military service owed to a feudal lord by a *knight in return for land. It was gradually commuted to a money payment and was abolished in 1662.

knight's fee. After the Norman Conquest all the land in England was owned by William I, who by a process of *enfeoffment granted most of it (except the royal *demesnes) to *earls and *barons, who in turn granted it to *knights in return for *knight service. England had about 5,000–6,000 knights' fees.

knitting. During the late Elizabethan period the traditional country craft of hand-knitting was transformed into a flourishing rural industry.

L

Labourers, Statute of (1351). This Act attempted to hold wages at their pre-*Black Death level by imposing severe penalties for infringement. The shortage of labour thwarted attempts to keep down wages, however, for demand was greater than supply.

labour party. The Labour Representation Committee, which was formed in 1900 as a loose federation of *trade unions and socialist societies, changed its name to the Labour Party upon winning 29 seats in the election of 1906. Its constitution was drawn up in 1918.

labour services. The obligation of medieval peasants to work for certain periods on the *demesne of the *lord of the manor.

lace-making was an Elizabethan project which took root in the south midlands and Devon. It survived as a handcraft ('pillow' lace-making) for females until the Victorian period in Bedfordshire, Buckinghamshire, Northamptonshire, and Devon. Machine-made lace originated in Nottingham in the late 18th century.

Lady chapels. *Chantry chapels in parish churches dedicated to Our Lady, St Mary. Chantry chapels were dissolved in 1547, but since Victorian times many of them have been restored as chapels for private prayer.

Lady Day. 25 March, the official start of the year until 1752. Rents were commonly paid twice a year, at Lady Day and *Michaelmas.

laithe houses. A term coined to distinguish a type of farmhouse found in northern England, especially on the Pennines, from the medieval *longhouse. The dwelling house and laithe (barn) are built on a long axis and share the same roof, but unlike the longhouse they have separate entrances and no internal connection.

Lambarde, William (1536–1601). Author of *The Perambulation of Kent* (1576), the first county history.

Lambeth Palace Library. Founded in 1610 in a wing of the palace, this public library houses many of the documents of the Archbishopric of Canterbury, e.g. enquiries about *benefices, *tithes, buildings, etc., the *marriage licences of the Faculty Office and Vicar General's Office, and the *probate records of the Court of *Arches and certain *peculiar jurisdictions in London. The library is now administered by the Church

Commissioners. Application to search the records should be made in writing to the Librarian, Lambeth Palace Library, London SE1 7JU.

Lammas grazing. Some enclosed lands, which formerly lay within the *open-fields of a *manor, were still grazed in common after the gathering of the harvest. Before 1752, Lammas Day was 1 August; after the change of the calendar it was 13 August.

Lancaster, Duchy of. Created in 1351 when Henry, Earl of Lancaster, was made a duke, and revived in 1377 by a grant to John of Gaunt, the Duchy of Lancaster retained its distinctive judicial system and administrative structure after it reverted to the Crown in 1399. The dukedom had estates in almost every county of England and Wales. Its records are kept at the *Public Record Office.

land tax was first imposed in England and Wales in 1693 and abolished in 1963. At first it took the form of a national poundage rate on both personal and real property, but in 1698 the direct poundage rate was replaced by a system of quotas, at county, *hundred, and *parish or *township level. During the 18th century the tax evolved into a true land tax, assessed on land, buildings, and various forms of rents. Relatively few records survive before 1780, but from that date until the Parliamentary Reform Act of 1832 annual copies or 'duplicates' of the assessments owed by each owner of real property and by each of his tenants were lodged at *quarter sessions in order to establish qualifications for the vote at county elections. These duplicates survive in bulk amongst the quarter sessions papers at county *record offices. The only return that covers almost all of England and Wales is that of 1798, which is kept in 121 volumes at the *Public Record Office in class IR 23. The duplicates contain three categories of data, each arranged in a separate column: the name of each proprietor within the township; the names of the occupiers; and the amount of tax assessed.

The main problem is that huge proportions of smallholders are commonly and continually missing. Sometimes between 50 and 80 per cent of the smallholders of a township are not recorded. Duplicates do not provide accurate or even consistent counts, either in their tax entries or in the names they record, of the entire spectrum of the land-owning population.

lands. The *strips or *selions of an *open-field.

larceny. Stealing. Grand larceny, the theft of goods worth more than twelve pence from a person's house, was a *felony (therefore a capital offence) which was tried at the *assizes. Petty larceny was tried at the *quarter sessions. The distinction was abolished in 1827.

lathe. An ancient Kentish division comparable with the Sussex *rape, comprising several *hundreds.

Latin, medieval. With the exception of the period 1651–60, Latin was the language of legal documents until 1733.

lawn. Originally, a grassy plot in the wooded part of a medieval *deer park.

lay brother. The *Cluniacs and other monastic orders had used lay brothers during the 11th century, but the idea was developed in a new way and on a much greater scale by the *Cistercians. Lay brothers entered monastic life as adults, were usually illiterate, and took no part in the daily choral offices. They provided both the skilled and the unskilled manual work, as farmers and craftsmen. They greatly outnumbered the choir monks.

lay subsidy. A tax for a specific purpose, e.g. to subsidize a foreign war, which was distinguished from taxes levied on the clergy. The lay subsidy rolls of 1290–1334 are a major medieval source. The tax was commonly known as the Tenth and Fifteenth because it was levied on one-tenth of movable property in a town and one-fifteenth of similar property in the countryside.

   The records are held at the *Public Record Office under E 179. Some *county record societies have published their fullest returns. The collectors arranged the returns by *hundred or *wapentake and then by *vill or *borough. The number of exempted poor and the amount of evasion are unknown. The lay subsidy was revived by Henry VIII. The lay subsidy of 1546 is the last that is of use to local and family historians, though occasional assessments were made until 1623.

lead was mined and smelted during the Roman period. The great growth of the industry occurred after 1570, particularly in the 17th century. The industry experienced boom conditions in the 1750s and 1760s and again from the late 1780s until 1796. The lead industry underwent prolonged periods of depression in 1816–18 and 1824–33, but recovered again before the lead fields became exhausted during the second half of the 19th century. The depression of 1880–2 signalled the end of mining in many districts and a dramatic emigration.

league. A measure longer than a mile that varied from one part of the country to another.

lease. The conversion of *copyhold tenure to *leasehold occurred over a long period, particularly from the mid-16th century onwards. The conditions attached to leases varied from *manor to manor but, as a generalization, in the western half of England the favoured method was a lease for three lives determinable upon 99 years. The lessee paid an entry fine and an annual rent and his lease held good as long as one of the entered names was still alive. It was common to enter the names of husband, wife, and eldest son, though any names could be chosen. Fresh lives could usually be entered upon the payment of another entry fine. These fines were negotiable; during the first half of the 17th century lords usually managed to raise them to meet inflation. The method favoured in the eastern half of England, namely a lease for 21 years. Long leases, including some lasting 800 years or more, were offered on some estates; on the other hand, short terms, e.g. three years, could also be negotiated. *Estate records often include a good run of leases; *surveys of estates give an account of the various ways in which property was held.

lease and release. A method of transferring land from one party to another without the necessity of enrolling a deed. The purchaser first took a lease of the property for one year (thus avoiding the need to enrol), then on the following day the vendor conveyed to him the reversion of the lease. The records of the transaction consisted of two documents, the lease and the release. The method remained popular until 1845.

leasehold. Tenure by *lease, either for lives, or for a stated term, a method that began to replace *copyhold tenure in the early modern period and which was also used for *demesnes that a landowner did not wish to farm himself, but which he could recover at the end of the term.

leasow. A pasture, particularly in the West Midlands and Welsh Borders.

leather. The leather trades were important during the Middle Ages and the early modern period when garments, boots and shoes, bottles, belts, saddles, sheaths, etc. were made from tanned hides or dressed skins. Workers in leather formed a sizeable proportion of the work-force, especially in towns.

lectern. Medieval stone lecterns were normally fixed to the north wall of the *chancel of a parish church. After the *Reformation detached wooden, brass, or latten lecterns were installed in the *nave. In three-decker pulpits the reading desk formed the middle tier. The Victorians reintroduced the late medieval practice of supporting the Bible by the outstretched wings of an eagle, the symbol of St John the Evangelist.

lecturer. In the 17th century private individuals endowed lectureships at parish churches to encourage preaching. The idea was much favoured by *Puritans.

Leicester University, Department of English Local History. Founded in 1948 with W. G. Hoskins as reader and sole member, it quickly became a unique postgraduate department concerned with the comparative study of local history throughout the whole of England.

Leland, John (1506?–52). The first English topographer. His notes of his journeys have been published as Lucy Toulmin Smith (ed.), *John Leland: The Itinerary*, 5 vols. (1907–10, repr. 1964).

Lent. The period of fasting and penitence from Ash Wednesday to Easter-eve, in commemoration of Christ's 40 days in the wilderness. A forbidden period for marriages.

lentils. A leguminous plant, closely related to the vetch, sometimes called 'tills'. It was valued as excellent fodder for calves and young cattle, and also for pigeons.

Letters and Papers (Foreign and Domestic), Henry VIII. A full *calendar for the years 1517–47 has been published in many volumes between 1864 and 1932. This includes papers from the *Public Record Office, the *British Library, and archives from abroad.

Levant Company. Founded in 1581 and known also as the Turkey Company. Its members, who until 1753 had to be Freemen of the City of London, acquired a virtual monopoly of trade in that area until 1825. The records are kept at the *Public Record Office, under SP 105.

levée en masse. Lists of men aged 17 to 55 who might form a reserve defence force in 1803–4 were drawn up by parish *constables.

Levellers. A group who advocated sweeping political reforms of a democratic nature in the 1640s and 1650s.

Lewis's *Topographical Dictionary*. Samuel Lewis published *A Topographical Dictionary of England* in seven editions between 1831 and 1848–9, the last edition being in 4 volumes and an atlas. He also published *A Topographical Dictionary of Wales* in 1833, 1844, and 1849, in 2 volumes and an atlas, *A Topographical Dictionary of Scotland* (1846), in 2 volumes and an atlas, and *A Topographical Dictionary of Ireland* (1846) in 2 volumes and an atlas. Brief historical details of each town and village were given and the civil and ecclesiastical arrangements noted.

leyerwite. A fine payable by a medieval *villein to the *lord of the manor upon his unmarried daughter becoming pregnant.

leys, grass. The *open-field system of farming was far more flexible than was once thought. Individual arable *strips were often converted to grass, on a temporary basis, in order to provide sufficient feed for livestock. These leys could last for varying periods, from two years to seven or eight years; if longer still, they seemed permanent.

Lhuyd, Edward (1660–1709). Welsh and Oxford antiquary, natural historian and philologist.

Liberal Party. The mid-19th-century successor to the *Whig Party. A split between groups led respectively by Asquith and Lloyd-George was a major cause of the decline of the party after the First World War. In 1988 the Liberals merged with a majority of the Social Democratic Party to form the Liberal Democrats.

Liberate Rolls. Writs authorizing royal officers to make payments on behalf of the Crown, from 1226 to 1426. The records are kept at the *Public Record Office. A *calendar has been published for the period up to 1272.

liberty. A *manor or group of manors, or other area, that lay outside a *sheriff's jurisdiction.

libraries, public. The first 'circulating libraries' were formed during the first half of the 18th century. Public lending and reference libraries became widely available during the second half of the 19th century after an Act of Parliament of 1850 authorized local authorities to provide them. The generosity of Andrew Carnegie (1835–1918), the Scots-born American multi-millionaire, allowed many small authorities throughout Britain to provide a 'free library'. The Public Libraries Act (1919) enabled the County Councils to form County Libraries.

licences. After the *Reformation schoolmasters, midwives, physicians, and surgeons had to prove that they conformed to the beliefs of the *Church of England and had attended communion. Licences to practice were then registered in the diocesan records.

Licences to pass beyond the seas were an early form of *passport issued from the late Elizabethan period until 1677. The records, which are kept at the *Public Record Office under E 157, include registers of soldiers serving in the Low Countries, 1613–24; people going to Holland and other places, 1624–37; and passengers to the colonies, 1634–9 and 1677.

liege. The lord of whom a man held his principal property was his liege-lord, to whom he owed military service.

lighthouses. The earliest survivors date from the 17th century. Electric arc lamps were used from the 1860s.

lime kilns. Some date from the 16th and 17th centuries, but most are from the 18th and 19th. Their chief use was to produce lime that farmers could spread on acid soils.

linen. In the early modern period linen weaving for garments, sheets, tablecloths, and sailcloth was a widespread rural industry wherever *flax could be grown in the British Isles. The industry began to be mechanized in the late 18th century.

List and Index Society. Established by readers and staff at the *Public Record Office to publish cheap finding-aids to records.

literary and philosophical societies. During the second half of the 18th century and the first half of the 19th, Britain's major towns founded 'lit. and phil.' societies to discuss the intellectual issues of the day and to sponsor cultural activities.

livery and maintenance. The medieval practice of maintaining large numbers of retainers who wore their lord's badge and livery. These retainers were expected to respond to a call for military service in return for the lord's protection. The practice was widespread from the 14th to the 16th century, but from the reign of Henry VII it required a royal licence.

livery companies. The medieval *guilds of the City of London. The records of most of the companies are kept at the *Guildhall Library, which also has a number of published histories.

Local Historian, The. Founded in 1952 as *The Amateur Historian*, its name was changed in 1968. Since 1961 it has been the official journal of the *Standing Conference for Local History and its successor, the *British Association for Local History. It is published quarterly and contains articles and reviews that are scholarly but accessible to a wider readership. As such, it is the principal journal for local historians.

Local History Magazine. A privately run national magazine for local historians, which has been published bi-monthly since 1984. It contains articles, reviews, and notices of events throughout the country.

Local Population Studies. A journal founded in 1968, devoted to the study of population history.

locative surname. A surname derived from a place-name.

lodges. In the Middle Ages small and simple hunting lodges provided temporary accommodation for a lord and his party. Between the 16th and 18th centuries lodges were fashionable retreats set in a *park. Some were rebuildings of old hunting lodges, others were new structures of superior quality and unusual design, often on new sites.

lodgings. In the 14th and 15th centuries the provision of lodgings altered the plans of palaces, *castles, and manor houses. Whole new ranges were built to accommodate retainers as well as guests and their retines. At the same time, urban terraces provided lodgings for *vicars-choral, *chantry priests, and students at universities. In the 19th century the word became associated with the rooms rented by migrant or unmarried workers in industrial towns.

Lollards. Followers of John Wycliffe (*c.*1329–84) who rejected the authority of priests and attacked abuses in the church, including the system of confession, penance, and indulgence. Wycliffe wrote popular religious tracts in English, translated the Bible, and organized a body of itinerant preachers who insisted on the importance of inward religion rather than the mechanical observance of established practices. His followers were persecuted from 1382, but his influence lasted down to the *Reformation.

London Gazette. This official news sheet was first published in 1665 as *The Oxford Gazette,* but from number 24 onwards (5 February 1666) it bore the name of *The London Gazette.* At first it was published each Tuesday and Friday, but it now appears daily. It reached most parts of the country from its earliest years. A complete set is available in the *Guildhall Library.

long-and-short work. A method of arranging the *quoins of a late Anglo-Saxon building, particularly in *Mercia. The quoins were laid alternately upright ('long') and sideways ('short').

longhouse. A house with opposed entries and an unheated lower room which was once used for accommodating livestock or as a workshop or storage-place. Humans and animals entered the building via a common door and passage. The longhouse was a common form of farmhouse in the Middle Ages. In the early modern period livestock were removed from the lower ends of longhouses and the space was used instead for service rooms.

lord of misrule. During the twelve days of *Christmas the traditional social hierarchy in a palace, *castle, or manor house was turned upside down by the appointment of a lowly member of the household as lord of misrule, with licence to organize boisterous activities and to make fun of his social superiors.

lord of the manor. *Manors varied considerably in size and their importance declined over the centuries. A lord of the manor could therefore be a medieval *baron, titled landowner, or just a well-to-do local farmer, businessman, or *attorney. Lords frequently did not reside on their manors and left the administration of the manor court to a *steward.

lords lieutenant. In 1551 king's lieutenants were placed in charge of the county militias, with responsibility for *musters and *beacons. As they were noblemen, they came to be known as lords lieutenant. They became a valued means of passing on local news to the central government. Records of their activities (mostly from the second half of the 18th century and the early 19th century) are available at county *record offices. The duties of the office are now ceremonial.

lordship. The larger feudal territories, e.g. a *castellany. Some were compact estates, others consisted of scattered *manors.

lorimer. A maker of bits, spurs, and the metal parts of harness.

Lowland zone. The concept of a Lowland zone was advanced in Sir Cyril Fox, *The Personality of Britain* (1932). It has greatly influenced historical geographers, archaeologists, and landscape historians. The populous, wealthier, and more advanced lowland areas, east and south of a line drawn from the Tees to the Exe, are contrasted with settlements in the *Highland zone. The concept has been refined by the study of *pays*.

Lowside window. A low window on the south side of the *chancel of a parish church, whose purpose is mysterious.

lucerne. One of the artificial grasses imported from France during the later 17th and 18th centuries.

Luddites. The machine-breaking activities of the Luddites occurred during 1811–12, with fresh outbreaks in 1814 and 1816. The central records are kept at the *Public Record Office under HO 40.

lych-gate. A term coined by Victorian ecclesiologists from Old English *lich*, meaning corpse, for a roofed structure at the principal entrance to a *churchyard. Here priests met burial parties at 'the church style' to commence prayers for the dead. Most surviving examples date from the 18th and 19th centuries.

lynchet. A landscape feature that is particularly noticeable on pasture land in limestone districts. Fields formed on slopes tended to have their upper and lower limits defined by scarps (lynchets) formed by the build-up of soil from ploughing. Some are prehistoric, but the type known as strip-lynchet is medieval.

madder. A plant whose roots produce a red dye, introduced into *market gardens around London in the 1620s.

Magna Carta. The great charter of 1215 by which King John, under pressure from his barons, conceded certain liberties, including the right of a freeman not to be imprisoned except by due process of law. It was much quoted in the constitutional struggles of the 17th century and came to be regarded as the foundation of English liberties.

mainprise. A writ requiring a *sheriff to obtain securities for the appearance of a defendant in court.

majority, age at. The age at which a person is legally considered to be an adult was 21 until 1969, when it was lowered to 18.

Malthus, Thomas R. (1766–1834). Clergyman and economist, whose *Essay on the Principle of Population* (1798; greatly enlarged in a new edition, 1803) argued that the natural tendency of population was to increase faster than the means of subsistence. The term 'Malthusian crisis' is used by demographers.

mandamus, writ of. An order to a public officer to carry out his duty.

manners, reformation of. The term is used in a broad sense to mean the *Protestant, and more particularly the *Puritan, attempt to create a godly society in the late 16th and 17th centuries. It is also used, more specifically, to refer to the renewed concerns of clergymen and churchgoers, especially in towns, in the late 17th century. In 1691 a Society for the Reformation of Manners was founded in London. Its title was changed to the *Society for the Promotion of Christian Knowledge in 1698.

manor. By the time that the *Domesday Book was compiled the manorial system was established throughout most of England. It was subsequently imposed on other parts of the British Isles that came under Norman rule.

A manor may be defined as a territorial unit that was originally held by *feudal tenure, by a landlord who was not necessarily noble, and who himself was a tenant either of the Crown or of a *mesne lord who held land directly of the Crown. In the Middle Ages the manor was an economic unit, which included the *demesne which the lord farmed himself (usually by paying wages and by *labour services or *boon work), and the rest of the land, which was farmed by tenants or used as common pasture and waste. There was much regional variety of practice; indeed, neighbouring manors differed in their customs. The manor became less of an economic unit in the early modern period, but retained its legal functions.

manse. The residence of a *Nonconformist minister, e.g. a *Congregationalist or a Scottish *Presbyterian.

manuscript. A document or book written by hand; abbreviated as MS, or MSS in the plural.

maps and mapmakers, early. The first English map of the British Isles was drawn by Matthew Paris, *c.*1250, followed about a century later by the anonymous 'Gough' map. By the beginning of the 15th century the principles of cartography were sufficiently understood for the making of maps to accompany local surveys.

During the 1570s maps of all the counties of England and Wales were made by Christopher *Saxton. Saxton's achievement provided the framework in which other topographers, such as John *Speed, John *Norden, and the Dutch mapmaker, Jan Blaeu, could work. During the late 16th and the 17th centuries written *surveys or descriptions of *manors or estates were often accompanied by a map. Such maps and surveys were concerned primarily with establishing ownership, boundaries, field names, and, occasionally, land use. The usual term for such maps was 'platt'.

march. Derived from the Old English *mearc*, meaning 'boundary', march denoted a tract of land along a border, notably the marches of Wales and Scotland.

mark. A metal unit of accountancy, worth 13*s*. 4*d*., two-thirds of a pound.

market charter. At the *Quo Warranto enquiries of the late 13th century manorial lords often claimed a prescriptive right to hold markets and fairs. The granting of royal charters for such foundations began in the late 12th century. A prescriptive right was one that dated from before that time, often going back to the early years of Norman rule, and sometimes into the *Anglo-Saxon era. In 1889 the *Royal Commission on Market Rights and Tolls*, i. 108–31 listed 2,713 grants of market and fair charters made between 1199 and 1483, records of which had been preserved in the *Public Record Office.

market gardening. Commercial gardening was introduced into southern and eastern England by *Protestant refugees from the Low Countries in the second half of the 16th century. In the second half of the 17th century market gardening spread to new areas, well away from London and East Anglia.

marl. A mixture of mud and *lime, which was dug out of pits and spread on fields to counteract acid soils and to improve the water retention of sandy soils, whether they were used for arable or grass.

marquess, marquis. The rank of nobility between *duke and *earl. The first man to receive the title was Robert de Vere, Earl of Oxford, who was made Marquess of Dublin in 1385. The French spelling 'marquis' is often preferred. The wife of a marquess is a marchioness. The heir to a dukedom sometimes has the courtesy title of marquis.

marriage. While it was a fairly common practice amongst the medieval and early modern *nobility to arrange marriages whilst the partners were children, the great majority of the people of Britain remained unmarried until their mid-twenties.

The record of marriages in *parish registers indicates that the peak periods when people married coincided with the ending of annual service contracts, i.e. at springtime in pastoral farming districts and in the late autumn in arable regions. During the Middle Ages the Church had forbidden marriage during *Advent, *Lent, and *Rogationtide. Advent remained unpopular until the late 17th century and Lent stayed a prohibited period. The calling of banns could be avoided by obtaining a licence to marry from the diocesan consistory court. The records of licences are kept at diocesan *record offices. They include the *allegations made by one of the parties, normally the bridegroom.

Marriage Act, Lord Hardwicke's (1753). The Act required marriages to be performed in the churches and chapels of the *Church of England (except for *Quaker or *Jewish marriages) and to be registered in a prescribed form in books which were kept separate from the registers of baptisms and burials. It came into effect in 1754.

Marriage Duty Act (1695). A tax on 'Marriages, Births and Burials and upon Bachelors and Widowers for the term of five years' lasted 11 years, from 1695 to 1706.

Marshall, William (1745–1818). Agricultural writer who produced a number of regional reports in his *Rural Economy* series between 1777 and 1796.

Martello towers were built during the *Napoleonic wars on the eastern and southern coast of England, from Suffolk to Sussex, in a similar manner to the earlier Tudor coastal *forts. They were named after, and designed like, the Torre della Mortello, an impregnable Corsican fort. Of the 103 towers that were built between 1804 and 1812, 43 have survived.

maslin. A mixture of the two winter-sown cereals, wheat and rye.

masons' marks. Each mason had his own distinctive mark to indicate which stones he had dressed. Marks are of a variety of simple designs, usually about two inches long.

masques. Costly and extravagant spectacles at court or a nobleman's house, either inside or in the open air, or a combination of both. They were much in favour at the court of Elizabeth I, James I, and Charles I.

Matins. Originally the office for the night, observed in monasteries; now the service of Morning Prayer in the *Church of England.

Matrimonial Causes Act (1857). The Act cleared up the previous confused laws of *marriage and separation. Jurisdiction for matrimonial affairs was removed from the *ecclesiastical courts and placed under a new court headed by the Lord Chancellor. The Act did not make radical changes in procedure or in the legal basis of the grounds for *divorce, and the financial cost of divorce remained high. The Act did not apply to Ireland. The records of the court established by the Act of 1857 are kept at the *Public Record Office under J 77 as the Principal Probate Registry Divorce Files, 1858 to 1937. These are indexed by the names of parties, subject to a 30-years closure rule.

Maundy Thursday. Christ's washing of the disciples' feet at the Last Supper is commemorated by the Maundy service on the day before Good Friday.

meadow. Meadows for the growing of hay were a precious part of farming systems until the modern practice of cutting silage for storage in a silo became widespread. In *open-field systems meadows were divided into *doles, which were sometimes reallocated on an annual basis. Meadows were valued highly in *surveys. During the 17th and 18th centuries artificial water-meadows were created.

measles. A children's disease, which often led to pneumonia and death before it was controlled in the 20th century.

Mechanics' Institutes. From the 1820s onwards mechanics' institutes were founded in most large towns and in many of the smaller ones. They represent the first serious efforts at adult working-class education.

Memoranda Rolls. Financial accounts, especially of monies owing to the Crown, kept by the *Exchequer and the Lord Treasurer's Remembrancer. The rolls are housed at the *Public Record Office under E 159, 368, and 370.

memorial (heraldry). A formal application for a grant of arms.

merchant. The term used in the medieval and early modern periods for a businessman, especially one involved in overseas trade.

merchant seamen. The Board of Trade records of men in the merchant service are kept at the *Public Record Office under BT. See the Public Record Office Information leaflet no. 5, 'Records of the Registrar General of Shipping and Seamen'.

merchet. A payment from a *villein to his *lord of the manor upon the marriage of the villein's son or daughter.

Mercia. The kingdom of the Angles, which in the 7th century stretched south of the Humber and west of the Trent as far as the forests of the western midlands. Mercia was at its most powerful in the second half of the 8th century under Offa, who was supreme among English kings south of the Humber.

mere. 1. A boundary, often commemorated in a place-name.
2. A place-name element for a glacial lake or pool.

Merton, Statute of (1235). This statute authorized lords to enclose part of the manorial wastes, provided they left sufficient pasture for their tenants.

mesne lord. A lord in the middle of the *feudal hierarchy, i.e. a *lord of a manor who held land from a superior lord and who let the land to a tenant.

Mesolithic. The middle period of the *Stone Age, *c.*10,000–5,000 BC, between the *Palaeolithic and the *Neolithic.

messuage. A term used in deed to signify a dwelling-house and the surrounding property, including outbuildings. A large residential property was referred to as a capital messuage.

Methodists. In 1738 John Wesley (1703–91) and Charles Wesley (1707–88) began the movement which soon acquired the nickname of Methodism. The Methodist Society was founded two years later. In 1744 circuits for Wesleyan preachers were established and the first national conference was held. The Wesleys' message was that salvation was possible for every believer, and that communion with God did not need the intervention of a priest.

The Methodists did not break from the *Church of England until 1784. Their rapid expansion did not begin until the 19th century, with a particularly successful decade in the 1830s. They then overtook the older Dissenting sects in terms of membership, and by the time of the 1851 *ecclesiastical census were the chief rivals to the Church of England.

In 1797 the Methodist New Connexion was formed from congregations that wished to have control over their own affairs. The Primitive Methodists broke away in 1812 and soon became the second strongest of the Methodist sects. The 'Ranters', as they became known, were humble people, especially the farm labourers of eastern England, the urban poor, and the miners in the new pit-villages. Smaller breakaway groups included the Independent Methodists, who left in 1807, the Bible Christians (O'Bryanites) of south-western England, who became independent in 1815, the Protestant Methodists, who became a separate body in 1827, and the Wesleyan Reform Movement, who set up a national headquarters in Sheffield in 1849. In the 20th century most of these groups have come together again. In 1907 the New Connexion joined with the United Free Methodist Churches to form the United Methodist Church. Then, in 1932, the Wesleyans joined the rest to form the Methodist Church in Great Britain.

The early Methodists accepted Church of England baptism, marriage, and burial. Only a few Methodist registers survive before the 1790s. Most start in the second decade of the 19th century, and even then the majority recorded only baptisms. In 1837 these early registers were deposited at the *Public Record Office. Later ones are mostly kept in local *record offices.

metronymic. A surname derived from a mother, e.g. Marriott, Megson, or Maude.

Michaelmas. 29 September, the feast of St Michael the Archangel, the time when half-yearly rents were due.

Middle Ages. The term is used to mean the long period between the fall of the Roman Empire and the *Reformation. However, many British historians restrict its usage to the period after the Norman Conquest.

migration, subsistence. A term coined by Peter Clark for the long-distance migration of poor people in the period between the *dissolution of the monasteries and the Civil War, which was distinct from the 'betterment migration' of others.

miles. The statute mile of 1,760 yards was defined by Act of Parliament in 1593, but various customary miles long continued in use in most parts of Britain. The statute mile was first adopted on maps by John *Ogilby, *Britannia Depicta* (1675), and became usual in the 18th century both on maps and on the milestones erected by the *turnpike trusts.

militia records. An Act of 1757, modified by subsequent legislation, set out the procedures for raising the militia. From time to time *constables were ordered to draw up lists of all the able-bodied men of a certain age in their *parishes or *townships. A ballot was then held to decide which of these men should be called upon to serve or else pay for a replacement.

The Act of 1757 instructed the constables of each township to list all men aged between 18 and 50, according to rank or occupation and incapacity, and to send their list to the *Lord Lieutenant of the county who supervised the ballot. In 1762 the age limit was reduced to 45. Those excused service included peers, clergymen, articled clerks, apprentices, seamen, soldiers, those who had served previously, and the constables. In some ballots judges, medical practitioners, *Quakers, and licensed teachers were also excused. Although the men in these exempted groups were supposed to be recorded by the constable when he drew up his return, this complete listing was not always carried out. Exemption from service was also granted on the grounds of infirmity or poverty, for it was held that, if such men were called to serve, their wives and children would have to be provided for out of the poor rates.

An Act of 1802 which divided the able-bodied into four classes, who would be called upon in order if the occasion arose: (1) men under 30 having no children; (2) men above 30 having no children; (3) men aged between 18 and 45 with no children under 14; and (4) men aged between 18 and 45 having children under 14.

mills, water and wind. Water-powered corn mills had been installed in many parts of Britain before the Norman Conquest; at least 6,000 English ones are recorded in the *Domesday Book. Water power was also used for *fulling mills by the last quarter of the 12th century, the period when windmills made their first appearance. Windmills are thought to have been an English invention of c.1180, and they spread rapidly during the next half-century.

ministers' accounts. The accounts of revenue and expenditure for Crown lands. They are kept at the *Public Record Office under SC 6 and have been indexed in *Lists and Indexes*, vols. 5, 8, and 34.

minster churches. The *Old English word *mynster* was derived from the Latin *monasterium*, for minster churches were served by communities of priests before the medieval system of *parishes was created. Many churches which were, and are, called 'minster' were ancient foundations. A number of place-names, especially in southern England, refer to former minster churches. Such churches were long-established and were regarded as 'mother churches' to which people over a large district paid dues. Their parishes remained significantly larger than neighbouring parishes, which had been carved from them.

However, it is difficult to prove that all minsters were ancient ecclesiastical centres. Minsters were a feature of the Anglo-Saxon period for which little documentation survives.

misdemeanour. An indictable offence that is less serious than a *felony.

misericord. A wooden seat which can be tipped up to provide a rest for someone who appears to be standing. The name is derived from the Latin word *miserere*, meaning 'to have pity'. Misericords date from the later Middle Ages and are found in the *choirs of cathedrals and monastic or *collegiate churches and the *chancels of some parish churches. The underside of the seat (which is visible in its upright position) was carved with figures taken from folklore, bestiaries, and moral tales, or with heraldic devices.

missal. A book of devotions, often illuminated, containing the words and directions for the celebration of the mass.

mister, mistress, miss, ms. In *parish registers and other records of the early modern period most people were recorded only by their Christian name and surname. A 'Mr' was someone of at least minor *gentry status (though many did not possess a *coat of arms). Mistress or 'Mrs' was used for a woman of similar status, whether or not she was married. The use of 'Miss' for an unmarried woman came into use during the early 18th century. In the later 20th century 'Ms' has become increasingly popular as the female equivalent of 'Mr', which has been the style for any untitled adult male since the later 18th or early 19th century.

moat. The digging of deep ditches, which were then usually filled with water, around *castles, manor houses, and some smaller properties was a common medieval practice. Most date from the 13th and 14th centuries, particularly the period from 1250 to 1325. Security obviously played a part, but moats could act only as a temporary hindrance to a determined attacker. Prestige was the main reason for their construction, though they were also useful for keeping *fish.

modus. The conversion of a *tithe payment in kind (i.e. a tenth of produce) to a fixed sum of money.

moiety. A half. The term was used, for instance, when the right of *advowson was split between two heiresses.

Monmouth's rebellion. The attempt in 1685 of the Duke of Monmouth to depose the new Catholic king, James II, was supported enthusiastically by Protestant craftsmen and labourers in Dorset and Somerset.

monogram. A character formed by interweaving two or more letters.

moot. An *Anglo-Saxon legislative assembly; hence, a moot-point is a subject for debate. The supreme council was the Witenagemot. Each *hundred and *borough also had its moot.

Moravians. A Protestant sect founded in Moravia and Bohemia by the followers of Jan Huss in the early 15th century. In 1728 Count Zinzendorf sent three missionaries from Saxony to London and Oxford. The earliest surviving register is that of the Fetter Lane congregation in London, beginning in 1741.

Morden, Robert (died 1703). London map- and globe-maker. He is best known for *The New Description and State of England, containing the Maps of the Counties of England and Wales, in fifty-three copper plates* (1701, and later editions).

Mormon Branch Libraries. The *Mormons have established a number of branch libraries, attached to a local church, in various parts of Britain. Their aim is to foster genealogical research by the provision of microfiche, microfilm, etc. of records from all over Britain, and from other parts of the world. The basic source is the *International Genealogical Index, but a range of other records are made available in reproduction form. The facilities are made available to all searchers, regardless of whether or not they are members of the Mormon Church.

Mormons. The Church of the Latter Day Saints of Jesus Christ, founded in the USA by Joseph Smith (1805–44). Members base their beliefs on the *Book of Mormon* (1830), claimed to have been written by a prophet of that name.

Morris, Joseph. Author of numerous topographical guides, including the series of 'Little Guides' to the counties of England, published by Black in the first third of the 20th century.

mortality, bills of. During the 17th century the practice grew up in London and the major provincial cities of collating information on burials recorded in *parish registers. This allowed municipal authorities to keep a check on the progress of *plague and other diseases and enabled them to identify infected parishes. Bills of mortality were published for many towns in the 18th and 19th centuries, but the figures must be used with caution.

mortgage. In the early modern period obtaining a loan upon the mortgage of property was a common form of *credit. Large collections of *deeds relating to mortgages can be found in the various *registries of deeds and in local *record offices.

Mortmain, Statute of (1279). This statute added to existing penalties for the transference of land to an ecclesiastical body without the lord's permission. The tenants of such land were free from the payment of *escheats and *reliefs, to the financial disadvantage of the lord.

mortuary. A fixed payment to the *rector or *vicar by a parishioner upon the death of a member of his or her *household. The poorest parishioners were exempt.

motte-and-bailey. An early type of *castle introduced by the Normans. Mottes were artificial mounds of stone and earth, which were round or oval at the base and flattened at the top so as to provide a look-out point and sometimes a temporary residence. Baileys varied enormously in size and shape, according to the scale of the enterprise and the restrictions imposed by the local topography. The bailey contained the outbuildings and was separated from the motte by a ditch. The whole complex was surrounded by a deep ditch and rampart.

mud walling. In areas where suitable building stone was unavailable mud was used from the Middle Ages to the 19th century in the construction of farmhouses and *cottages, barns and other outbuildings, and field walls.

mullion. A vertical post, usually of stone, which divides a window. They gradually went out of fashion after the invention of *sash windows.

mummers. The local men who performed a traditional play at *Christmas in the larger houses of their parish.

municipal boroughs. The Municipal Corporations Act (1835) reformed the ancient constitutions of 178 *boroughs and provided for the incorporation of others. The Municipal Corporations Act of 1882 revised and added to the Act of 1835. Municipal corporations were abolished in 1974.

muniments. Title *deeds, etc. that confer rights and privileges. The term is used to refer to a collection of archives relating to an estate.

murrain. Infectious disease in cattle.

museums. The British tradition of collecting began in the 16th century. The British Museum was founded in 1753. After the success of the *Great Exhibition, the South Kensington Museum was founded in 1852; by the end of the century it had developed into the separate Science Museum, Natural History Museum, Geological Museum, and the Victoria and Albert Museum. The Imperial War Museum moved from South Kensington in 1936. The National Maritime Museum was founded at Greenwich in 1937. The two major national museums of Scotland—the National Museum of Antiquities of Scotland and the Royal Scottish Museum, both based in Edinburgh—were amalgamated in 1985.

The civic museums which were created by municipal enterprise in the second half of the 19th century copied the national museums in the scope of their collections and in their style of presentation. The first such 'open-air' museum was the Welsh Folk Museum at St Fagan's (1947).

muster rolls. The name given to *militia lists of the 16th and 17th centuries. All able-bodied men aged 16 to 60 were liable for military service, armed with their own weapons and armour according to their income. Muster rolls are now kept at the *Public Record Office, mostly in the *State Papers Domestic. See the Public Record Office Records Information leaflet no. 46, 'Militia Muster Rolls, 1522–1640'.

mystery plays are so called because they were performed by the trade *guilds, or 'mysteries', of medieval towns. They were performed at *Corpus Christi. Each guild was responsible for financing, producing, and acting a particular scene.

nail-making. The making of nails was an ancient handcraft in the industrial villages of the west midlands, south Yorkshire, north Derbyshire, and central Lancashire, which expanded greatly after the introduction of *slitting mills in the 17th century.

Napoleonic wars. The initial enthusiasm for the French Revolution in some parts of Britain turned to hostility during the prolonged wars with France from 1793 to 1815. Napoleon I became First Consul of France in 1799 and Emperor in 1804.

narrow cloths. Cheap, coarse cloths, half the length and width of *broadcloths.

National Register of Archives. Founded in 1945 as a branch of the Royal Commission on *Historical Manuscripts, to collect and disseminate information about manuscript sources for British history outside the public records, the NRA aims to make this information available for public use as quickly and as widely as possible. Its coverage includes the papers of individuals of note, families and estates, businesses, churches, local authorities, societies, and other organizations. The Register may be consulted on Mondays to Fridays from 9.30 a.m. to 5 p.m. at The Royal Commission on Historical Manuscripts, Quality House, Quality Court, Chancery Lane, London WC2A 1HP.

National schools. The National Society for the Education of the Poor in the Principles of the Established Church was founded in 1811 to take over the schools of the *Society for the Promotion of Christian Knowledge and to build new ones. They operated under the monitorial system.

naturalization. Applying for naturalization was a troublesome and costly business and many aliens did not bother, especially when they married an English woman, for their children then automatically became British nationals. Before 1844 naturalization could be accomplished only by private Act of Parliament; from 1844 it could be gained by a certificate from the Home Secretary. The records are kept in the *Public Record Office under HO.

nave. The public part of the parish church, where parishioners congregate during services. Parishioners were responsible for the upkeep of the nave and its aisles, tower, and porch.

navvies. The 'navigators' who constructed the *canals and *railways.

Navy records are kept at the *Public Record Office under the reference ADM. Nearly every class of naval records mentions individuals by name, but the chief sources are the Ships' Muster and the Ships' Pay Books. Ships' musters survive from 1667 under ADM 36–39, 41, 115, 119. From 1764 they sometimes give a man's age and place of birth. Description Books, particularly those of the 19th century, record a man's age, height, and complexion, and note any scars or tattoos. Ships' Pay Books from 1669 (ADM 31–35, 117) provide confirmation that a man served in a particular ship.

neatherd. The cowman who drove the cows of all villagers in one herd to the pastures.

negative proof. A term much used in genealogical research. It denotes the attempt to prove that a name found in a *parish register, etc. is the one being sought by searching all other records in the neighbourhood to make sure that no one else of that name is recorded.

Neolithic. The last phase (*c.*5000–2400 BC) of the *Stone Age, following the *Mesolithic.

nephew. Before the 18th century this could mean a descendant or kinsman and not just the son of a brother or sister.

New Draperies. In the 16th century craftsmen from France and the Low Countries were invited to settle and practise their trade in southern and eastern England. The most successful of these projects was the enlargement of the cloth industry by the introduction of lighter-weight cloths, known collectively as the New Draperies, using innumerable combinations of long *wool, *silk, and *linen yarn.

newspapers, local. The first newspapers were published in the 17th century. Large collections of early newspapers are kept at the newspaper library of the *British Library at Colindale, north London, and at the *Bodleian Library, Oxford. The larger provincial towns began to publish their own newspapers in the first half of the 18th century. Local news began to feature prominently only in the later 18th century. The chief interest of local newspapers in the 18th century is often in the advertisements.

niece. Until the 17th century this word was used in a wider sense than 'daughter of a brother or sister' to mean either a male or female descendant or a younger relative.

nobility. The term was originally applied to all ranks above commoners, so as to include *earls, *barons, *knights, and *esquires. The establishment of the House of Lords created a clear distinction between the hereditary nobility (the peerage) and lower ranks, but in the 17th century the *gentry were still thought of as noble. By the 19th century the exclusion of the gentry from the nobility led to the use of the inclusive term aristocracy.

noble (coin). A gold coin worth 6s. 8d., or half a *mark. It was first minted in 1351.

Nonconformity. A Nonconformist or Dissenter was originally one who refused to conform to the Acts of the 'Clarendon Code' passed after the *Restoration of Charles II, in particular the Act of Uniformity, which came into force on St Bartholomew's Day, 24 August 1662, and which required all English and Welsh clergy to consent to the entire contents of the *Book of Common Prayer. For refusing to conform, over 2,000 clergymen, about one-fifth of the entire body of ministers, were ejected from their livings. For short periods in 1669 and 1672 Nonconformist meetings were tolerated as 'licensed conventicles'.

In 1689, after the *Glorious Revolution, Protestant Nonconformists were allowed to license their meeting-houses for public worship at the quarter sessions, but they were still banned from holding public office and excluded from the universities.

The early Nonconformist registers are mainly records of baptisms. For marriages and burials (and often duplicate baptisms) Dissenters used the *Church of England. *Civil registration, from 1837, heralded a relaxation of the insistence that Church of England baptism was a necessary requirement for the holding of public office; Nonconformist registers deposited with the *Registrar-General (and now kept at the *Public Record Office) were allowed as legal evidence by the Non-Parochial Registers Act (1840).

Norden, John (1548–1625?). Writer of county histories, surveyor and mapmaker, and author of devotional or religious works.

Northumbria. The most northerly of the *Anglo-Saxon kingdoms. The original Anglian migrants formed the two kingdoms of Bernicia and Deira. In the early 7th century Aethelfrith united the two territories into one kingdom, which remained intact until the Danish conquest of 865.

notary. A professional scribe and compiler of legal documents.

Notes and Queries. A periodical first published weekly in 1849, and now published quarterly by Oxford University Press. It contains much valuable information on all subjects, mostly supplied by readers in reply to other readers' queries. The main subjects are literary and historical, but much genealogy and local history are included. There are cumulative indexes, but not for the more recent volumes. It is available in most of the large public libraries.

novel disseisin. A medieval legal action for claiming recent dispossession.

nuncupative. A will made by word of mouth only, before 'credible witnesses' who later made sworn statements before a probate court.

nunnery. Small religious houses, with usually only up to 12 nuns under a prioress. Most were founded in the 12th or 13th centuries.

nuptiality. A measure of the extent to which women marry.

o

oasthouses. Kilns for drying *hops in south-eastern England and the south-west midlands.

Ogilby, John (1600–76) is remembered best for his *Britannia Depicta* (1675), which contained 100 strip-maps of the 73 principal highways of the kingdom, the first set of road maps produced in Britain.

old age pensions. Introduced from 1 January 1909 by David Lloyd-George, the Chancellor of the Exchequer of Asquith's Liberal Government. At first, the state pension was for people over 70.

Old English. 1. (linguistic). Term used to embrace all the dialects of the *Anglo-Saxons up to *c.*1150. These developed into Middle English (to *c.*1500) and Modern English.
    2. (Irish). Term used to distinguish English people who settled in Ireland before the new settlers of the 16th and 17th centuries.

old style. The dating of days and months before the replacement of the *Julian by the *Gregorian calendar in 1752 and the change from 25 March to 1 January as the official start of a new year.

one hundred years' rule. The rule to preserve confidentiality of certain records, e.g. *census enumerators' returns, by prohibiting access before 100 years have passed.

One-Name Studies, Guild of. A group which encourages the registering of all available information about individuals sharing a particular *surname and which seeks to study past and present distributions of such names. The guild was founded in 1979, is based at the Society of *Genealogists, and holds regular meetings.

open-fields. The widespread system whereby the agricultural land of a *parish was farmed in large fields which were divided into *strips. The number and extent of the fields varied. They were normally farmed communally under regulations agreed at the manor *court.

open hall. In the Middle Ages and after manor houses were arranged around a central hall which was open to the rafters. Smoke from a central fire escaped through a louvre in the ceiling. The hall served as a communal dining-area and as sleeping accommodation for some of the servants. The lord's family and guests sat at a table on a raised dais at the end of the hall that had access to the private withdrawing rooms and chambers. The other end of the hall was shielded from the service rooms by a screen.

oral history. Oral history is a term imported from the USA to describe a historical approach that is based on the use of personal reminiscences.

The pioneer work in Britain is *Ask the Fellows Who Cut the Hay* (1956) by George Ewart Evans. In this and subsequent books Evans established the value of personal testimony in providing an understanding of the old farming economy of the era of horse power and hand tools. No written sources could match the wealth of detailed explanation of this former way of life. He showed that oral evidence could be treated just as rigorously as evidence from other sources.

The year 1971 marked the appearance of the first issue of *Oral History*, the annual journal of the Oral History Society.

orator. A plaintiff or petitioner, referred to in legal documents as 'your orator'.

oratory. A medieval chapel which was licensed for private use. Upon toleration in the 19th century, a *Roman Catholic society of priests which was founded at Rome in 1564 built oratories for preaching and the holding of popular services.

ordeal. Until 1212 legal suits could be decided by three types of ordeal; by combat for *knights, by fire for freemen, and by water for *villeins.

ordinary. 1. In *heraldry, a reference book that lists the heraldic descriptions of shields of arms.

2. In ecclesiastical law and administration, one having authority, e.g. a bishop.

Ordnance Survey. The threat of invasion from France in the late 18th century caused the Board of Ordnance, based at the Tower of London, to map the south coast of England on the scale of one inch to one mile. This grew into a series covering the whole of Britain.

The Ordnance Survey became a separate organization in 1841. The six-inch series was started in 1840; the 25-inch maps covering all but the wildest areas date from 1853 to 1896. Large-scale maps for urban areas began with the five feet to one mile survey of the 1850s, which was abandoned in 1858 in favour of a 10 feet to the mile survey; this was discontinued in 1894. The latest series of 25-inch maps was begun in 1948 and completed in the early 1980s.

outfangtheof. The right of a manorial lord to arrest a thief beyond the manorial estate and to hold the trial at his own court.

outlaw. One who had escaped custody or who had failed to appear before a court to answer criminal charges. After four summonses an absconder's goods were confiscated and he was declared beyond the protection of the law; therefore an outlaw could be legally killed by anyone who met him. Outlawry was not abolished until 1879.

ovens, common. In the Middle Ages and the early modern period many towns and villages had a common oven for the baking of bread. These were usually provided by manorial lords.

Owen, William, *Book of Fairs.* The most popular of the 18th-century guides to *fairs, arranged under counties. First published in 1756, the sixth edition of 1770 is the fullest and most accessible.

Oxford movement. An intellectual movement in the *Church of England, centred on Oxford University in the middle decades of the 19th century. It was concerned at first with doctrine and ecclesiastical authority, but soon became associated with the move to restore ritual in the Anglican church. The movement was inspired by a romantic medievalism, which led to many internal changes in parish churches, involving *stained glass, screens, choir stalls, elevated chancel floors, etc.

Oxford University archives. The archives of the University, including *wills proved at the court of the Chancellor of the University, are kept at the *Bodleian Library. The individual colleges have their own archives.

oxgang. See BOVATE.

oyer and terminer, commission of. In the Middle Ages and after, justices of the royal court were occasionally commissioned by the Crown to hear and determine specific cases of treason, murder, and other serious crimes within a particular county. The records are kept in the *Public Record Office under JUST 1.

packhorses Although specialist breeds of horse were sometimes used, the term 'packhorse' was applied loosely to any horse that carried a pack. By the 18th century the normal weight of a pack of cloth was 240 lb. and the distance covered in a day was up to 30 miles.

pains. The regulations issued by the jury of a manorial *court leet, the breach of which incurred a fixed penalty.

palaeography. The handwriting of documents from the 18th century onwards does not present too many difficulties in terms of unfamiliar forms and styles, though, as today, individual writers vary in their clarity. The script used in the 16th and 17th centuries was radically different, however, even if it was in English rather than Latin.

Several manuals provide guidance on how to read medieval Court Hand, the Secretary Hand of the Elizabethans, and the Italic Hand, which was introduced in the 16th century from Italy and which became general after the *Restoration and was the forerunner of modern styles.

One of the greatest difficulties in reading old documents is caused by the use of abbreviations. These were developed in the Middle Ages, but long continued in use. At first, they consisted of various signs above the line to indicate the exact nature of the shortening, but by the 16th century they had often degenerated into dashes, flourishes, or squiggles. They cause particular problems when the declension of a Latin word is obscured by an abbreviated ending.

Palaeolithic. The Old *Stone Age, the earliest period of human activity following the last Ice Age.

palatine means 'pertaining to a palace'. Palatinates were huge lordships established for the defence of border regions.

Pale. 1. A territory under a particular jurisdiction, e.g. the English Pale in the hinterland of Calais, or the Pale in Ireland over which the English had jurisdiction. This sense has given rise to the expression 'beyond the pale'.

2. A stake in a fence, e.g. around a *deer park.

palimpsest. A manuscript on which the original writing has been replaced by new. The word was recently used by W. G. Hoskins to describe the successive layers of history that are revealed by a study of the land-scape.

Palladian. The villas, churches, and other public buildings of Andrea Palladio (1508–80) in Vicenza, Venice, and the surrounding country-side, together with his *Four Books of Architecture* (1570), were enormously influential in western European countries and their former colonies. The style was based on the strict proportions and decorative features of the major surviving buildings of ancient Greece and Rome.

Pallot's Index of Marriages and Births. An index begun in 1818 by a firm of record agents, whose successors included Messrs Pallot & Co. The index includes the marriages of 101 of the 103 ancient *parishes of London and of many Middlesex parishes for the period 1800–37, with a smaller number from elsewhere, together with 30,000 baptisms. The index is now held (and catalogued) by the *Institute of Heraldic and Genealogical Studies, Canterbury.

palmer. One who wore a representation of a palm branch as a token of a pilgrimage to the Holy Land.

pannage. The right to graze pigs on acorns and beech mast on the *commons of a *manor.

pantiles are the curving, orange-coloured roofing tiles which were introduced into eastern England from the Netherlands during the 17th century.

paper-making. The earliest-known paper mill was in production at Hert-ford in 1495, but the industry was insubstantial until the second half of the 17th century. Water power was used for beating until well into the 19th century.

parchment. Many old documents were written on both sides of the treated skins of sheep or goats.

pardoner. A seller of *indulgences.

pargeting. The decorative plasterwork on external walls of houses in Suffolk, Essex, and parts of adjacent counties.

paring and burning. A technique used to kill weeds and fertilize the land with potash before bringing it into cultivation.

parish. The majority of England's medieval parishes were formed by 1200. The antiquity of parish boundaries has been a matter of much de-bate. Many parishes preserve the outline of pre-Conquest estates. The shape and size of a parish varied from one part of the country to an-other.

The pattern of parishes in urban areas is markedly different from that in the countryside. London had over 100 parishes by the end of the Middle Ages, while leading provincial cities such as Norwich or York had over 40 each. On the other hand, the new industrial towns, such as Manchester or Sheffield, were served by single parishes which included large sections of the surrounding countryside. These huge urban parishes were not divided up into numerous new ones until the second and third quarters of the 19th century.

The Tudor governments gave responsibilities for the poor, the highways, and for petty law and order to civil parishes, which often covered the same area as the ecclesiastical parishes. Where ecclesiastical parishes were large, their subdivisions (the townships, or groups of townships) became the civil parishes. Information on the size and shape of these civil parishes can be obtained from 19th-century *directories, the large-scale maps of the *Ordnance Survey, and the relevant volumes of the *Victoria County History*. The Local Government Act (1894) divided England and Wales into some 14,000 parishes, whose boundaries generally followed those of the old civil parishes. Anomalies caused by divided parishes and detached portions were removed.

Scotland had acquired a similar structure of ecclesiastical and civil parishes by the 16th century. The medieval parishes of Ireland were often made redundant by the land reallocations of the 17th century. The parishes of the *Church of Ireland are usually amalgamations of the ancient parishes, but the Catholic Church had to create a new parish network in the 18th and 19th centuries.

parish registers. In 1538 Thomas Cromwell ordered each *parish in England and Wales to keep a register of baptisms, marriages, and burials. At first the normal practice was to record such events on loose sheets, many of which have been lost or destroyed. In 1597 it was ordered that from the coming year each parish should keep a bound register and that older records should be entered into that register, the accuracy of the transcript being attested at the foot of each page by the minister and two churchwardens. Only a minority of parishes have records as far back as 1538; many parishes began their copies in 1558, the year that Elizabeth I came to the throne. These *bishop's transcripts are now kept at diocesan *record offices.

Since 1979 (and in individual cases long before) parish registers have normally been deposited at the appropriate local record office, unless a church has adequate facilities to ensure their safe keeping.

A great number of parish registers have been published. No standard form of entry was imposed on English and Welsh parish registers until Lord Hardwicke's *Marriage Act (1753) and *Rose's Act (1812). The style of entry therefore varies from place to place and over time. Often, only the barest details are given, i.e. the date of the event and the name of the person who was buried, or the names of the groom and bride, or the name of a baptized child with the name of the father. In the earliest registers this information is often recorded in simple Latin. Most registers have occasional gaps.

An Act which came into force at *Michaelmas 1653 transferred responsibility for keeping the register to an elected official, known as the Parish Register [sic], though in practice the minister or clerk was often elected and the arrangements continued as before. The Act ordered the recording of births rather than baptisms, but this instruction was frequently ignored. During the later 17th and 18th centuries various attempts were made by central government or the bishops of some dioceses to improve the quality of registration. Rose's Act (1812), which came into effect on 1 January 1813, insisted on standard entries in bound volumes for all events. Henceforth, a baptismal entry noted the name of the child, the date of baptism, the full names of the parents, their place of residence, and the occupation of the father. Marriage entries recorded the names of both partners, their parishes, the date of the ceremony, and the names of witnesses. Burial entries noted the name and age of the deceased, his or her place of residence, and the date of the burial.

In Scotland the older system of parish registration goes back to 1552. The quality of these registers was never as good as in England and Wales. The 4,000 or so registers that survive have been deposited in the Scottish General Register Office and have been microfilmed for the Mormon International Genealogical Index. In Ireland the records of almost 1,000 parishes were destroyed by fire in 1922. However, transcripts survive for some parishes, and a number of original volumes are intact because they were not deposited centrally.

park. The meaning of the word 'park' has changed considerably over time. It is derived from the *Old English *pearroc* 'an enclosed piece of land', a meaning which is retained in some field-names. In the Middle Ages it was used exclusively for *deer park. The 18th century was the great age of landscaped parks, the 19th century of the municipal recreational park.

Parliament: the franchise. The right to vote at parliamentary elections was gradually extended by the Reform Acts of 1832, 1867, and 1884, until in 1918 all men over 21 and all women over 30 were enfranchised. In 1928 the age at which women were allowed to vote was lowered to 21. The age for both males and females was lowered to 18 in 1969. Voting was a public affair until the Secret Ballot Act (1872).

Parliamentary papers. The 'blue books' of the late 18th and 19th centuries, a comprehensive collection of which may be consulted at the

*British Library. Reprints by the Irish Universities Press are available at major public and university *libraries.

parlour. A ground-floor sitting-room and bedroom. In many parts of Britain it remained the best bedroom into the 18th century. By the 19th century it had acquired the meaning of best front room.

parterre. A level flower-bed in a formal *garden, especially one designed in the late 17th and early 18th centuries after French and Dutch examples.

partible inheritance. A system whereby all children, or in some cases all sons, received a share of an estate, in contrast to the system of *primogeniture. Particular types of partible inheritance included *Borough English and *gavelkind.

passenger lists of emigrants to the colonies of the British Empire are incomplete. Most are kept in the *Public Record Office under BT 27. The fullest give name, age, place of origin, occupation, and the family relationship of each passenger; but many are simply a list of names. Bristol Archives Office has a detailed register of passengers who embarked at Bristol for America between 1654 and 1679.

passports. From the late 16th century to 1677 the government issued *licences to pass beyond the seas. A register of passports from 1795 onwards is kept at the *Public Record Office under FO 610. Indexes of names are available for 1851–62 and 1874–98 under FO 611. The modern type of passport with a description and photograph of the holder was introduced in 1921.

pastor. In Britain the word is used for a *Nonconformist minister.

patent. From 1617 the sovereign, *Privy Council, or Parliament granted the right to use an invention. The Patent Office for the *United Kingdom was established in 1852.

Patent rolls. The registered copies of Letters Patent issued by the Court of *Chancery from 1201 to 1946, kept at the *Public Record Office under C 66.

patronymic. A surname derived from a father.

pattern books. Local builders and other craftsmen obtained their knowledge of the latest styles through pattern books that were published in France, Italy, the Netherlands, etc. and in Britain from the 16th to the 19th centuries.

pavilions. The term had a specialist meaning in the 18th century to denote the balancing wings of a country house.

pays. A framework of explanation of social and economic development focused on distinctive countrysides, best described by the French word *pays*.

Although it was recognized that *pays* underwent change, studies have stressed the long continuity of major characteristics such as farming systems, land-ownership and manorial control, social structure, rural industries, and religious and political attitudes.

peas were formerly grown as a fodder-crop for animals as well as for human consumption.

peasants. In France *paysan* is used to denote a small farmer, but in Britain the term has acquired derogatory connotations. Medieval historians find the term an appropriate one, but early modern historians prefer the contemporary terms *husbandman and *yeoman.

Peasants' Revolt (1381). The major uprising of the Middle Ages, also known as the English Rising, for it occurred in towns as well as in the countryside. The main area of revolt was southern and eastern England.

peculiar jurisdiction. For a variety of reasons, certain *parishes, *manors, and *liberties were exempt from the jurisdiction of the bishop and archdeacon in whose *diocese and *archdeaconry they were situated. They include the separate or 'peculiar' jurisdictions of another archbishop or bishop, the *dean and *chapter of a cathedral, the Knights *Templar and Knights *Hospitaller, and of chapels royal, e.g. St George's, Windsor. A knowledge of such jurisdictions is necessary when searching for *wills and probate *inventories before 1858. In practice, the records of most peculiars are found in diocesan *record offices alongside those that were proved through the archdeaconry courts.

pedigree. A genealogical table. The first collections of pedigrees were made in the 15th century.

pedlar. In the early modern period pedlars provided a distribution system that connected all parts of Britain. Pedlars sold ribbons, gloves, *lace, tape, points, pins, thread, looking-glasses, necklaces, bracelets, brooches, hats, *ballads, *chapbooks, etc.

pele-towers. Characteristic *tower houses found on both sides of the Scottish border, dating from the 14th to the 17th century, by which the typical arrangement of service-rooms, living-quarters, and bedrooms was expressed vertically rather than horizontally. Such buildings afforded short-term defence against marauders.

penance. At the *Reformation instead of having works of penance imposed, the guilty person was ordered to stand in the presence of the congregation at church, dressed in a white sheet, bare-headed, bare-legged, and bare-foot, carrying a wand, and to confess the fault, express penitence, and pray for forgiveness. The minister and churchwardens signed a certificate, which was sent to the bishop's office, to say that the penance had been performed. These certificates are kept at diocesan record offices. The practice fell into disuse in the later 17th century.

pence. Silver pennies were first minted in the 8th century, when they were known as *deniers* after the Roman *denarii*, hence the abbreviation *d*. Twelve old pence made one shilling, twenty shillings made one pound. Pence were often counted (and written down) in amounts up to two shillings, e.g. as 16*d*. or 20*d*.

pens. The quill pen that was used until the 19th century was made from a goose feather, shaped by a penknife to form a nib. Metal nibs were first made in the mid-19th century and fountain pens from the end of the century.

peppercorn rent. A nominal rent acknowledging the tenancy.

perambulations. Until the *Ordnance Survey published large-scale maps which marked the boundaries of *parishes, it was a common practice at *Rogationtide for groups of parishioners to walk their boundaries and to mark stones and trees. A number of written accounts of such perambulations have survived in manorial records, dating from the 16th to the 18th centuries, which record each boundary point in turn.

perch. A square measure. 40 perches made one *rood (a quarter of an *acre). Old *maps and *surveys express measurements in the form of, e.g., '7 a[cres]. 3 r[oods]. 21 p[erches]'.

Perpendicular architecture. The last of the *Gothic styles of the Middle Ages and the only one to be peculiarly English. The style is distinguished by the straight mullions of the windows, by ranges of clerestorey windows surmounted by battlements and pinnacles, and by splendid *towers.

perpetual curate. A priest who was nominated by a lay *rector, and licensed by a bishop, to serve a *parish which did not have a *vicar. Once appointed, such a curate had lifelong tenure.

personalty. Personal estate that, under common law, did not pass to the heir upon the death of an owner but could be bequeathed by a *will.

petty sessions. Courts of summary jurisdiction held by two or more *Justices of the Peace or magistrates for trying lesser offences or to enquire into indictable offences. The proceedings of the 17th and 18th centuries are not well recorded. They are now sittings of magistrates' courts.

pews were not widely used in the early Middle Ages, when most people stood during church services, or squatted on the floor. The 'weak went to the wall' to sit on a stone bench. Wooden benches were introduced into English churches during the 14th century. They became widespread during the 15th century, though they occupied only part of the available space.

During the 17th century it became the fashion to fill the nave of a parish church with box-pews. In rural parishes, in particular, the ownership of these pews passed with that of the farm or *cottage to which it belonged. The arrangement of the pews reflected the social structure of the parish, with the rich at the front, the middling sort in the centre, and the poor at the sides and the back. In corporate towns the mayor and corporation occupied the best pews. During the 18th century many churches became crammed with pews and galleries. Most of these were replaced during the Victorian period by new pews.

pewter. An alloy of *tin, *lead, and *brass, which was cast in moulds, then turned and hammered. From the early 14th to the 18th century pewter was widely used in Britain for plates, mugs, tankards, etc.

pheasant shooting was a minority sport of the rich which became organized in a big way during the reign of Victoria.

photographs. Photography was invented independently in France and England in the first half of the 19th century. Photographs become a major source of information for local and family historians in many parts of Britain in the 1840s and 1850s. Many places had their early enthusiasts who have left invaluable records. Most public reference *libraries or *museums have large collections of local photographs. Many old photographs are undated, and few of those collected in family albums have been identified for future generations.

Picts. During the *Roman occupation of Britain the *Picti* were hostile tribes north of the Antonine wall. They were assimilated with the Scots in the 9th century.

piece halls. The *clothiers of the West Riding of Yorkshire brought their finished pieces of cloth to market at the close of each week. During the 18th century several clothing towns built halls to protect sellers and buyers from bad weather.

piece work. The system by which a worker was paid by the 'piece', or finished good, rather than by a regular wage.

Piepoudre, Court of. Especially in the Middle Ages, the court by which the owner of the right to hold a market or *fair settled disputes, regulated measures, and maintained order.

Piers Plowman. The great Middle English poem written by William Langland in the late 1370s, which *inter alia* provides much information about medieval agriculture.

pightle. A small, irregular shaped piece of land, usually at the edge of cultivation. The word was corrupted into various forms, e.g. pingle.

Pilgrimage of Grace (1536). A rebellion that began in Lincolnshire and the East Riding of Yorkshire and which quickly spread to other parts of the country. It was sparked off by opposition to the *dissolution of the monasteries, but its underlying causes were high prices and resentment directed against certain landlords.

pillboxes. In 1940 thousands of small concrete defences, from which Bren machine guns could be fired on all sides, were built under the threat of German invasion.

pillory. Whereas the *stocks fastened an offender by the legs, the pillory secured a standing person by the neck and arms, thus leaving him vulnerable to objects thrown by spectators. Pillories stood in market places and offenders were placed there by order of the *Justices of the Peace. The pillory was abolished in 1837.

pillow mounds. Long, raised banks of soft earth with artificial burrows were deliberately created for *rabbits by the keepers of *warrens, especially in the 16th century.

pinder. The manorial officer in charge of the *pinfold.

pineapples. The fruit was introduced from central and south America in the early 18th century. The 'pineapples' used in decorative carving in the 17th century were based on the cones of pine trees.

pinfold. A pound in which stray animals were locked. Manorial *court records record fines and disputes.

Pipe Rolls. The annual accounts of Crown revenues, which were sent by *sheriffs to the *Exchequer, where they were rolled around rods ('pipes') for storage. They are now housed in the *Public Record Office under E 372. They survive from 1130–1, with an almost continuous series from 1155–6 until 1832. Some have been published by the Pipe Roll Society.

piscary, right of. The common right to fish in the pools, etc. of a *manor.

piscina. The stone basin in which a priest washed his hands and the vessels after mass. They are normally set in the wall to the south of an *altar.

plague. Plague was endemic in Britain from at least the *Black Death of 1348–50 until its mysterious disappearance after 1666.

Plantagenets. A family, French in origin, to which the Kings of England from 1154 (Henry II) to 1399 (Richard II) belonged.

Plantations. The new settlements in Ulster and other parts of Ireland, Virginia, New England, and the West Indies in the late 16th and early 17th centuries.

plashing. The formation of stock-proof hedges by skilful pruning and intertwining of branches.

plasterwork, decorative. The *nobility and leading members of the legal profession started the fashion for decorating ceilings and walls with plasterwork mouldings in the second half of the 16th century. The fashion spread to *gentry families and then to wealthy *yeomen.

playstow. A recreational area or playground, commemorated in minor place-names.

Plea rolls. Records of actions brought under the common law in the courts of *Common Pleas, *Exchequer, *King's Bench, etc., from the late 12th century until 1873. A *Calendar of Pleas and Memoranda Rolls* is available for the early rolls down to 1482.

pleaching. See PLASHING.

Plot, Robert (1640–96). Oxford scholar and first keeper of the Ashmolean museum, who was influential in moving the *antiquarian tradition of county studies in a new direction with his emphasis on natural history: *Natural History of Oxfordshire* (1677) and *Natural History of Staffordshire* (1686).

Plough Monday. The public holiday on the Monday following 6 January. In the Middle Ages farm-workers in eastern England raised money for the local parish church by dragging a plough around the streets. The associated performance of a play involving song, dance, verse, and ad-libbing is not recorded before the 1760s.

ploughs. The design of ploughs was highly varied, since, until the late 18th century, most were made locally, were adapted to local soil conditions, and conformed to local preferences.

plurality. The holding of more than one *benefice by a clergyman.

Plymouth Brethren. A *Nonconformist sect founded in Ireland in the late 1820s by The Revd J. N. Darby and established at Plymouth in 1830. It has no formal creed or ministers; each local church is autonomous. In 1849 the Open Brethren split from the Exclusive Brethren.

Pococke, Dr Richard (1704–65). Irish bishop famous for his travel writings.

police. The first police force was established at Bow Street, London, in the early 18th century. In 1829 Sir Robert Peel, the Home Secretary, appointed police commissioners to take over responsibility from the magistrates. An Act of 1839 allowed the *Justices of the Peace at *quarter sessions to create a county force of chief and petty constables. This was made compulsory in 1856.

Polish immigrants. Many Polish *Jews emigrated to Britain in the late 19th century to escape Tsar Alexander III's pogroms. The main period of Polish immigration was during and immediately after the Second World War.

poll books. Until 1872 elections to Parliament were not held in secret. An Act of 1696, designed to prevent fraud on the part of returning officers, authorized the publication of copies of the poll, showing how each elector had voted. Returning officers soon afterwards allowed local printers to publish poll books of county elections as a commercial venture.

poll tax. A tax on heads, or polls, was first levied in England in 1377. It was levied again in 1379 and 1381, but the hostility aroused by the tax caused the government to abandon it after the *Peasants' Revolt. The tax returns are kept in the *Public Record Office under E 179.

In 1377 the tax was levied at 4*d*. per head for all lay people over the age of 14; clergy paid a shilling. It is not clear how many people were exempt or under the age of 14 or who evaded payment, so different multipliers have been used to calculate population totals. The 1377 returns are considered to be the most complete, being less subject to the large-scale evasions of 1379 and 1381. The return of 1379 is useful, however, in grading the tax according to the wealth of people above the age of 16. The basic rate remained 4*d*., but many craftsmen and tradesmen paid 6*d*., 1*s*., or 2*s*., and the more substantial people paid higher rates, culminating in the £4 paid by an earl; clergy were now exempt.

The poll tax was reintroduced in 1641 and again upon the *Restoration of Charles II. It was levied on eight occasions between 1660 and 1697. Few returns survive in central records, but a number of local returns are housed in local *record offices.

pollarding. The cropping of trees, especially oak, beech, elm, and hornbeam, at their heads (Norman French *poll*), in order to obtain poles for fencing, etc.

polyfocal settlements. The old idea that the original *Anglo-Saxon settlers lived in villages has been discredited. It is now realized that villages arose in the late Anglo-Saxon / Scandinavian period either through a deliberate act of replanning or by the gradual coalescing of small settlements or isolated farms, which did not originally have a single focus.

pontage. A toll levied at a bridge for its maintenance.

poor, overseer of. The officer chosen at a *vestry meeting of a *township or civil *parish to administer the *Poor Law for the ensuing year. The overseer was empowered to raise taxes ('assessments' or 'rates') in order to meet demands for poor relief. He had to submit his accounts at the end of his year of office for the approval of the vestry. The system started in Elizabeth's reign and was consolidated by the Poor Law Acts of 1597–1601. It lasted until the Poor Law Amendment Act (1834).

Overseers' records were kept in the parish chest and are now housed at local *record offices. Quarter sessions records in the form of depositions, indictment books, and order books are the other major source of information.

Poor Law. The history of poor relief in England and Wales is divided into two periods, separated by the Poor Law Amendment Act (1834). During the first period the civil *parish was the unit of administration. The Acts of 1597 and 1601 ordered the annual election of overseers of the *poor, who were answerable to the parish *vestry and to the *Justices of the Peace. The overseers were empowered to raise revenue from local rates.

The Act of *Settlement (1662) defined the ways in which a parish was responsible; this led to large numbers of cases being heard before the *quarter sessions. The Poor Law Amendment Act (1834) abolished the old system and introduced a new one based on unions of parishes, run by boards of elected *guardians.

port. 1. The place-name can mean either harbour, market town, or gate.
2. The Exchequer port books, housed at the *Public Record Office under E 190, are an important source for the history of local overseas trade and of coastal traffic in the early modern period. They survive in large numbers for many ports for the period 1565–1799, though there are gaps in the Civil War and *Commonwealth and for some ports the records cease in the mid-18th century.

portcullis. The heavy grating, made of iron or wood and iron, that defended the entrance of a medieval *castle, manor house, or town.

portico. A range of columns supporting a pediment, which provided a formal entrance to a classical-style building.

Portland stone. The white oolitic limestone of the Isle of Portland (Dorset).

portraiture. The fashion for hanging portraits of family and friends developed in the reign of Elizabeth I.

postcards were used from about 1870 onwards. Picture-postcards with views of streets and rural scenes became popular towards the end of the 19th century and were used on a very large scale during the first 20 years of the 20th century.

post-medieval archaeology. The archaeology of the centuries between 1500 and 1800.

Post Office. The office of Postmaster of England was created by James I (1603–25), who in 1609 created a monopoly, the Royal Mail. By the middle of the 17th century towns throughout England and Wales were connected by a postal service. The system was subsequently extended to Scotland and to Ireland after unification. The Post Office has an Archives and Records Centre at Mount Pleasant House, London ECIA IBB.

potatoes. During the early 17th century the potato was introduced from America into Ireland and by the middle of the century was also successfully established in western Lancashire and Cumbria.

poultry. The keeping of poultry was traditionally regarded as the responsibility of the farmer's wife, the profits being used as spending money. For this reason poultry (or 'pullen') were often not recorded in probate *inventories.

prebendary. A member of a *chapter of a cathedral or *college, who held the revenues of a prebend, e.g. the *tithes and dues of a parish that formed a *peculiar jurisdiction.

precentor. The officer in charge of musical arrangements at a cathedral.

precognition. In Scotland, the written report of the evidence of witnesses to a crime, taken in order to prepare a case before it comes to trial. These survive from 1812 onwards amongst the Lord Advocate's records at the *Scottish Record Office, under AD 14 and 15. The records are arranged within years by the name of the accused. A card index, arranged alphabetically, is available up to 1900.

Premonstratensians. An order of regular *canons, founded at Premontré, near Laon (France) in 1120. The first house in Britain was established at Newhouse (Lincolnshire) in 1143. Soon the Premonstratensians had 31 abbeys and three nunneries, mostly in remote places. The heyday of the order was in the 12th century. All were dissolved in the late 1530s.

prerogative courts. The probate courts of the Archbishops of Canterbury and York, which proved the *wills of testators who left considerable goods in more than one *diocese or *deanery. Wills proved in the Prerogative Court of Canterbury (the senior of the two) from 1383 to

1858 are kept at the *Public Record Office, under PROB 11 and 12. Indexes have been published down to 1700, and the Society of *Genealogists has a slip index for 1750–1800. Surviving probate *inventories are collected under PROB 2 to 5. During the years 1653–60 all wills in England and Wales were proved through this court. The probate records of the Prerogative Court of York are housed at the *Borthwick Institute of Historical Research, York, alongside the records of the *archdeaconry of York. The Yorkshire Archaeological Society Record Series has published indexes from the 1380s down to 1688; typewritten indexes are available for later periods.

Presbyterians. The Presbyterian Church rejected government by bishops in favour of a hierarchy of general assembly, synod, presbytery, and kirk session, on each of which sit ministers and elders of equal rank. The doctrines of the church were strongly influenced by Calvinism. At the *Reformation the *Church of Scotland became Presbyterian.

The number of English Presbyterians grew in the 1570s and 1580s. They became one of the most influential *Puritan sects in the first half of the 17th century. After the *Restoration the Presbyterians became the most respectable *Nonconformist group, with an educated ministry and a prosperous membership. In 1972 the Presbyterian Church of England joined with the Congregational Church of England and Wales to form the United Reformed Church.

presentment. A statement made on oath by a jury concerning matters within its knowledge, e.g. the ownership of property, or by a churchwarden at a bishop or archdeacon's visitation.

presents (by these). A formal start to a legal document, meaning 'by this document'.

press-gang. Once a man had accepted the 'King's shilling' from a recruiting party for the navy or army he was obliged to serve. Such payments did not entice enough volunteers, so military parties forcibly pressed others into service. The system was used sporadically from the 16th to the 19th centuries.

priest. In Christian teaching, an ordained minister above the level of *deacon and below that of bishop, authorized to celebrate the mass and hear confession. After the *Reformation, use of the term declined within the Reformed Churches, being associated with the *Roman Catholic and Orthodox Churches, but in the *Church of England it was readopted in some parishes for clergymen associated with the *High Church movement.

priest holes. Secret hiding-places in the homes of *Roman Catholic families for protecting chaplains and itinerant priests from persecution during the late 16th and early 17th centuries.

Prime Ministers, lists of. See pp. 280–2.

primogeniture. The system of *inheritance whereby an estate passed to the eldest male heir. In practice, the distinctions were blurred, for younger children received some provision.

Principal Probate Registry. Founded in 1858, to take over responsibility for proving *wills. The registry is at *Somerset House, London.

priory. A monastery or *nunnery headed by a prior or prioress, which was a lower rank than abbot or abbess. In practice, some priories were larger than some abbeys.

prise. The compulsory purchase of provisions for a royal household on the move and the requisition of means of transport. The Statute of Purveyors (1362) attempted to remedy abuses.

prison. The *Public Record Office keeps records of prisoners from 1770 to 1894 under PCOM. These include registers, photographs, minute books, and visitors' books. From 1824 to 1876 quarterly prison returns record offence, date, place of conviction, and length of sentence. The PRO also has registers for the Fleet and King's Bench prisons and for Newgate Gaol (HO 10). A card index of people in debtors' prisons in London from 1775 can be consulted at the Corporation of London Record Office at the *Guildhall. Some county gaol records up to 1877 are retained amongst quarter sessions papers in county *record offices.

Privy Council. This group of royal advisers emerged in the 14th century and exercised great power during the 16th and 17th centuries, as the forerunner of the Cabinet. The council dealt with all matters of state, and members sat upon the bench at sessions of the courts of *Star Chamber, *Requests, and *High Commission. In Elizabeth I's reign, in particular, many local matters came to its attention. See *Acts of the Privy Council of England* (several vols., 1890–1964), which print the register from 1542 to 1631. The most important classes in the *Public Record Office are PC 1 and LIS 24 and 35.

Privy Seal. From the 12th century the clerks of the King's chamber attached a private seal to documents. By the 14th century the authority of this seal rivalled that of the *Great Seal.

probate accounts. About 30,000 probate accounts survive in various *record offices. A year or so after the death of a testator, accounts of the

estate were submitted to an *ecclesiastical court by an executrix or
executor, or by the person who had received letters of *administration
in cases of intestacy. By that time, an inventory of the personal estate
had been drawn up, debts had been paid, and expenses were known,
leaving the residue to be divided according to the terms of the will or
the wishes of the administratrix. Nearly three-quarters of all probate
accounts were filed by women. These records therefore provide unique
information on women's experience in handling property and the history of property relations between men and women.

prodigy-houses. The name for the huge country houses that were built
in the Elizabethan and Jacobean age by the members of the government
circle.

proof of age. Before documentary evidence was available in the form of
*parish registers, etc. proof of age, e.g. of a minor, was established by a
sworn jury making a presentment. Records are kept in the *Public
Record Office under C 132–42. See also the published volumes of
Calendars of Inquisitions.

prospect towers. 18th- or 19th-century towers which commanded a
prospect or distant view from a hill or a landscaped *park. Some commemorate historical events or characters.

Protectorate, the. The period 1653–60, when Oliver Cromwell, followed in 1658 by his son Richard, had the title of Lord Protector of the
Commonwealth.

Protestant. Member of any of the churches that repudiated the supremacy of the pope at the *Reformation or which emerged later from
that tradition.

Protestation returns. In 1642 Parliament ordered all males in England
and Wales over the age of 18 to take an oath 'to live and die for the true
Protestant religion, the liberties and rights of subjects, and the privilege
of Parliaments'. Lists were made by churchwardens and *constables of
all who signed and of those who refused to sign.

The *Appendix* to the *5th Report of the Historical Manuscripts Commission*
(1876), 120–34, notes all the areas for which returns survive in the
*House of Lords Record Office.

proto-industrialization. A concept advanced by F. F. Mendels argued
that the origins of the *Industrial Revolution must be sought in rural industries which produced goods for external markets. The success of
these industries provided economic opportunities for earlier marriages
and therefore more children, and encouraged the rise of commercial
agriculture, two necessary conditions for rapid industrial growth. Critics

have pointed to the eventual failure of some flourishing rural industries and to the role of towns in the industrialization process.

provost. 1. In Scotland, the head of a municipal corporation or *burgh, cf. the English mayor.

2. In the *Church of England, the head of a *chapter of a cathedral founded in the 19th or 20th century, cf. the *dean of older establishments.

3. The head of a *college.

psalter. A written or printed book containing the Psalms.

pseudo-gentry. A term coined by Alan Everitt to describe those 17th-century townsmen who were as wealthy as the rural *gentry but who did not have a landed estate to support a claim to gentility.

public health. The Public Health Act (1848) established local boards which were responsible to the General Board of Health. The Public Health Act (1872) established urban and rural sanitary authorities, and the Public Health Act (1875) empowered local authorities to make by-laws governing the building of new houses and streets. Each of these authorities has extensive records, deposited in local *record offices. The reports by government inspectors on local conditions, which were published for about 300 places between 1848 and 1857, were often very detailed.

Public Record Office. The Public Record Act (1838) established the Public Record Office as a central depository for 'all rolls, records, writs, books, proceedings, decrees, bills, warrants, accounts, papers, and documents whatsoever of a public nature, belonging to Her Majesty', together with those records previously deposited in the Tower of London, the Chapter House at Westminster, and elsewhere. In 1838 purpose-built premises in Chancery Lane, London, with reading space in the Round Room, the Long Room, and the Rolls Room, were opened to the public. In 1977 new purpose-built premises were opened at Kew, with a main reading room, a microfilm room, and a room for large documents and maps. These rooms were provided with a new computerized system and mechanical delivery.

For Scotland, see the SCOTTISH RECORD OFFICE. The Public Record Office for the Republic of Ireland (now the National Archives) is housed at Bishop Street, Dublin. The Public Record Office of Northern Ireland is at 66 Balmoral Avenue, Belfast.

pulpits. Stone or wooden pulpits were introduced into the *naves of parish churches in the 14th century. The *Reformation brought a greater emphasis on preaching and reading the *homilies, which was reflected in the prominent position given to the pulpit. The late 17th and 18th centuries was the age of the 'three-decker pulpit', with the clerk positioned below and the minister seated at the reading desk in the middle, until he ascended to the top tier to preach. During the *High Church movement of the Victorian period many of these 'three-deckers' were replaced by new pulpits designed in the medieval manner. In *Nonconformist chapels the pulpit is often the focal point.

Purbeck marble. A dark limestone from the Isle of Purbeck (Dorset).

Puritan. The word 'puritan' was in use in England by the late 1560s amongst both supporters and opponents. It came to mean a variety of things, but was originally a label for those radical *Protestants who were not content with the Elizabethan settlement of 1559. Before the 1630s Puritanism was not seen as separatist, anti-episcopalian, or revolutionary. Puritans were content to work for further reforms in the *Church of England.

The events of the Civil War and the *Commonwealth have been labelled 'The Puritan Revolution'. The 1640s and 1650s saw an outbreak of millenarian beliefs. Upon the *Restoration, the former puritan sects formed the basis of *Nonconformity.

purlieu. Land on the edge of a *forest which had once formed part of that forest and which still came partly within its jurisdiction.

purpresture. An encroachment in a *forest or other royal land.

purlin. A horizontal post in a roof-truss, which supports the weight of the rafters.

purveyor. One who purchased provisions for the Crown. The system caused resentment because of abuses.

putting-out system. A system by which manufacturers or middlemen sub-contracted work to pieceworkers, e.g. in the textile or cutlery industries.

Q

Quakers. The popular name for members of a *Nonconformist sect. George Fox (1624–91), founder of the religious Society of Friends, began preaching in 1647. Quakers rejected formal church services and the sacraments (including baptism), paid ministers, and the authority of the scriptures, and emphasized instead the 'inner voice of God speaking to the soul'. They faced great hostility and much prosecution in *ecclesiastical courts (for interrupting church services and insulting clergymen and magistrates, for forming illegal *conventicles, and for non-payment of *tithes) and at *quarter sessions (for refusing oaths, military service, etc.) until the Toleration Act of 1689 allowed Nonconformists to worship in public.

A structure of monthly and quarterly meetings had been established by 1654. By 1670 most monthly meetings, and a few particular ones, were keeping registers. The early Quaker meeting-houses had burial grounds, but the Society forbade the erection of *gravestones until the yearly meeting decided in 1850 that stones of a uniform size and design should be allowed.

The registers of births, marriages, and burials were not kept according to a standardized form until 1776. The Friends' Library, which was established in London in 1673, preserves many early records. It is rare to find a list of members before the late 18th century; many meetings did not make such lists until 1836. In the following year the registers of surviving Quaker meetings were copied for the *Registrar-General. They are now kept with other Nonconformist registers at the *Public Record Office.

quarter sessions. The system of quarterly meetings of the *Justices of the Peace for each county and county *borough began in 1361. Under the Tudors the responsibilities of JPs were extended to include not only the enforcement of law and order but conformity to the established religion, the regulation of trade, commerce, and employment, the maintenance of the poor, and the upkeep of *roads and *bridges. The elected *county councils which were created in 1888 took over the administrative functions of the quarter sessions, but the judicial and licensing powers were retained, and until 1971 the quarter sessions continued to serve as a criminal court.

Surviving quarter-sessions records may be consulted at county *record offices. They date from the late 16th or 17th century and the more formal ones are written in Latin until 1733. Most counties have a series of indictment and order books, which record the cases under discussion and the decisions that were made. These form the basis of the quarter sessions records that have been published by various county record societies. Informal papers, including petitions and depositions, provide much more human detail where they survive. Associated documents include *jurors' lists, *prison records, lists of licensed *brewsters (keepers of *inns and *alehouses) and of *badgers, *drovers, and other itinerant traders, together with *land tax assessments, and maps and plans associated with *enclosure awards, *turnpike roads, and other public works.

At the quarter sessions JPs tried crimes that were not capital offences, regulated wages, enforced *apprenticeship regulations, licensed *Nonconformist meeting-houses and received *sacrament certificates, ordered the repair and rebuilding of 'county' bridges, and forced parishes to maintain their highways. A major part of their time, however, was spent on overseeing the operation of the *Poor Law, dealing with complaints from aggrieved parties, and judging *settlement disputes between contending parishes.

quarto. A quarter sheet, or a book consisting of such sheets.

Queen Anne's bounty. From 1704 the incomes of the poorer clergy of the *Church of England were supplemented by a fund which drew upon ecclesiastical revenues confiscated by Henry VIII and payments made by clergymen with larger incomes. The records are kept in the *Public Record Office under QAB 1; an index of parishes is available. In 1948 the scheme was taken over by the Church Commissioners.

queen post. A vertical post extending upwards from a *tie-beam towards horizontal timbers which help take the weight of a roof. This elaborate style was a particular feature of the Wealden houses of south-eastern England.

querns. Stones for grinding corn by hand.

Quia Emptores, Statute of (1290). A law ensuring that feudal obligations were preserved when a *mesne lord sold land for a nominal sum.

quit rent. A small fixed annual rent whose payment released a tenant from manorial services. Such payments were abolished in 1922.

Quo Warranto enquiries. From 1278 to 1294 the Crown made a series of enquiries into the privileges that lords claimed to hold, e.g. the right to hold a market and fair, so as to ascertain by what warrant they were held. A statute of 1290 accepted undocumented rights that had been held since before the accession of Richard I in 1189. These have been published by the Record Commission.

quoin. The external corner-stones of a building.

rabbits. The rabbit was introduced into Britain by the Normans. The word 'rabbit' was originally applied only to the young of the species; adult rabbits were known as *coneys. At first, rabbits had to be carefully reared in specially created *warrens until a hardier breed was able to withstand the damp British climate. It was not until the 18th century that rabbits successfully colonized the wild.

rack. Medieval and early modern instrument of torture by stretching to obtain a confession.

rack rent. In the 18th and 19th centuries landowners increasingly tried to maximize their incomes by moving away from long leases to annual agreements with their tenants. Such 'rack rents' came to be regarded as extortionate, but in practice landowners were able to get only what the market would stand.

radio-carbon dating. A method of dating organic material from archaeological deposits, based on the knowledge that the radiocarbon content of dead animals and plants decays at a regular rate. However, radiocarbon years are not the same as calendar years and conversion formulae remain controversial. Dates arrived at by this method are only rough approximations.

Ragged schools. Founded in 1818 by John Pounds of Portsmouth, as free schools for poor children, they formed an unofficial union in 1844 under the patronage of Lord Shaftesbury.

railways. The earliest railways were horse-drawn wooden waggonways, which were used in the Northumberland and Durham coalfield in the 17th and 18th centuries.

Richard Trevithick, a Cornish engineer, built the first steam loco-motive for a railway, in 1804. John Blenkinsop and William Hedley were other pioneers, who used steam locomotives to move coal. George Stephenson was part of this tradition. He built the engine *Locomotion* for the Stockton and Darlington railway, which was opened in 1825 for both passenger and goods traffic. However, this railway also used horses and stationary engines, and passenger traffic remained of minimal importance. The Manchester to Liverpool railway of 1830 was the first to convey passengers and goods entirely by mechanical traction. Stephenson's *Rocket*, which won the famous Rainhill trials in 1829, was the first steam locomotive designed to pull passenger traffic quickly.

By 1852 nearly all the main lines of the modern railway system in England were authorized or completed; progress in Scotland, Wales, and Ireland was less rapid. By Act of Parliament which came into effect on 1 January 1923 the nation's railways were amalgamated into four large companies: the Great Western; the London, Midland, and Scottish; the London and North Eastern; and the Southern. These companies were nationalized as British Railways in 1948.

The *Public Record Office Records Information leaflet no. 32, 'Records Relating to Railways', outlines the national records of the former railway companies: these include maps and plans, reports and returns, *Parliamentary papers, minutes and accounts, staff records, etc. Important collections of railway records are also housed at the *House of Lords Record Office, the *Scottish Record Office, the Greater London Record Office, and the National Railway Museum, York.

rake. A vein of lead.

rape seed was once grown all down the eastern side of England. It was valued for its industrial oil and as fodder for sheep. The seed was crushed at windmills or water *mills.

rapes. Ancient divisions of Sussex, comparable to the *lathes of Kent.

rate books. A few rate books, or assessments, survive amongst the records of the Old *Poor Law, naming householders and the rate paid. After the Poor Law Amendment Act (1834) the names of both owners and occupiers were recorded. Borough rate books from the 19th and 20th centuries are an important source of information about owner-occupiers and those who lived in rented properties. They are arranged in columns and typically list occupants and owners, then describe the property and name the street in which it was situated, and note the rental value and rate to be paid.

Rebecca riots. Riots in south Wales which formed the most dramatic and successful of the 19th-century rural protests. The name is derived from a passage in Genesis about Rebecca 'possessing the gates of those which hate them', for the protesters were principally concerned to remove the gates erected on the new *turnpike roads, and the leaders of the riots dressed in women's clothes. The riots began in 1839 and lasted until 1844. The targets of the rioters included the *workhouses of the New *Poor Law and *Church of England clergymen who demanded the payment of *tithes.

recognizance. A bond kept by the *clerk of the peace to secure the appearance at *quarter sessions of defendants, prosecutors, and witnesses.

record offices. See Reference Section, pp. 270–8.

recorder. The person who presided over *borough *quarter sessions.

Recovery rolls. A fictional method of conveying property in use from the 15th century until 1833. The rolls are kept at the *Public Record Office under CP 43.

recto. The right-hand page of a book, the opposite of *verso. In folio numbering, the reader is guided by the use of the superscript 'r'.

rector. The person who was appointed to the *benefice of a *parish and who thus received the *tithes of the parishioners. At first, the rector was the incumbent who was responsible for the church services and the spiritual welfare of his parishioners, and for maintaining the *chancel of the parish church. In time, many parishes were appropriated to monasteries or *colleges, who kept the great tithes and spent the small tithes on the appointment of a *vicar to serve in their place. After the *dissolution of the monasteries the rector's rights were purchased by lay people. If a parish church is, or has been, served by a vicar, then its tithes must have been appropriated in the past.

reddle, ruddle, raddle. Red ochre dug out of pits and used for marking sheep, staining fences, etc.

reeve. A man elected by his fellow tenants to act as intermediary with the *lord of the manor and to undertake certain customary duties. In some manors he was known as the greave or grave.

Reformation. The Protestant Reformation of the English Church began in 1534 with Henry VIII's decision to renounce papal supremacy and become head of the *Church of England. This was soon followed by the *dissolution of the monasteries between 1536 and 1540 and the suppression of the cults of some local saints, which considerably reduced the number of minor holy days.

In 1538 a new set of royal injunctions brought about the first major alteration in local worship at the parish church. These injunctions ordered the churchwardens of every parish to purchase a Bible, to extinguish all lights in the church that were used for a religious purpose rather than for practical illumination, except for those on the *altar, in the *rood loft, and before the Easter sepulchre. The candles and lamps which had burned before the images of saints were extinguished. The injunctions also instructed churchwardens to remove any images which had been 'abused with pilgrimages or offerings', not to venerate holy relics, and to regard the surviving representations of saints simply as memorials. Meanwhile, in Scotland the Protestants were destroying most of the institutions and liturgy of the medieval Church and were establishing a new *Church of Scotland.

Upon the death of Henry VIII and the accession of Edward VI the pace of change quickened considerably. On 31 July 1547 the government of Lord Protector Somerset ordered the destruction of all shrines and pictures of saints, and of all images to which offerings had been made or before which candles had burned. They limited the number of lights in the church to two upon the high altar, they banned the blessing of wooden crosses, and they forbade processions in or around the church when mass was celebrated, thus cancelling one of the principal Palm Sunday ceremonies. They ordered churchwardens to buy the *Paraphrases* of Erasmus, a work much admired by the reformers.

In the autumn of 1547 the government dissolved *chantry chapels, religious *guilds, and endowed masses known as perpetual obits, and confiscated their properties. Another change in liturgy allowed the laity to share the communion wine with the priest. On 6 February 1548 a royal proclamation forbade four of the major ceremonies of the religious year: the blessing of candles at *Candlemas, of ashes upon Ash Wednesday, and of foliage upon Palm Sunday, and 'Creeping to the Cross'. The dissolution of religious guilds meant the end of *Corpus Christi celebrations. In mid-February 1548 the *Privy Council ordered the removal of all remaining images in parish churches. Together, these measures had a profound impact on religious observance at the local level. In 1549 the *Book of Common Prayer set out the new liturgy: services were now held entirely in English, prayers to individual saints and for intercession on behalf of the dead were prohibited, and many old feast days and ceremonies were abolished.

The progress of the Protestant Reformation came to a sudden end in July 1553 with the death of Edward VI and the accession of the Catholic queen, Mary Tudor. However, in November 1558 Mary died and her Protestant sister Elizabeth came to the throne. In April 1559 Parliament passed a statute prescribing the use of a new Protestant liturgy, based on that of 1552. The impact upon ritual was even swifter than that of Edward's measures, but the removal of the physical surroundings of Catholic worship was slower, churchwardens being naturally reluctant to destroy the images and fittings that had been paid for so recently and when the survival of the new regime was not certain. *Ecclesiastical visitation and court records and churchwardens' accounts show that many altars were not taken down until well into the 1560s.

Regency. The term is applied to the period 1810–20, when the future George IV was Prince Regent during the final years of the reign of

George III, who was ill, but it is also used to denote the Regency style of classical architecture which continued in use in the 1820s and 1830s.

regional novels. The first regional novel was Maria Edgeworth's *Castle Rackrent* (1800). Relatively few regional novels were published in the first half of the 19th century, but they grew in popularity during the late Victorian and Edwardian periods. During the 20th century, such writing declined during both World Wars, but gained new impetus from the 1950s onwards.

Registrar-General. The civil servant in charge of the *General Register Office, created in 1836 to oversee the *civil registration of births, marriages, and deaths in England and Wales. From 1841 he has also been responsible for *census returns. In 1970 the department was remodelled as the Office of Population Censuses and Surveys. Scotland has its own Registrar-General, whose records are kept at the New Register House, Edinburgh, part of the *Scottish Record Office.

registries of deeds. Middlesex and the three Ridings of Yorkshire established registries of *deeds in the early 18th century, upon a voluntary basis. Deeds were copied in bound volumes and indexed by personal name and by place-name.

regrate. The buying of food and other goods outside the market place. Market toll-owners frequently passed by-laws to prohibit this practice.

regular. A person bound by vows to a communal religious life (living 'by the rule').

relics. The venerated material remains or possessions of martyrs and other saints. The cult reached its peak during the *Crusades, when many spurious relics were brought back from the Holy Land. The relics were often kept in richly decorated reliquaries. On the most important holy days the reliquaries were carried at the front of processions. Many superstitious beliefs were associated with them until their destruction at the *Reformation.

relict. Widow.

relief. 1. A customary payment to a *lord of the manor by an incoming *freeholder.
    2. Payments to parish paupers by the over-seers of the *poor.

remainder. The residue of an estate. The term is often used in title *deeds and *wills.

removals. Under the Act of *Settlement (1662) a person who needed poor relief was the responsibility of the *parish or *township in which he or she was legally settled. The over-seers of the *poor of a parish or township could apply to the *Justices of the Peace for an order to remove such a person to the parish of settlement. Such orders were on printed forms with spaces in which the particular details of the case were filled. Removal orders survive amongst parish records deposited at local *record offices; they give the name(s) of the people removed, the names of the parishes involved, and the date of the order. Such cases were frequently disputed at *quarter sessions, where records survive in the form of indictment and order books and depositions.

rental. Manorial accounts and *estate records sometimes include details of rents collected each year, usually at *Lady Day and *Michaelmas, though sometimes at Christmas and Midsummer. These normally give only the tenants' names and the amounts of rent paid. It is often the case that the person who actually occupied the property was a *sub-tenant who is not recorded.

Requests, Court of. Court for the recovery of minor debts; abolished in 1642. The records are kept at the *Public Record Office under REQ 1–3.

reservoirs. In the 18th and 19th centuries private water companies constructed small reservoirs on the outskirts of towns to provide drinking water. Groups of millowners sometimes obtained private Acts of Parliament to build reservoirs to ensure a constant supply of water to turn the water wheels of their mills.

During the Victorian period the demands for water from the growing industrial towns led to municipal authorities gradually taking over responsibility for the provision of water for drinking and for industrial purposes.

resiants. The term used in the call lists of manorial *court rolls to describe those heads of *households who were not tenants. Resiants included *sub-tenants, ex-tenants who were still resident within the *manor, and some householders who eventually became tenants. Call lists of tenants and resiants cover most of the households within a manor, except the poorest ones.

residence, certificates of. The practice in the 16th and 17th centuries of issuing certificates to show that people who had paid their *lay subsidy and had then moved elsewhere should not be charged again. The certificates are kept in the *Public Record Office under E 115 and are calendared by surname.

Restoration. The restoration of the monarchy in 1660 after the Civil War and *Commonwealth. Contemporary records date the start of the reign of Charles II not from 1660 but from the execution of his father, Charles I, in 1649.

Restoration houses. Country and town houses built in a classical style during the reign of Charles II (1660–85). These were greatly influenced by the houses in France and the Low Countries. Restoration houses were formal and compact, with classical proportions and details.

retours. Scottish record of heirs, from about 1530 to the present day. Those dating before 1700 are summarized (in Latin) and indexed in *Inquisitionum Capellam Regis Retornatarum Abbreviatio* (3 vols., 1811–16). Original documents are kept with the Chancery records in the *Scottish Record Office, under C 22 (to 1847) and C28. They are indexed by the name of the heir.

ridge-and-furrow. In many parts of Britain the evidence of former ploughing is preserved in patterns of ridge-and-furrow in fields now used for pasture. In some cases these patterns are a few hundred years old. M. W. Beresford and J. K. St Joseph showed that ridge-and-furrow on aerial photographs could be correlated with the *strips of *open-fields of 16th-century maps, in terms of length, breadth, and position.

Ridge-and-furrow patterns are particularly visible in the Midland Plain. The ridge-and-furrow patterns in former open-fields curve like an inverted S, to allow the oxen team to turn as they reached the *head-land. They did not simply mark the strip boundaries but were useful for drainage.

Not all ridge-and-furrow is as old as this. Land taken in from the *commons and wastes by parliamentary enclosure, particularly during the period of the *Napoleonic wars, was newly ploughed with straight, narrow patterns of ridge-and-furrow.

ridgeway. Ancient upland routes of prehistoric origin. Most of their present names are modern inventions.

riding. A Viking word meaning 'a third part', used from the time of the *Danelaw until 1974 to divide Yorkshire into East, North, and West Ridings (with York separate from each). Lindsey, the northern division of Lincolnshire, was also divided into North, South, and West Ridings.

ringwork. An early Norman defensive earthwork in the form of a mound surrounded by a ditch.

Riot Act (1715). A *constable or other figure of authority who was faced with 12 or more persons whom he considered to be gathered unlawfully or riotously was empowered to read a specified section of the Act, whereupon those who refused to disperse within an hour were considered to be felons.

riparian rights. Rights to river water possessed by the owners of land bordering a river, above the tidal point.

river traffic. Even in the Middle Ages, rivers were often navigable far inland. The road and water transport systems were complementary rather than rivals. The navigability of the major rivers was improved by companies authorized by private Acts of Parliament during the 17th and early 18th centuries.

roads. Many roads are prehistoric in origin. The Romans built many new roads for military purposes, but they also adapted older roads. Many of the minor roads and lanes of later times were probably in existence by the Romano-British period.

No further roads were planned until the 18th century. The medieval and early modern roads were partly ancient ones that continued in use and partly new ways that connected the medieval planned towns. The names of the traders in particular commodities are often attached to these routes. Others were 'church ways' or 'kirk gates'. The old words for such routes were the Anglo-Saxon 'way' and the Scandinavian 'gate', together with 'lane' and a variety of dialect words for minor tracks. The word 'road' was rarely used before the later 17th century. The early turnpike authorities took over existing highways and improved them, sometimes with new diversions from the old course; entirely new roads were not constructed by such bodies until the end of the 18th century.

Rogationtide. The Monday, Tuesday, and Wednesday before Ascension Day. Before the *Reformation this was a time of fasting and supplication for the coming harvest; afterwards it remained the time of year for the *perambulation of the parish boundaries by the parishioners.

Roman Britain. Recorded history begins in Britain with the Roman occupation. The area that was most intensively settled by the Romans lay south of the river Thames and the Bristol Channel. Some major medieval towns and cities grew on Roman foundations. Yet other important Roman sites disappeared entirely.

Population levels were much higher than was once thought. Archaeological evidence, especially that provided by aerial photography, has confirmed that lowland Britain was farmed intensively during the Roman period.

Roman Catholicism. Until the *Reformation, people throughout the British Isles worshipped according to the rites of the Catholic Church. During the reigns of Elizabeth I and James I, English Catholics formed only a small, persecuted minority. In certain rural areas, however, where local Catholic *gentry families provided leadership, they were stronger.

In England and Wales, the fear of persecution meant that few Catholic registers were kept before the middle of the 18th century. Most Catholics opted for Anglican registration of their vital events. From 1791, more Catholic registers were kept, but most surviving ones date from the 19th century. In 1858 Catholic registers from Northumberland, Durham, Yorkshire, and some other places were deposited with the *Registrar-General and can now be consulted at the *Public Record Office, under RG 4. In recent years many Catholic registers have been deposited in local *record offices.

The English Catholic population was small before the 19th century. A number of Catholic chapels were opened between 1791 and 1814. The *Catholic Emancipation Act (1829), after which many more parish churches and a few cathedrals were built. *Irish emigration brought a great rise in the numbers of Catholics living in England, Lowland Scotland, and parts of Wales.

Romanesque. Architecture in the Roman manner. In Britain the style is divided into the Anglo-Saxon and the Norman, with a period of overlap in the 11th century.

Romanticism. A movement in European literature and art, from about 1770 to 1848, which asserted the importance of intense individual experience and valued a sense of the infinite.

rood. 1. (measure). A quarter of an *acre.
  2. (ecclesiastical). The crucifix which was supported by a loft on top of the rood screen that separated the *nave of a parish church from the *chancel. The carved and painted figure of Christ on the cross was usually flanked by images of the Virgin Mary and St John the Evangelist. Most roods, with their lofts and screens, were removed at the *Reformation, under orders of 1547 and 1561, but new ones were installed in Victorian times under the influence of the *High Church movement.

Rose's Act (1812). The Act which came into operation on 1 January 1813, by which the forms of entry of baptisms, marriages, and burials in Anglican churches were standardized in bound volumes.

rotten borough. A *borough which still returned members to Parliament despite the decay of the settlement. Such boroughs, which were often controlled by a single landowner, were abolished by the Reform Act of 1832, which redistributed the seats to the growing industrial towns.

rough music. The use of a rude cacophony of sound and simple dramatic performance to ridicule or express hostility towards those who had offended against communal values and moral standards. Rough music was just one of the terms used for such activities; regional variations include '*skimmington' and 'riding the stang', and Continental historians use the term 'charivari'.

round tower. 1. Irish monastic bell-towers, probably designed as watch-towers and defences against *Viking raids. Some are over 100 feet high.

    2. East Anglian church towers of the late Saxon and Norman periods, constructed of flint. The lack of adequate stone for quoins meant that a round form had to be used.

Royal Air Force. Formed in 1918 by combining the Royal Flying Corps and the Royal Navy Air Service. See the *Public Record Office Records Information leaflet no. 13, 'Air Records as Sources for Biography and Family History'.

royal arms. Painted representations of the royal arms on square or lozenge-shaped boards were placed above the *chancel arch (upon the removal of *rood lofts and screens) to symbolize loyalty to the Crown as head of the *Church of England. Surviving Tudor ones are relatively rare; they can be distinguished by the Tudor griffin in place of the Stuart unicorn. Most date from after the *Restoration of Charles II. Where they survive, they are now found hanging in many different parts of a church.

Royal warrant. From Elizabethan times tradesmen who provided personal services to members of royal households (and from the 19th century those who provided particular products) advertised the fact that they operated 'By appointment to His [or Her] Majesty'.

Royalist composition papers. In 1643 the Parliamentary Committee for the Sequestration of Delinquents' Estates was formed to confiscate the lands of those who fought on the Royalist side in the Civil War. In 1653, after the war was ended, a new Committee for Compounding the Estates of Royalists and Delinquents was established. Those Royalists who pledged their loyalty to the new government were allowed to compound for their estates, i.e. pay a fine for their recovery, on scales depending upon the extent of their involvement in the war. The records of the two committees are kept at the *Public Record Office under SP 20 and 23.

rubble. Stones of different shapes and sizes, often uncut, used in *vernacular buildings. The term distinguishes such materials from *ashlar stone, but does not necessarily imply poor quality.

runes. Letters used by *Anglo-Saxon and *Viking inscribers of *crosses and memorial stones.

runrig. In the Highlands and Islands of Scotland, and in parts of Ireland, the communal farmers of a permanent *infield and temporary outfields used *ridge-and-furrow for drainage, the patterns of which are still visible.

Rural District Councils. Elected councils which were created in 1894, at the same time as *Urban District Councils. They took over the responsibilities of the old rural sanitary authorities, and later assumed responsibility for rural council housing. RDCs were abolished by local government reorganization in 1974. Minutes of the council and administrative records are kept at local *record offices.

Rural History Centre. University of Reading. A national centre for the study of the history of farming, food, and the countryside, particularly since 1750. Its library contains 30,000 books and periodicals, over 1 million photographs, numerous water-colours and drawings, and 40,000 computerized bibliographical references.

rustication. A method used by the architects of the Italian Renaissance and widely adopted in Britain, at first by Inigo Jones and later by the *Palladians, by which the basement and ground storey of large houses were constructed of stones with deeply recessed joints to suggest that the building was emerging from the natural rock below. In contrast, the first floor (the *piano nobile* of the Italians) and upper storey were constructed in smoothly jointed stone.

Rylands, John, Library, Manchester. It has a considerable manuscript collection, including a wide range of charters and deeds, manorial records, and family muniments, particularly those of the landed families of Cheshire and Greater Manchester.

sacrament, certificate of. Amongst the provisions of the Test Act (1673), which excluded from civil or military employment all except members of the Church of England, was the requirement that a certificate, signed by a minister, churchwarden, and two witnesses, should be presented to *quarter sessions by the holder of a civil or public office to acknowledge that he had received communion in the *Church of England.

saffron, safflower. Saffron was grown as a dye, a condiment, medicine, and perfume in the 16th and 17th centuries, especially around Saffron Walden (Essex), Walsingham (Norfolk), and in Suffolk and Cambridgeshire, on a variety of soils.

sainfoin. One of the new grasses, introduced from Normandy in the second quarter of the 17th century as a fodder crop.

St Catherine's House. Home of the *General Register Office, which holds the records of *civil registration from 1 July 1837 to the present day. The address is 10 Kingsway, London WC2. It is open on weekdays from 8.30 a.m. to 4.30 p.m.

Saint Peter's Pence. Annual tribute by householders to the Papal See, stopped by Henry VIII in 1540, but still collected in Catholic churches.

Saints' Days, calendar of. Up to the 17th century documents were often dated by reference to saints' days. The major ones (and other Christian celebrations) are given on p. 282.

salt. The making of salt from sea water, or from the brine springs of Cheshire and Worcestershire, goes back to at least Roman times. Numerous minor place-names, e.g. Saltergate, Salter Hill, Saltersford, indicate the routes of ancient *roads by which salt was carried to market towns. Deep brine pits were in use at Droitwich and Nantwich in the Middle Ages and later. Rock salt was mined at Northwich, Middlewich, and Nantwich from the 1690s.

Salt, William, Library. The library at 19 Eastgate Street, Stafford, which contains the antiquarian collection of William Salt, and forms part of the Staffordshire Record Office.

sanctuary. The medieval right of sanctuary was claimed by fugitives from justice. The area of sanctuary was originally only around a bishop's throne, but it was later extended to include the whole of a church and an area around it defined by crosses. The fugitive had 40 days in which to appear before a coroner to confess his crime, to abjure the realm, and to accept banishment. In 1540 the privilege of sanctuary was restricted to seven towns. Sanctuary for those accused of crime was abolished in 1623 and for civil cases in 1773.

sarcophagus. A stone coffin from the Middle Ages, sometimes seen in *churchyards or church porches, shaped to take a body, and with a drainage hole.

sash windows. Sashes were introduced from France and Holland in the 1670s. The so-called Yorkshire sash, where the sashes slide sideways without the use of weights, was also introduced in the late 17th century, and, despite its name, is found in many parts of Britain.

Sasines, Register of. In Scotland copies of legal transactions involving the ownership of heritable property are registered in one of the registers of sasines. The Secretary's Register of 1599–1609 was the forerunner of the system inaugurated in 1617. Registers of sasines for royal *burghs were kept from 1681. The registers are kept in the *Scottish Record Office. Indexes up to 1780 have been published for most parts of Scotland.

Saxo-Norman overlap. Churches built in the 11th century cannot usually be dated to either side of the Norman Conquest, as techniques that had been developed by Saxon masons, e.g. the use of *herringbone masonry, continued in use.

Saxton, Christopher (*c*.1542–*c*.1611). The maker and publisher of the first atlas of England and Wales (1579) and the first wall map of England and Wales (1583). These were based on his series of county *maps which appeared individually between 1574 and 1579.

scagliola. Marble chips imported from Italy in the 18th and 19th centuries, which were cemented together to imitate true marble. The columns of many a great house have a hollow ring to them when rapped, for they are not of solid marble.

scolding. Women who scolded their neighbours received rough justice in the form of the *cucking stool in the early modern period. Cases of scolding were sometimes brought before the *ecclesiastical courts or *quarter sessions.

scot ale. A dinner given to tenants on the occasion when they paid their rents.

scot and lot. Parish rates; scot was collected for the poor, lot for church maintenance.

Scotch Baptists. The Scotch Baptists differed from the *Baptist church in their rejection of a trained or paid ministry. Originating in the 1760s, they spread throughout Scotland and into parts of England during the next half-century.

Scotchmen. In the 17th century Lowland Scots *pedlars hawked cheap *linen in many parts of England. Local authorities occasionally attempted to restrict the activities of such 'Scotchmen'. In time, the name was applied to any pedlar who specialized in linen, regardless of whether or not he originated from north of the border.

Scotland, National Library of. A copyright library occupying two sites in Edinburgh. The Department of Manuscripts and the Department of Printed Books are at George IV Bridge, Edinburgh EH1 1EW; the Map Room is at 137 Causewayside, Edinburgh EH9 1PH. The Department of Manuscripts inherited the collection of private papers in the Advocates' Library (dating from 1680), a catalogue of whose material has been published as the *Summary Catalogue of Advocates Manuscripts*. Five catalogues of later holdings have also been published, but many other catalogues are not available in print. The collections are principally of *estate and business papers; *trade union records are also strongly represented. The Map Room has collections of maps from the middle of the 16th century, including comprehensive holdings of all *Ordnance Survey series from the earliest surveys to the present day.

Scottish Episcopal Church. The Scottish church that retains the episcopal system of government, as in the *Church of England. The church's archives are kept at the *Scottish Record Office under CH 12. The SRO also has microfilm copies of Episcopal Church registers, arranged by diocese.

Scottish Record Office. HM General Register House, Edinburgh EH1 3YY has been the home of the Public Records of Scotland since the late 18th century. It was opened for public searches in 1847. The General Register House occupies a prime site at the east end of Princes Street and is open on Mondays to Fridays from 9 a.m. to 4.45 p.m. A second building, West Register House, in Charlotte Square a mile away, is also open during those hours. (The New Register House, which is adjacent to the General Register House, but is not part of the Scottish Record Office, serves as the *General Register Office for Scotland, housing the *civil registration records and *census returns.

screens passage. Through passage, dividing the *open hall from the service end of a manor house or other large building. The entry into the hall was through a screen, which was carved and decorated and some-times supported a minstrels' gallery above.

scutage. The annual money payment by which military service that was owed by *knights to a feudal lord was commuted.

seaside resorts. The fashion for sea-bathing started with the aristocracy and *gentry in the mid-18th century and soon spread to the middle classes. Transformed by the railways, the appeal of the seaside changed from an emphasis on health to the provision of pleasure amongst all social groups. The golden years were those of the late Victorian and Edwardian era.

Secretary hand. The style of handwriting of the 16th and 17th centuries.

Seebohm, Frederic W. (1833–1912). His *The English Village Community* (1883) was enormously influential in the development of local agrarian studies.

seed drills. Jethro Tull, the author of *The Horse-Hoeing Husbandry* (1733), invented the first seed drill, but its spread from his native Berkshire was slow. It did not begin to replace *broadcasting of seed in most districts until the 1830s and 1840s.

seigneurial borough. A *borough which did not have a mayor and cor-poration, but which had a measure of independence from the local *lord of the manor. The lord, however, remained a dominant figure in his *castle nearby; he often retained the right to the market tolls and ex-ercised authority through his manorial *court.

seisin. Possession of property, as distinct from ownership.

Selden Society. A national record society founded in 1887 'to encourage the study and advance the knowledge of the history of English law' by annual publications.

selion. A strip of arable land in an *open-field. This is the term usually favoured in documents.

Sephardic Jews. Those Jews whose ancestors lived in Spain became known as Sephardic from a medieval Hebrew word meaning Spaniard. Most of the 16th- and 17th-century Jewish migrants to England were Sephardic Jews, who came mostly from Portugal. During the following century others came from various Mediterranean countries, but the 19th-century Jewish immigrants were mainly of *Ashkenazic origin from central and eastern Europe.

sequestration (Scottish). The temporary possession of an estate or *benefice because of debt or vacancy.

serf, serfdom. Serfs were the unfree peasants of the Middle Ages. Their obligations to a *lord of the manor varied in detail from one *manor to another, but had a basic similarity. Generally, they paid modest money rents and frequently some rents in kind. They owed seasonal *boon works, which normally consisted of a few days' ploughing, harrowing, threshing, haymaking, and harvesting, and perhaps some carting, fencing, ditching, and cutting thatch. Their heaviest obligation in many places was 'week-work', a regular obligation to work the lord's land. The severity of these services was reduced considerably between the late Anglo-Saxon period and the 14th century. In many places services were commuted into money rents during the mid-12th century, only for serfs to face new exactions in the later 12th and 13th centuries, before a general relaxation again in the late 13th century. The great loss of population in the *Black Death created a situation in which such services were abolished once and for all, though vestiges of serfdom survived into the early modern period.

sergeant-at-law. Member of a superior order of barristers which was abolished in 1880.

serjeantry. A type of medieval tenure by which land was held in return for various personal services below that of *knight service.

service rooms. The kitchen, dairy, etc., which in larger houses were separated by a *screens passage from the living and sleeping quarters.

Session, Court of. The highest civil court in Scotland. The arrangement of the records in the *Scottish Record Office is complicated and poorly indexed. The archives date from 1478 and include Registers and Acts of Decreets from 1542 to the present day, Minute Books from 1557, Register of Deeds from 1554, and Extracted and Unextracted Processes, by which claims and counter-claims were lodged.

settlement. (legal). The complex arrangements for passing on property, adopted by the major landowning families after the *Restoration.

Settlement, Act of (1662). The *Poor Law Acts of 1597–1601 established the *township or civil *parish as the unit of local government that was responsible for relieving the poor. The Act of 1662 set out the ways in which a poor person could claim to be legally settled. Anyone entering a township to occupy a property worth less than £10 per annum might be challenged by the overseers of the *poor within 40 days of arrival, and after an order from two *Justices of the Peace be removed by the *constable to the place where he or she was legally settled, unless security for indemnity against becoming chargeable to the parish could be provided. Children obtained settlement in the place where they were born, even if they were illegitimate; overseers were therefore anxious to remove pregnant, unmarried women before the birth of a child. A new settlement could be obtained through *apprenticeship, or through service for more than a year. Upon marriage, a wife took her husband's place of settlement.

The practice of issuing certificates, signed by churchwardens and overseers, and confirmed by JPs, whereby responsibility for an individual was acknowledged, began in 1691. Disputes about settlement occupied much of the business at *quarter sessions. The records of settlement examinations concerning applicants for poor relief, or of those thought liable to become a burden on the poor rates, may be found amongst parish records in local *record offices. They include much information about the length and conditions of service and about the movement of individuals. An Act of 1795 laid down that removal could take place only when a person became chargeable to the parish. The 1662 Act was repealed by the Poor Law Amendment Act (1834), which created unions of parishes as the responsible authorities.

severalty. Private possession of land. The term is used to describe enclosed lands beyond the *open-fields of a village.

Sewers, Commissioners of. An Act of 1531 authorized the appointment of commissioners charged with the drainage of low-lying land that was liable to floods. Courts of sewers conducted their administrative business in a judicial manner, before a jury. They were abolished in 1930, when their work was transferred to bodies which now form part of regional water authorities. Their records are to be found at local *record offices.

Shambles. The name was commonly applied to that part of a market place or adjoining street where the butchers (and sometimes the fishmongers) had their stalls or shops.

sheila-na-gig. A naked female figure, with legs wide open, which is incorporated in the decorative sculpture of some medieval churches and (in Ireland) secular buildings such as *castles and mills. The term is an Irish Gaelic expression for an immodest woman. They first appear in the British Isles amongst the *Romanesque carvings of 12th-century Herefordshire churches, where their purpose was to portray sin.

shell keep. A circular or polygonal stone enclosure, which in the later 12th century began to replace the wooden palisades on the tops of *mottes. They contained domestic quarters and were not strong defensive structures like the square and polygonal towers that often replaced them.

sheriff. The 'shire-reeve' was the chief official of a county after the Norman Conquest. His legal responsibilities passed to the *Justices of the Peace in the 14th century and his responsibility for the *militia passed to the *lords lieutenant in the 16th century. The office is now ceremonial.

sherman. A sheep shearer.

shieling. A summer settlement for farmers practising *transhumance in Scotland and northern England, so as to rest their winter pastures. These men lived in stone or turf huts known as *bothies, and cultivated a small field of oats or rye, while tending their cattle and sheep. Place-names such as -erg, -scholes, and -sett commemorate these settlements. The Welsh 'hafod' and the Irish 'buaile' have the same meaning. Shielings also acted as territorial markers on disputed moorlands.

shilling. A silver coin, introduced in 1504, bearing the portrait of Henry VII, and at first known as the testoon. It was worth 12 old pence; 20 shillings were worth £1.

shingles. Wooden tiles, usually of oak, were used for medieval roofs, especially in southern England. In domestic buildings, they were gradually replaced by clay tiles from the 16th century onwards, because of the fire risk, but they have continued in use on church spires.

ship money. The collection of a tax, based on the previous practice of raising money in time of war, but used in the 1630s by Charles I for other purposes without recourse to Parliament, was based on assessments levied on counties and towns. There are no detailed records naming individuals.

shires. See COUNTIES, ORIGINS OF. In the kingdom of *Northumbria smaller units than counties were also known as 'shires', e.g. Blackburnshire, Hallamshire, Howdenshire.

shops. Gregory *King estimated that in the late 17th century England and Wales had about 40,000 shopkeepers. Most of these were based in towns, but a contemporary tract claimed that shops were also to be found 'in every country village'. Most shopkeepers were known as grocers, drapers, etc., but their inventories show that they sold anything they could and that shops were often general stores.

During the second half of the 19th century the centres of major towns and cities ceased to be residential areas and became retail and entertainment districts. The process whereby shops replaced old houses can be followed in trade and commercial *directories and by the use of old *photographs.

shot, shutt. A block of *strips in an *open-field, a *furlong.

shows, agricultural. Numerous local farmers' societies were founded in the late 18th and 19th centuries, especially from the 1830s to 1840s onwards.

Shrove Tuesday. The day preceding Ash Wednesday, which together with the preceding two days forms Shrovetide, the period of confession before *Lent. Long after the *Reformation, Shrove Tuesday remained the day when *apprentices were boisterous in the streets (indulging in crude sports such as stoning cocks), and when traditional sports were held.

side-alternate quoins. The large corner-stones used in Anglo-Saxon churches. The early Norman churches used smaller stones in similar arrangements. Later churches used buttresses instead.

silk. The silk stockings that were fashionable in Elizabethan times were sometimes made of Spanish silk, but were increasingly made from yarn produced by Flemish weavers working in London, especially Spital-fields. Canterbury was another important silk weaving centre at the same period, accommodating French immigrants. The importation of French silks was banned in 1698, and of Indian and Chinese silks in 1701, in order to encourage the native industry.

The first provincial silk spinning, or 'throwing', mill was that erected in 1702 on the river Derwent at Derby by Thomas Cotchett. This small mill was overshadowed by the one built alongside it in 1718–22 by Thomas Lombe, on an Italian model. Lombe's mill, which produced yarn of a superior quality, broke London's ancient monopoly.

Luxury silk garments were worn by the wealthy in the 18th and 19th centuries, and the silk top hat became fashionable in the 1840s; in the first half of the 20th century silk garments became fashionable amongst wider sections of society.

simony. The buying or selling of a *benefice or other ecclesiastical office.

Sir. The title of *baronets and *knights, and, until the *Reformation, of a priest who was not a university graduate.

sister. The term was also used to mean sister-in-law.

skimmington ride. Public disapproval of an adulterous couple was expressed by the parading of effigies and *rough music, especially in the 18th and 19th centuries. The performance was also known as 'riding the stang'.

slitting mill. Water-powered mills for the slitting of iron into rods were introduced from the Continent into the west midlands by the 1620s.

slubber. An occupation in the West Riding scribbling and *spinning mills, whereby loose cardings were drawn out and slightly twisted so that they could be wound on to bobbins.

smallpox was the major killer disease of the late 17th and 18th centuries. Survivors were disfigured by pock-marks on their skins. Smallpox was believed to be eradicated throughout the world in 1977.

smithy. 1. The small forge of a blacksmith, cutler, nail-maker, etc.
  2. A term used, often in the plural, in the 16th and 17th centuries for a much larger site for the forging of iron.

smoke-penny. An Easter due payable to the incumbent of a *parish by the occupier of a house with a fireplace.

smuggling. The duties charged on foreign imports such as tobacco, wine, proof spirits, *tea, and *sugar from the 16th to the 19th centuries made smuggling a profitable if dangerous enterprise for the inhabitants of remote coastal communities. Smugglers have attracted a romantic literature, but so secret a trade has left little firm evidence.

soap was originally made from animal fats, vegetable oils, ashes, and lime, boiled in large pans. Its domestic use was rivalled by its use in the cloth industry. Soap-making was both an urban and a rural occupation, often combined with that of making candles.

socage. A form of *feudal tenure in which land was held not by service but by a money rent.

Society for the Promotion of Christian Knowledge. Founded in 1698 to reform manners and to encourage the provision of charity schools under the auspices of the *Church of England. The manuscript records of the society include letters and minutes from 1699 to 1729 (and later). Annual *Reports* were printed from 1705 to 1732.

sojourner. A temporary resident.

soke. Land in the *Danelaw which was held by free peasant tenants who owed suit of court and other customary dues to the *lord of the manor. They are recorded in the *Domesday Book. A soke was a dependent free territory scattered over many villages. By the end of the Middle Ages soke had come to mean simply an administrative division of a *lordship. The Soke of Peterborough, consisting of 32 *townships, was a separate county until 1974.

solar. A private chamber on the sunny side of a house.

Solemn League and Covenant. An agreement made by members of the House of Commons in 1643 to defend *Protestantism and the rights of Parliament, to which in the following year all males over 18 were expected to subscribe. A few lists survive in county *record offices.

Somerset House. The Principal Probate Registry, containing all *wills proved in England and Wales after 1858. Indexes may be consulted free. The address is Strand, London WC2. It is open on weekdays between 10.00 and 4.30.

son-in-law. The term was often used to mean 'stepson'. A 'son-in-law' was often referred to as 'son'.

South Sea bubble. The huge financial speculation, encouraged by the Government, which burst in September 1720 ruining many families.

sovereign (coin). Introduced by Henry VII (1485–1509) at the value of 20 *shillings. During the second half of the 16th century it was worth 30s. Discontinued in the early 17th century, it was reintroduced from 1817 to 1917, when it was again valued at 20s.

spas. The fashion of visiting spa centres for the supposed healing properties of sulphur and chalybeate springs was imported from Belgium, France, and Germany in the 16th and 17th centuries, but took a long time before it flourished in the 18th and 19th centuries.

Speed, John (1552–1629). Cartographer and antiquarian. Between 1605 and 1610 he produced a new set of 54 maps of the counties of England and Wales, which remain popular to this day. In 1610 he published the six maps of the *Kingdome of Scotland*. The following year he published *Theatre of the Empire of Great Britaine*.

Speenhamland system. In 1795 the overseers of the *poor in the parish of Speenhamland (Berkshire) adopted a method of supplementing low wages with an allowance paid for out of the rates. This allowance varied according to the cost of bread. The system was widely copied in southern England, but as local farmers deliberately kept wages low, in the knowledge that allowances would be given by the *parish, the number of people on poor relief actually rose. The system was discredited before the *Poor Law Amendment Act (1834).

spelling, phonetic. In documents of the Elizabethan period and later it is common to find the same word spelt in different ways only a line or two apart and to find that people spelt their own names in different ways as the spirit moved them. Spelling gradually became standardized during the 17th and 18th centuries as the amount of printed literature increased.

spice. Spices from the East came via the Mediterranean in the Middle Ages. The *East India Company was the major provider once a sea route around Africa was established.

spinning. The spinning of yarn was traditionally a woman's domestic employment. Spinning was mechanized during the late 18th century, long before *weaving. Women and children formed most of the workforce of the water-powered *cotton and woollen mills.

square panelling. The method of arranging the posts of *timber-framed buildings that was favoured in the western half of England.

squarson. A word used in the 18th and 19th centuries for a clergyman (parson) who was also the *squire of his village.

squatters. The increase in the national population in the late 16th and early 17th centuries meant that large numbers of families sought space on which to erect *cottages. They were attracted to the edges of *commons in *forests and fens, and on the moors. An Act of 1589 tried to ensure that new cottages had at least four acres of land attached, but this statute was enforced only sporadically. Some manorial lords allowed new settlements and obtained rents by the roundabout method of annual *fines for *encroachment. Squatting was tolerated where labour was needed on farms or in industries. Many other squatters remained through the negligence of the authorities. Growing concern was expressed as resources dwindled during the population growth of the 18th century. The *enclosure of most of the remaining commons and wastes in the late 18th and early 19th centuries removed the opportunities for squatting and channelled the rural poor towards the towns.

squire. The dominant landowner in a *parish.

stables. Commodious stables first became an architectural feature of country houses during the 17th century.

stained glass. Only small pieces of Anglo-Saxon stained glass survive. During the late 12th and 13th centuries English churches adopted the designs and techniques used in French *grisaille and richly coloured glass. The *Reformation destroyed the living of many artists, but some, notably Henry Giles of York, found new patrons amongst the aristocracy and *gentry for heraldic glass. William Peckitt and others kept the tradition of stained glass alive during the 18th century. The Victorian period saw a major revival under William Morris, Edward Burne-Jones, and C. E. Kempe. The later 20th century has seen another revival.

staith. A wharf. The word is of Viking origin.

standard (tree). Many *coppice woods included a number of standard trees that were allowed to grow to a full height for timber. Legislation that tried to enforce a minimum number of standards per acre was difficult to enforce.

standard abbreviations (genealogy).

b.	born
bapt.	baptized
d.	died
d.unm.	died unmarried
d.s.p.	died without children
dau.	daughter
div.	divorced
l.	left descendants
s.	son
unm.	unmarried
	= married

Standing Conference for Local History. Founded in 1948, under the aegis of the National Council for Social Service, the SCLH was the forerunner of the *British Association for Local History, and former publisher of The *Amateur Historian*, later The *Local Historian*.

Stannaries. The *tin-mining district of Cornwall, which was regulated through the Stannaries Court.

Star Chamber, Court of. So-called from the chamber at the royal palace of Westminster with painted stars on its ceiling, where the *Privy Council met in the 14th and 15th centuries. The court was revived by Henry VII in 1487 and at first was popular because it provided quick redress cheaply, but it was associated with the exercise of the royal prerogative under the early Stuarts and was abolished in 1641. Its records are kept at the *Public Record Office under STAC 1 to 9. The court dealt with a number of local disputes and received lengthy depositions.

State Papers Domestic. All the state papers from the accession of Edward VI (1547) to the second year of Queen Anne (1704) have been published in official *calendars. They are a rich mine of information on everything under the sun, and have reasonably, but not consistently, good indexes. The *List and Index Society has published a Calendar of State Papers (Domestic) for the reign of George I (1714–27). The term 'Home Office' was used for domestic, as distinct from foreign, affairs later in the century.

statute labour. An Act of 1555 ordered the annual election of overseers of the *highways for each *township or civil *parish, and obliged every householder to work under the supervision of the overseer for four days a year (or to pay for someone else to perform the work) on repairing and maintaining the local highways. An Act of 1563 increased this liability to six days a year. The better-off inhabitants were also obliged to provide carts and draught animals. 'Statute labour' or 'the common days work' system formed the basis of road maintenance for the next three centuries. The system was not replaced by *turnpike roads (for statute labour was used to supplement the work-force there, and minor roads were not turnpiked).

steam engines. Those of the late 17th and early 18th century designed by Savery, Newcomen, and Trevithick were used for pumping water out of mines, and later for draining the fens. They are marked on 18th-century county *maps as 'Fire Engine'. James Watt's single-action engine of 1769, his rotative engine of 1783, and other improvements made steam the principal source of power in many industries in the late 18th and 19th centuries, particularly in the blast *furnaces and the textile mills.

steel. In the early modern period steel was imported from abroad, firstly from Bilbao, then via Cologne, or Danzig. The first steel to be made in England was in the Forest of Dean in the early 17th century. The English cementation steel industry was largely dependent on imported Swedish ores. A purer form of steel was invented by Benjamin Huntsman in Sheffield *c*.1742. Huntsman reheated cementation steel in clay crucibles to a high temperature.

A new stage of the steel industry began in 1856 when Henry Bessemer invented a convertor. Further advances were made by the Siemens open-hearth furnace, the James Nasmyth steam hammer, and the techniques of Robert Mushet and Robert Hadfield for making special steels. In 1912–13 Harry Brearley invented stainless steel.

steward. In the later 17th and early 18th centuries landowners began to employ land stewards to supervise their estates during long periods of absence. These stewards became a highly professional group during the 18th and 19th centuries.

stint. A share. The term was applied by manorial *courts to the amount of livestock that a tenant was allowed to graze on the *commons.

stocks. The stocks were an ancient punishment for petty offenders, who were subject to ridicule by having their feet locked in a wooden structure which was placed in some public space, such as a village green or market square. The use of the stocks died out during the middle years of the 19th century.

Stone Age. Popular term for the *Palaeolithic, *Mesolithic, and *Neolithic, the earliest periods of prehistory.

Stow, John (1525–1605). Author of the famous *Survey of London and Westminster* (1598).

strapwork. A fashionable ornamentation of the Elizabethan and Jacobean age, imported from the Netherlands for use on the roofs and garden walls of great houses, on chimney pieces and tombs, and in other decorative arts. The name came from the resemblance of the ornamentation to curved leather straps.

straw plaiting. The plaiting of straw hats, bonnets, and mats was a cottage industry for women and girls, especially in the south midlands. The numbers employed declined rapidly in the last quarter of the 19th century.

strays. A term used by family historians for events that are recorded in unexpected places.

street names. Many street names are medieval in origin, but others did not become fixed until Victorian times. Alternative forms can be found on successive maps. Once signs were erected, the names of streets became settled. The Victorians took this opportunity to rename streets which had offensive or lowly connotations.

street numbering. The early *census enumerators' returns and trade *directories show that in the mid-19th century the houses in most towns and nearly all villages were still not numbered. The fashion spread during the later 19th century, but it is common to find inconsistencies between one census return and the next, as houses were renumbered.

string course. A horizontal, projecting course, usually half-way up a wall, used for decorative rather than constructional purposes.

strips. The term used by agricultural historians to describe the long, narrow divisions of *open-fields that farmers usually called *lands. These had a sinuous, reverse-S shape to allow the plough-team to turn as they approached the *headland. Strips were individually owned, but initially the open-fields were farmed in common, allowing communal grazing over all the land after harvest.

stucco. The application of plaster to the exterior of a building to simulate stone.

stud. An upright post in a *timber-framed building, serving a minor purpose.

stylobat. The stone footing for a principal post in a *timber-framed building.

subinfeudation. The granting of a *fee by a *tenant-in-chief or *mesne lord to a *sub-tenant.

sub-manor. The lords of large medieval *lordships sometimes granted favoured retainers the right to hold manorial *courts for small districts within their jurisdiction. In time, these sub-manors usually became completely independent, with their own manor houses, *deer parks, etc.

sub-tenant. *Surveys and *rentals usually record the name of the tenant but, as the matter was of no financial importance to the landowner, they do not usually name any sub-tenants. A misleading picture of a local community may be drawn from such evidence, if much of the land was tenanted by absentees who sub-tenanted their properties to the men who actually farmed them.

suburbs. The major medieval and Tudor cities were largely confined within their walls. The early suburbs housed the poor immigrants. As towns became more crowded, so the middle classes moved out of the centres into spacious streets and squares at the edges. This evacuation of town centres became a mass movement during the 19th century.

sugar. Sugar cane was imported from the Mediterranean from the 16th century. During the 17th century it became the major product of the new *plantations in the West Indies. In the 20th century a large supply has come from sugar beet.

suicide was held to be a crime by the *ecclesiastical courts. Those who had committed suicide were buried either in unconsecrated ground on the north side of a *churchyard or at cross-roads with a stake driven through the heart to destroy evil spirits. Suicide rates were low in the early modern period. For later times, see *coroners' inquests, and *newspaper reports.

sulung. A measure of land used in south-eastern England, about twice the size of a *hide.

summoner. An *apparitor who summoned people to appear before an *ecclesiastical court.

sumptuary laws. Medieval and early modern laws which attempted to restrict private expenditure on dress and to confine the use of certain materials to the *nobility. In England a series of Acts were passed from 1463 onwards. Until 1600 'excessive apparel' was controlled by seven Acts and ten proclamations. In 1566 four 'sad and discreet' persons were stationed at the gates of the City of London to watch for people who might be wearing prohibited styles of hose.

sundials. Parish churches used sundials to enable clergymen to judge the times of services and for public use long before clocks were installed in church towers. A few Saxon sundials survive. In the Middle Ages 'scratch dials' were inscribed on a buttress or wall close to the porch of a parish church. Later sundials were mounted on stone posts in the *churchyard. From the 17th to the 19th centuries churchyard and private sundials became increasingly ornate. Many are inscribed with reminders of mortality.

surety. One who stood as security for the repayment of a *bond or for the proper performance of duties.

surnames. The fashion for families to have fixed, hereditary surnames began at the top level of society and spread slowly down the social scale. The fashion spread in southern England and East Anglia during the second half of the 13th century and the first half of the 14th century, but took another century to become widespread in northern England and Lowland Scotland. By the 15th century most English people had acquired fixed, hereditary surnames, but Welsh names did not take an English form until the 16th century.

'Surnames', The. The kinship groups of Northumberland and Cumberland which offered some measure of protection to their members and which had some affinity to Scottish *clans. They became an anachronism after the union of the English and Scottish crowns under James I and VI.

surrender. A document that extinguishes an owner's right in a property. Conditional surrender refers to the practice of mortgaging *copyhold land, for if the loan was not repaid the mortgagee could enter the property only if the *lord of the manor agreed to accept him as his tenant.

surrogate. A deputy presiding over a court.

Surtees Society. Founded in 1834, the society has published a wide range of records relating to County Durham and Yorkshire, in annual volumes.

survey. During the late 16th and 17th centuries landowners often employed a land surveyor to make a survey of their estate, showing the extent of each property, the form of tenure by which it was held, and often the use to which it was put, i.e. arable, *meadow, pasture, or wood. The most detailed surveys also described each building, by its size (expressed as so many bays), purpose, and sometimes by its building materials. The entry *fines and rents and customary payments were always noted, sometimes with the 'improved rents'. Surveys were often made upon a change of ownership, with the intention of discovering the value of the estate in detail and of assessing ways in which the yield to the owner could be increased. The written survey was usually accompanied by a map, which is often the first large-scale map of the area.

swaler. The alternative name in the north midlands for a *badger, i.e. a dealer in meal, corn, butter, and eggs.

sweating sickness. The name given by contemporaries to the epidemic of the late 1550s, which was probably a virulent form of *influenza.

Swing, Captain. The name given to the widespread rural incendiarism and destruction of *threshing machines of 1830–1, which started in Kent and spread over southern and eastern England. *Agricultural labourers demanded improved wages, reductions in *tithe payments, and the removal of machinery which caused under-employment.

syke, sick. The steep slopes of land by streams were difficult to plough and were therefore not incorporated in *open-fields, but were used for hay which was auctioned to local farmers.

Synod of Whitby. The church synod of 664 which determined the outcome of the clash between English and Irish churchmen over the dating of Easter, a symbolic battle about whether the Roman or the Celtic form of Christianity would be the dominant one in Britain. The Roman form was triumphant.

tallage. A medieval tax, levied by a feudal lord upon his *villeins at *Michaelmas, by the king upon towns and his *demesne manors, or by a *borough upon its *burgesses. It was replaced by other taxes by the 14th century.

tallow chandler. A candle-maker.

tally. A stick notched as a record of accounts and then split down the middle so that the two halves 'tallied'.

tatty hawker. An itinerant, Irish potato-seller.

Taxatio Ecclesiastica (1291). A tax valued at one-tenth, published by the Record Commission as *Taxatio Ecclesiastica Angliae et Walliae, auctoritate Papae Nicholai IV, c.1291* (1802).

tea. Tea was brought from the Far East from the late 17th century.

teasels. Plant with large prickly head, used for the finishing of cloth.

telephone directories are a prime source for establishing the modern distribution patterns of *surnames. The *United Kingdom is divided into 103 districts. The whole series from 1879 is available for consultation at The British Telecom Archives and Historical Information Centre, 2–4 Temple Avenue, London EC4Y OHL.

Templar, Knights. Founded in 1119 as the Order of the Poor Knights of Christ and of the Temple of Solomon to protect pilgrims in the Holy Land, the knights became established throughout Europe by the late 13th century. In 1312 their possessions were transferred to the Knights *Hospitaller.

temporalities. Ecclesiastical income that came from secular sources, e.g. rents, as distinct from spiritualities.

tenant-in-chief. Under the *feudal system a person who held land directly from the king.

tenements. Originally, any rented property. In his account of Myddle (Shropshire) in 1700–2 Richard *Gough used the term to describe the holdings of *yeomen and *husbandmen, which were smaller than farms but larger than the properties of *cottagers. In the Victorian period the word was used to describe the working-class houses which were subdivided horizontally in the major industrial towns.

tenters. After a piece of woven cloth had returned from the *fulling mill, it was hung on frames known as tenters to be stretched and dried.

terraces. 1. (housing). By the first half of the 19th century the typical accommodation of a working-class family was a two-storey house that formed part of a terrace.

2. (gardens). Terraced gardens were introduced into England and Wales during the reign of William III (1689–1702).

thane, thegn. An Anglo-Saxon landowner who held his land by charter in return for military service. King's thegns were substantial men, but petty thegns were hardly distinguishable from ordinary farmers.

theatre. Travelling bands of actors are recorded in provincial towns and cities from the 1530s. The Vagabonds Act (1572) forced companies of travelling players to seek royal or aristocratic patronage and thus forced them to be based in London.

Theatres were banned by the *Puritans during the *Commonwealth, but were re-established in London after the *Restoration. During the next century provincial urban drama flourished as never before.

thirdborough. An alternative name for *headborough or *tithingman.

threshing. Hand-threshing by *flail survived well into the 19th century, and later on the smallest holdings. Experiments with threshing machines had begun in the late 18th century. Steam-powered threshing machines were made from the 1840s.

tie beam. The horizontal beam which connects the principal posts of a *timber-framed building and which helps to support a roof-truss.

tied housing. In the 19th century and later, farmers and other employers often provided rented accommodation for their work-force, whereby such housing was 'tied to the job'.

timber-framed buildings. Until the late 16th or 17th century the majority of *vernacular buildings were constructed with timber frames. *Dendrochronology has allowed the precise dating of numerous timbers. It is clear that many surviving timber-framed houses are medieval rather than Tudor. The earliest vernacular examples are 13th century.

time immemorial. From 1291 a person who had no *charter of authority for a franchise, e.g. the right to hold a market or *fair, had his claim allowed if he could prove that he and his ancestors, or predecessors in his position, had held that right since 'time whereof the memory of man runneth not to the contrary'. This was known for short as 'time immemorial', or 'time out of mind', and was fixed as the period before the accession of Richard I in 1189.

tin was produced in Devon and Cornwall from prehistoric times in its alloy, bronze, and since at least Roman times in its alloy, *pewter. The industry came to an end in the late 20th century.

tithe awards and maps. The bureaucratic structure that was created in 1836 to solve the *tithe problem was closely modelled on the *Poor Law Commission established in 1834. Between 1836 and 1852 the Tithe Commission quietly brought about a major redistribution of English and Welsh property. During that time they made apportionments for 11,395 districts (which were either *parishes or smaller *townships); in 7,147 cases (63 per cent) the agreements were made voluntarily. Only a few of the remaining cases dragged on, some until the 1880s.

The commissioners appointed surveyors to make large-scale maps and schedules. These were drawn up in triplicate: the copy made for the tithe office is now kept at the *Public Record Office; the ones for the parish clerk and the bishop of the diocese are normally kept at an appropriate county or diocesan *record office. The maps often the earliest surviving large-scale maps for a given area. The reference numbers on the tithe maps correspond to those in the accompanying tithe apportionment.

A preamble to the apportionment notes the extent and use of the arable land which was liable to tithe, the names of all tithe owners, and all customary payments which were made in lieu of tithe. After the preamble, the tithe apportionment lists all landowners and tenants and their fields; it is therefore a principal source for the study of landowner-ship and of field-names. The apportionment goes on to note the land use of each field (usually as arable, meadow, or pasture). Nevertheless, about 79 per cent of England and Wales is covered by tithe maps.

The tithe files in the Public Record Office consist for the most part of the working papers of the assistant commissioners. About half the civil parishes in Ireland were valued between 1823 and 1830; the rest were valued between 1832 and 1837. The valuers' notebooks, known as tithe applotment books, note the names of tenants and *townlands, and record the area, value, and tithe payable.

tithes. The great tithes of corn and hay, and the small tithes of livestock, wool, and non-cereal crops, went to the support of the *rector of a *parish, who in return maintained the *chancel of the church and saw to the provision of church worship. Where the resident minister was not the rector but an institution such as a monastery or *college, or a layman, the small tithes were paid to the *vicar who served in the rector's place. Local customs varied greatly to complicate this general picture. At the *Reformation tithe-rights that belonged to monasteries were confiscated by the Crown and granted or sold to various owners known as lay impropriators. From this time, about a third of all tithes became owned by lay people; moreover, some clergymen and ecclesiastical institutions leased the collection of tithes to laymen. This lay involvement created opposition to the payment of tithes. In the mid-17th century *Quakers and *Anabaptists refused to pay tithes to any owner. By the early 19th century the growth of *Nonconformity had increased opposition to the payment of tithes to the Established Church.

Originally, tithes were payable in kind. In most English parishes the precise customs to be followed in collecting tithes were set out in detail in *glebe terriers. In some parishes it had become the practice by the early modern period for farmers to pay a fixed *modus instead. After periods of inflation, tithe-owners frequently challenged the legality of such arrangements, either in diocesan courts (which tended to favour the tithe-owners) or in the equity courts of *Chancery and *Exchequer (which were expensive and dilatory). The records of such cases contain depositions which are often informative about local customs. Contests over the payment of tithes on new crops, e.g. *potatoes, indicate when such crops were first grown in a parish.

Parliamentary *enclosure provided an opportunity for ending strife by allotting land to the tithe-owners in lieu of tithe. Over 60 per cent of the 3,700 or so Acts passed between 1757 and 1835 dealt with tithes in this way. The Tithe Commutation Act of 1836 converted tithes into rent charge payments based on the prevailing price of grain. New Tithe Acts, notably those of 1891, 1925, and 1936, dealt with changed circumstances. Rent charges finally disappeared in 1936 when landowners began to pay an annuity over 60 years in order to redeem all tithe by 1996.

In Scotland, tithes were abolished at the *Reformation. In Ireland an Act of 1823 allowed the voluntary commutation of tithes into a money payment; an Act of 1832 made commutation compulsory. In 1838 the tithe payment was reduced by 25 per cent and transferred from the tenant to the landowner. Tithes were abolished in Ireland in 1869.

tithing. The medieval system whereby groups of ten *households were responsible to the manorial *court leet for the good conduct of each member.

tithingman. The elected representative of each *tithing who was responsible for presenting the misdemeanours of his members or their families to the manor *court leet.

toft. A plot of land to the rear of a building, often bounded at the rear by a back lane. The regularity of tofts in some medieval villages suggests a planned settlement.

Toleration Act (1689). After the *Glorious Revolution of 1688 had ousted the Catholic King James II, congregations of Protestant *Nonconformists were allowed to worship openly provided they licensed their meeting houses at *quarter sessions.

Tolpuddle Martyrs. The six Dorset *agricultural labourers who were sentenced to *transportation to Australia in 1834 for being members of a secret society which aimed to improve their wages. They subsequently became symbolic heroes of the *trade union movement.

tomb chest. A form of *funerary monument, dating from the 13th to the 17th century, and from the *Gothic revival of the 19th century.

toot-hill. Look-out points used to watch for raiding armies in the *Anglo-Saxon and *Viking era.

topographical guides. The first topographical guides were published in the late 18th century to cater for the increasing numbers of visitors to the Lake District, Snowdonia, and the Highlands of Scotland.

topographical surname. A surname derived from a feature in the landscape, e.g. Green, Wood, or Hill.

toponymic. The term is used to describe the classes of surname that are derived from places.

Tories. The word (derived from an Irish word for 'outlaw') was first used as a nickname to distinguish a group of aristocratic politicians from their *Whig opponents in the late 17th century. They adopted the name *Conservative under Sir Robert Peel in the mid-1830s.

Torrington, Viscount. The Hon. John Byng, 5th Viscount Torrington, kept diaries of his tours through England and Wales between 1781 and 1794. These have been published as C. B. Andrews (ed.), *The Torrington Diaries*, 4 vols. (1935–6).

torture was commonly used in the Middle Ages and the early modern period to get a confession to a charge of treason. Common methods were to stretch suspects on a rack, or to press them with heavy weights on their chests, or to screw their thumbs. The use of torture by government declined during the 17th century.

total descent. A chart showing all ancestral lines, both male and female. In practice, such charts usually go back no further than the 16 great-great-grandparents.

tournament. Medieval tournaments were a mixture of sport and warfare, where rival groups of knights fought across open country, often with the loss of life and limb. The Tudor and Jacobean tournament was very different. It no longer served as a training ground for war, but was a carefully stage-managed public spectacle for political and cultural purposes.

tower houses were built on both sides of the Scottish border in the 14th and 15th centuries to protect the occupants from raiders.

town halls. The traditional town hall of the 16th and early 17th centuries consisted of a large room or rooms raised on columns above an open arcade. Such buildings served also as market halls and sometimes as the meeting places of manorial *courts.

Even more striking are the town halls of Britain's Victorian cities, which provided office space for staff as well as rooms and chambers for meetings and prestigious reception and dining areas. The architectural styles are eclectic and often incorporate both classical and *Gothic elements.

townfields. A term used in the north of England when referring to the *open-fields of a *township, particularly those relatively small openfields of upland areas.

townland. The ancient and basic unit of local government in Ireland. The average size of the 60,462 townlands is 350 *acres; the range is from a little over 1 acre to over 7,000 acres.

township. The smallest unit of local government, and an ancient one, largely synonymous with *vill. In many parts of England *parishes formed a single township, but in districts where parishes were large, e.g. the Pennines, they were subdivided into townships. In the 16th century townships or civil parishes were given responsibility for the poor and the highways. They were also units of taxation. Townships survived until the creation of *Urban and *Rural District Councils in the late 19th century.

trade token. The shortage of coins in the early modern period led to shopkeepers and other traders issuing their own tokens. Millions must have been produced until a royal proclamation of 1672 forbade their circulation after the introduction of copper *farthings and halfpennies.

trade unions. By the middle of the 18th century trade unionism was already well established among many groups of industrial workers. The main collections of trade union records are those housed at Warwick University and Nuffield College, Oxford. Many Scottish trade union records are kept at the Department of Manuscripts, the National Library of *Scotland. Some branches have deposited their archives at local *record offices.

trams and buses. Horse-drawn omnibuses were a Parisian invention. London's first service was opened in 1829. Horse-drawn trams, which ran on rails, were an American invention, which was introduced into London in 1870. They were soon replaced by electric trams, whose efficiency led to the decline of omnibus services except in suburbs where trams did not penetrate.

transcript. An exact copy of the wording of a document.

transept. An 'arm' which projects north or south from the space below a central tower in a church.

transhumance. The ancient practice whereby livestock that had been wintered in sheltered valleys were taken in summer to graze on upland or woodland pastures, accompanied by shepherds and cattle herders who lived in *shielings or similar structures.

transom. The horizontal division of a window; usually associated with *mullions.

transportation of convicts. In 1615 the *Privy Council authorized the transportation of criminals to America, particularly to Virginia, as an alternative to hanging. On arrival, prisoners were sold to the highest bidders. Transportation to the American colonies continued until the War of Independence in 1776. By then, an estimated 40,000 convicts had been transported to America.

After 1776 British gaols began to get overcrowded. Parliament therefore authorized transportation to Australia. The 'First Fleet' of 586 male and 192 female convicts, together with free settlers and seamen, set sail on 13 May 1787 and arrived the following January. Transportation ceased in 1868, by which time it is estimated that about 162,000 convicts had been transported to the other side of the world. The Public Record Office has convict transportation records arranged by ships (HO 11), contracts for the transportation of convicts who are named, with their place of trial and sentence noted (TS 18), lists of convicts on particular ships (PC 1), Privy Council registers (PC 2), lists of convicts at particular dates (HO 31/1), and thousands of petitions for release (HO 17). *Quarter sessions records are another major source of information.

travellers' accounts. Some discerning descriptions of England were written by early foreign travellers. Before the 17th century people rarely travelled for pleasure. A tour of the 'Wonders of the Peak' was one of the first recognized itineraries. The celebrated account of the travels of Celia *Fiennes is exceptional, not only in its 17th-century date and in being written by a woman, but in its breadth of interest in contemporary matters. Daniel *Defoe, *A Tour Through the Whole Island of Great Britain* (1724–6), the first attempt at a comprehensive account, was a compilation of observances made on journeys undertaken over many years, with additional information culled from other writers.

In the later 18th and early 19th centuries the fashion for travelling to remote places was at its height. The number of travel diaries that survive for this period is far in excess of earlier ones.

T.R.E. *Tempore regis Edwardi*, 'in the time of King Edward the Confessor', the *Domesday Book formula for the period before the Norman Conquest.

treasure trove. Discovered hoards of gold or silver coins or other precious objects that have been deliberately hidden by unknown owners. Ownership is determined at a *coroner's inquest.

trefoil. One of the artificial grasses whose cultivation in pastures and in an arable rotation was introduced from the Continent in the 17th century.

Tribal Hidage. A 7th- or possibly 8th-century document that appears to be a list of the tribute assessments paid to the kingdom of *Mercia by dependent peoples, some of whom are not known from other sources.

Trinitarianism. Belief in the Holy Trinity, especially by 19th-century members of the *Church of England, in opposition to *Unitarianism.

trow. A term used in the 17th and 18th centuries for various kinds of boats or barges that conveyed goods on rivers or along the coast. The precise meaning varied considerably from region to region.

truck. The system by which employers paid part of an employee's wage by vouchers that could be used only at a shop or store belonging to the employer. The system was open to abuse and was forbidden by the Truck Act (1831).

tumulus. A term, favoured by the *Ordnance Survey, for a prehistoric burial site.

turbary, right of. The right to dig peat for fuel on the *commons and wastes.

turnips. An improved variety was introduced from the Low Countries as a vegetable, and became a *market garden crop in the later 16th century. By the end of that century they were much grown in gardens by the poor. Farmers learned in the 17th century to value them as fodder for cattle, sheep, and poultry. From the late 17th century onwards turnips were increasingly grown by farmers in *open-fields, on light soils but not on heavy clays.

turnpike roads. Roads administered by trusts authorized by private Acts of Parliament, on which tolls were charged at gates.

The first turnpike trust was established by private Act of Parliament in 1663 to repair and maintain a particularly badly worn 15-mile stretch of the Great North Road between Wadesmill and Royston in Hertfordshire and Cambridgeshire, but this pioneering enterprise was not imitated elsewhere until 1696. The number of new turnpike Acts rose steadily from four in the 1690s, to 10 in the 1700s, 22 in the 1710s, and 46 in the 1720s. By 1750 most of the major through routes in England had been turnpiked, though no turnpike roads had yet been authorized in Cornwall, Devon, Dorset, or Wales, and the movement had only just begun in Scotland, and had achieved only limited success in Ireland. The most active period for the formation of turnpike trusts was between 1751 and 1772, when 389 new Acts were passed. The 1790s was also a busy period. By 1820 over 1,000 turnpike trusts controlled about 22,000 miles of British roads and charged tolls at some 7,000 or more gates.

The progress of a private bill through Parliament can be followed in the printed *Journals* of the *House of Commons and *House of Lords. Printed Acts, which name the trustees and outline their powers, are usually available at local studies libraries and local *record offices. A complete set of Acts is available in the *House of Lords Record Office, including renewal Acts which are available only in manuscript. Powers were normally granted for 21 years, after which a renewal Act had to be sought.

Tusser, Thomas (*c.*1520–80). East Anglian writer on agriculture, whose metrical *Five Hundrethe Pointes of Good Husbandrie* (1573), an enlarged version of his *A Hundreth Good Pointes of Husbandrie* (1557), went into numerous editions.

Tyburn. The gallows, known as 'Tyburn tree', was the place of public execution in London until 1783. The site is now occupied by Marble Arch.

typhoid. An infectious disease, once thought to be a variety of *typhus, whose main characteristic is catarrhal inflammation of the intestines.

typhus. A contagious fever transmitted to humans by body lice or rat fleas, and characterized by rose-coloured spots, prostration, and delirium. Outbreaks affected the urban poor and armies involved in siege warfare.

U

ultimus haeres. Under Scottish law, if a person died without a known heir, the Crown was deemed the *ultimus haeres* (last heir). The records are kept in the *Scottish Record Office. Those dating before 1834 relate to the granting of *ultimus haeres* to petitioners. After 1834 fuller records are kept under E 851–870.

uncle. In the early modern period the term had a wider meaning than brother of one's father or mother. It included more distant relatives and was used for an older man.

underdrainage. Although much land had been drained before the 19th century, the heavy clays could not be effectively drained until the invention of machine-made tiles *c*.1840 made the work cheaper and more efficient.

Unitarians. A *Nonconformist denomination that denies the Holy Trinity and accepts the humanity of Christ. During the second decade of the 18th century *Presbyterian and *Independent congregations split on the issue of the Trinity. In some places the Unitarian majority retained possession of the chapel, elsewhere they left to erect new meeting houses. The old name Presbyterian was retained by both groups. Unitarianism became legal only in 1813.

United Kingdom. The United Kingdom of Great Britain and Ireland was formed in 1801. In 1922 southern Ireland became independent, since when the UK has consisted of England, Scotland, Wales, and Northern Ireland.

Urban District Councils. When county *borough councils were created in 1888, responsibility for the public health of towns with under 50,000 inhabitants remained with urban sanitary authorities. In 1894 these and other functions were taken over by elected urban district councils and their officers. UDCs were abolished under local government reorganization in 1974. Their minutes and other records have been deposited with local *record offices.

urban renaissance. A term coined by Peter Borsay to chart the rise of provincial urban society after the *Restoration, together with the great improvement of the built environment, and the provision of leisure and intellectual activities on an unprecedented scale.

V

vaccary. A place for rearing cattle in hilly or moorland districts.

vaccination against *smallpox was introduced by Edward Jenner (1749–1823), a physician from Berkeley (Gloucestershire). Previous attempts to combat the disease had been by *inoculation.

vagabond. The Elizabethan *Poor Law Acts of 1597–1601 dealt harshly with sturdy *beggars, rogues, and vagabonds, whose numbers were greatly exaggerated by the government and commentators. Most vagrants were single men, who travelled alone or in twos, rather than in the gangs that worried the writers of pamphlets. After the *Restoration their numbers fell and they ceased to be a matter of national concern.

Valor Ecclesiasticus. An Act of 1535 impropriated the 'first fruits' and imposed an annual tax of one-tenth of the net income of all ecclesiastical *benefices. As a result, a detailed and exact valuation of church wealth was made. This has been published in six volumes as J. Caley and J. Hunter (eds.), *Valor Ecclesiasticus* (Record Commission, 1810–34). The survey gives details of the income of all parish churches, together with many chapels, *guilds, and *chantry chapels. The full report is missing for some counties, but summaries of incomes survive.

Valuation Office. The Finance Act (1910) proposed a tax on land values. The valuation survey that was carried out between 1910 and 1915 describes and assesses the value of land and buildings in both an urban and a rural context. Information on each unit of property was recorded in Valuation Office Field Books, which are now housed in the *Public Record Office under IR 58, and in the accompanying forms of return which were filled in by owners. The properties referred to in the Field Books can be identified from accompanying *Ordnance Survey sheets. Parish indexes are available in the Map Room at the Public Record Office, where a detailed finding sheet is available.

vassal. Under the *feudal system, a person who held land of a lord in return for sworn homage.

Vatican records. The medieval papacy received a constant stream of letters petitioning for privileges, confirming appointments, and dealing with disputes. The Vatican houses a mass of documentation of an administrative and legal nature that is of use to local historians who are concerned with the Middle Ages.

vellum. A fine type of parchment made from the skin of young calves and kids.

verderer. The medieval official who administered the *vert and venison of a *forest. Each forest had four verderers, who were elected by the *freeholders who had rights in the forest.

vernacular architecture. The term 'vernacular architecture' has been used by architects, historians, and archaeologists since at least 1839 to describe the minor buildings of town and countryside, but it is only in the second half of the 20th century that the term has been widely employed to define an area of interest that has attracted much scholarly and amateur study.

verso. The left-hand page of an open book, the opposite of *recto. In folio numbering, the reader is guided by the use of the superscript 'v'.

vert and venison. In a *forest, vert referred to the trees and shrubs which bore green leaves and thus provided food and shelter for livestock; venison referred originally to all livestock, not just deer.

vestry. A room attached to the *chancel of a church which is used for the keeping of vestments, etc. The vestry is now usually reserved for the minister, but it was originally the room where parish meetings were held. Membership of the vestry comprised the minister, churchwardens, and leading parishioners, who were either co-opted (under a 'close' or 'select' vestry system) or elected ('open vestry'). In the 16th and 17th centuries the vestry assumed many of the old functions of the manor *court, e.g. appointing the *constable, as well as taking on new responsibilities for the *poor and the *highways. The vestry lost these responsibilities during the 19th century, and in 1894 the civil functions of parishes were transferred to parish councils and parish meetings.

vicar. Originally, the minister who was appointed by an absentee *rector, e.g. a monastery or *college. The vicar received the small *tithes, whereas a resident rector received all the tithes. Parishes which today are served by a vicar must have paid their tithes to a religious institution such as a monastery in the Middle Ages.

vicars-choral. The body of choristers in a cathedral.

vicinage, common of. Rights on *commons claimed by owners of adjacent properties.

Victoria County History, The. The *Victoria History of the Counties of England* was founded in 1899. The series is divided into sets for each of the historic counties and, within each county set, into general and topographical volumes. The general volumes deal with natural history, prehistory, the *Roman and *Anglo-Saxon periods, the *Domesday Book, political and administrative history, ecclesiastical history and religious houses, social and economic history, *forests, endowed schools, and sport. The topographical volumes are arranged by *hundred or *wapentake, subdivided into *parishes and *townships, or by towns. The history of each township is traced by a general description, followed by sections on *manors and other estates, economic history, local government, church, *Nonconformity, education, and charities for the poor.

Vikings. Scandinavian invaders, settlers, and traders who spread throughout northern Europe between the 8th and the 11th centuries. They came to Britain as two groups: the Norwegians, who settled in the Orkney and Shetland Islands, the Hebrides and west Scotland, northwest England, the Isle of Man, and the eastern coast of Ireland; and the Danes, who settled in what became the *Danelaw in north-eastern and eastern England.

vill. A term often found in medieval records, e.g. central government taxation returns, for a *township.

villages, close. A term coined by the *Poor Law Commissioners to denote those villages where all the land was owned by a *squire, or a small group of landowners, from which poor immigrants were excluded in order to keep the poor rates at a minimum.

villages, estate. During the 18th and 19th centuries great landowners and country squires redesigned and rebuilt villages in an aesthetically pleasing manner. To do this they had to own all the properties. Some were resited outside the landscaped *park of the great house. They were often built in *vernacular styles, especially the Tudor or Jacobean, using traditional materials for walls and roofs.

villages, open. A term coined by the *Poor Law Commissioners to describe villages that were not dominated by a *squire, or a small group of farmers, and where control of movement, building, and religious and social preferences was therefore lax. Such villages were populous and contained large numbers of poor people. Many were industrial villages.

villeins. An unfree tenant of manorial land under the *feudal system. A villein held his land by agricultural services, by working on the *demesne, and by *boon work. The term was introduced by the Normans and gradually fell into disuse after the consequences of the *Black Death had altered the supply of labour.

virgate. A standard holding of arable land in the Middle Ages, of up to 30 *acres, scattered amongst the *open-fields of a *manor, with accompanying rights on the *commons.

viscount. The rank of the peerage between *earl and *baron, created in 1440.

Vitruvius Britannicus. The publication in 1715 by Colen Campbell, under the sponsorship of the Earl of Burlington, of two volumes of plans and elevations of contemporary country houses in Britain, to inspire others to follow best practice. It signalled the beginning of the *Palladian movement in Britain. Vitruvius was the greatest architect in ancient Rome. A further three volumes were subsequently published.

waggons and wains. The Old English word 'wain' and the Dutch word 'waggon' have a common root. They were translated as *plaustrum* in medieval Latin documents. The lighter, two-wheeled wain was in common use, even in highland Britain, in the Middle Ages.

John *Stow observed that 'long waggons' which brought goods and passengers to London from Canterbury, Norwich, Ipswich, Gloucester, etc., began to operate about 1564. This heavy, four-wheeled vehicle was introduced from the Low Countries. Its use was long confined to southern England.

waits, town. Musicians employed by urban authorities to play on ceremonial and other occasions, e.g. accompanying the watch at fair times. Extra employment was obtained by playing at weddings and other private gatherings. Waits appear in town records from the Middle Ages to the 18th century upon their appointment and upon the provision of cloaks, ribbons, badges, etc. Payments were also made for musical instruments, such as fiddles, bass viols, hauteboys, and bassoons.

Wales, National Library of. Founded by royal charter in 1907, and sited at Aberystwyth, the Library collects a wide range of manuscript, printed, cartographic, visual, sound, and moving-image material relating to Wales and the Celtic peoples. The collections are held in three curatorial departments: Printed Books, Manuscripts and Records, and Pictures and Maps.

Public records include the records of the Court of Great Sessions, established by the Second Act of Union 1542 and functioning until 1830. The extensive collections of *estate records, including correspondence, account books, *deeds, and *rentals, and associated manorial records, together with a wide range of ecclesiastical records, are valuable sources. The records of the Welsh *dioceses, the Presbyterian Church of Wales (previously Welsh Calvinistic Methodists), and other *Nonconformist churches have been deposited at the Library. Of particular importance are *bishops' transcripts, *parish registers, probate records, membership lists, and annual reports. A computer index to the pre-1858 probate records is available, as also is the post-1858 Calendar of Grants. Microform copies of the *census returns for the whole of Wales (1841–1991), the *General Register Office's indexes (1837–1983), and the 1988 edition of the *International Genealogical Index may be consulted in the microfilm reading area.

wall painting. The interiors of medieval parish churches were a blaze of colour. Wall paintings of scenes from the Bible and lives of saints were used as visual aids. At the *Reformation it was ordered that these paintings should be destroyed or covered with whitewash. Many have been recovered during the 19th and 20th centuries. About 200 British churches have paintings in a good state of preservation and very many more have fragments.

wall paper. The earliest British wall papers, dating from Tudor times, were printed from wood-blocks to imitate fabric designs. Wall paper became fashionable in the late 17th century. The standard roll size of that time, 36 feet long and 22 inches wide, remains in use to this day. From the 1690s until the 19th century Chinese hand-painted papers were particularly popular in great houses; as they were imported from China by the *East India Company, they were often known as 'Indian' papers.

wall plate. A horizontal post which rests on the *tie-beams of a *timber-framed building, to help support the weight of a roof-truss. The side-walls of a building reach from ground level as far as the wall plate.

Walter of Henley. 13th-century author of a treatise on husbandry, which provided practical advice for owners of estates of moderate size and for squires farming their own land.

wapentake. The *Danelaw equivalent of the Anglo-Saxon *hundred, i.e. a subdivision of a county for administrative and judicial purposes. The original meeting-places were open-air sites, often at river crossings or near major highways. Wapentakes survived as taxation districts (combining a number of *townships) into the early modern period and for calling out the *militia in the *Napoleonic wars, and did not finally disappear until the reorganization of local government in 1974.

war memorials. Memorials listing the dead, as distinct from earlier monuments commemorating victories or peace, were first placed in public places after the Crimean War. A number survive from the Boer War, but it was only after the First World War that monuments were erected by public subscription in every town and parochial centre.

War Office records. The appointment of a Secretary at War upon the *Restoration in 1660 led to the keeping of more systematic records. These are now kept in the *Public Record Office under WO. The returns of accommodation for men and horses at *inns and *alehouses in 1686 (WO 30) provide statistical information about such provision for each settlement in England and Wales.

ward. A division in the four northern counties of England and in some of the southern counties of Scotland. They appear to have arisen after the Norman Conquest. East Ward and West Ward (Westmorland), and Castle Ward (Northumberland), survived as the names of *civil registration districts.

Wards and Liveries, Court of. The court that administered funds received by the monarch for rights of *wardship, marriage, and livery. Established in 1541, it was abolished in 1660. Its records are kept at the *Public Record Office under WARD 1 to 7.

wardship. The right of the Crown to hold and administer the estates of heirs of *tenants-in-chief until they reached the age of 21, or 14 for an heiress. During this period the Crown received the revenues of the estate and could determine the marriage of the heir or heiress. These rights were enforced from Henry VII's reign (1485–1509) until the abolition of feudal tenures in 1660. Wardships were frequently sold to *nobility and *gentry, and were, of course, lucrative assets. Often wards were married off to a child of the person who got wardship; sometimes relations got wardship.

warrens. In the Middle Ages royal grants of *free warren allowed feudal lords to hunt small game in defined areas. Warrens which were enclosed for the rearing of *rabbits were widely established, on heaths, sandy wastes, and other land that was fit for little else, in the medieval and early modern periods.

wars, foreign. The first major foreign war in English experience was the prolonged war with France, begun by Edward III (1327–77), and known as the Hundred Years' War. It came to a temporary end in 1382, but was revived under Henry V (1413–22). By the mid-15th century the English retained no interest in France, except for Calais. Henry VIII conducted three expensive and inconclusive campaigns in France (1511–14, 1522–5, and 1542–6), and waged war against the Scots. During the second half of the 16th century the Continental balance of power changed and Spain became the major threat to England, until the defeat of the Armada in 1588. Another war with Spain lasted from 1656 to 1659. From the reign of Elizabeth I (1558–1603) onwards, the English were concerned to create and extend an empire, starting with Ireland, and then Virginia. This led not only to conflict with the Irish and the Native Americans, but to frequent skirmishes, and eventually to full-scale wars, with other western European powers engaged in similar activity. Three wars were fought against the Dutch (1652–4, 1665–7, and 1672–4), and two long wars were fought against the France of Louis XIV (1689–97 and 1701–14, the latter being known as the War of Spanish Succession).

In the 18th century the Union with Scotland (1707) and the defeat of the *Jacobite rebellions of 1715 and 1745 brought an end to wars between England and Scotland, but renewed struggle with the Catholic countries of Europe brought the War of Jenkins' Ear (1739), the War of Austrian Succession (1740–8), and the Seven Years' War (1756–63). Military activity took place not only in Europe, but in Brazil, the Caribbean, New England, Africa, and India. The American colonies were lost as a result of the War of Independence (1775–83). The major and prolonged conflict known as the French Revolutionary and *Napoleonic wars lasted from 1793 to 1815. France subsequently ceased to be the traditional enemy of the English and fought with the British against the Russians in the Crimean War (1854–6). British military activity was thereafter largely concentrated on consolidating an empire in India and Africa, culminating in the Boer War (1899–1902). (See the records of the two WORLD WARS (1914–18 and 1939–45).) The Korean War (1949–51), the Suez Campaign (1956), and the Falklands War (1982) have been the major wars involving British troops in the second half of the 20th century.

Wars of the Roses. A struggle for power between the rival aristocratic factions headed by the houses of Lancaster and York, both of which descended from Edward III (1327–77) and therefore claimed rights to the throne. Several battles were fought between 1455 and 1461. The Yorkist victory at Towton led to the crowning of Edward IV as king of England in 1461.

'waste' in the Domesday Book. After valuing a *manor as it had been in the time of Edward the Confessor, the *Domesday Book often concludes 'and now it is waste'. The frequency of this expression in entries for the north of England has led to the belief that such manors were laid to waste by William I's army during the 'Harrying of the North'. Such views are now largely discredited, despite the reality of the 'harrying'. 'Waste' seems to have meant land from which no tax was forthcoming, for whatever reasons. No fewer than 128 Yorkshire manors in the Domesday Book were described as 'waste', even though some had resources, population, or value recorded.

watch and ward. The medieval and early modern system whereby the security of towns was preserved by patrols. The watch kept a lookout at night, the ward was responsible for daytime security. Membership of the watch and ward was a duty for all male citizens by rotation.

water closet. The first water closet used in Britain was invented in the Elizabethan period by Sir John Harrington, but it was not until the late 17th century that water closets became installed in country houses.

wattle and daub. One of the principal ways of filling in the spaces between the posts of a *timber-framed building. The wattle came from *coppice wood, the daub was made from clay, cow dung, animal hair, straw, etc. and was usually whitened to improve the appearance.

weather cocks / vanes. Weather cocks are revolving metal structures on the tops of church towers and spires, which indicate the direction of the wind. The cockerel shape was preferred as the tails are well suited to catch the wind, but the emblems of patron saints were also favoured, as were idiosyncratic designs. Most examples are difficult to date, and in any case have probably been replaced frequently. The use of weather vanes is thought to have originated in France. The first in England were heraldic devices (the word is derived from *fane*, meaning banner), placed on domestic buildings, especially of the Tudor period. Pre-Victorian vanes were usually painted.

weatherboard. Timber cladding used to protect the external walls of houses, *mills, church towers, etc. in eastern and southern England.

weaving was a major source of employment in the Middle Ages and the early modern period, in both the towns and the countryside. The urban weavers were often members of *guilds; those in the countryside were usually smallholders who combined their craft with running a small farm. Weaving did not become mechanized as quickly as spinning, so when woollen and *worsted *spinning mills were erected in the late 18th and early 19th centuries the increased amount of yarn that was produced continued to be woven at handlooms in *cottages. The characteristic weavers' cottages that survive in parts of the Pennines mostly date from this time. They are distinguished by their row of windows on the second or top floor, which allow the maximum amount of light to fall on the looms. By this time, weaving was normally a full-time occupation. Weaving became mechanized from the 1820s and 1830s, and hand-weaving disappeared during Victoria's reign.

weights and measures. There was much regional variety in the use of customary weights and measures, even within a county, until the late 19th century. See pp. 283–5.

weld. A crop that produced a yellow dye.

Wellcome Institute for the History of Medicine. An archive and research centre at 183 Euston Road, London NW1 2BN.

wergild. The *Anglo-Saxon system of compensation for murder or malicious injury, payable by the malefactor or his family to the family of the murdered or injured person. Payments were on a scale according to a man's social position.

Wessex. The kingdom of the West Saxons, which became pre-eminent in *Anglo-Saxon England. During the period 685–840 Wessex became dominant in southern England. Under Alfred (871–99), Wessex successfully resisted the Danes. During the 10th century Alfred's descendants recovered much of England from the Danes. The name 'Wessex' was revived in the 19th century by the Dorset poet William Barnes, and by Thomas Hardy.

Western Rebellion. A rebellion in Cornwall and Devon during 1547–9 against the Edwardian *Reformation.

wheelhouses. Horse-mills under permanent cover. These are built in a semi-circular shape, one storey high with a sloping roof, against the wall of a barn in which machinery was housed. A horse walked round and round to power a gin for *threshing, cutting turnips and chaff, crushing *gorse for animal feed, etc.

Whigs. A nickname of uncertain origin applied to the aristocratic political party that was formed after the *Glorious Revolution of 1688 to keep a check on royal power.

whipping. The whipping of men and women, who were tied to a post or fastened to the tail of a cart which was led through the streets, was a punishment for criminals, *vagabonds, and *beggars until well into the 18th century. Whipping was also used to maintain discipline in the army and navy.

white coal. Wood fuel for lead smelters, burnt slowly in pits which often survive in *woods. The fuel was lighter in colour than *charcoal. It was used from Elizabethan times until it was replaced by coke in the late 18th century.

whitesmith. A worker in tin; also, a polisher and finisher of metalware.

wife-selling. The 'poor man's divorce' of the 18th and early 19th centuries. The sale was conducted according to recognized procedures: the venue was the market place or other public space, the event was sometimes preceded by a public announcement and was conducted by an auctioneer, the woman was led in by a halter round her neck to signify that she was the property of her husband, a nominal purchase price was agreed, and the woman left with her purchaser, who was her accepted lover.

Williams's, Dr, Library, 14 Gordon Square, London. A library and archive of *Nonconformity. Of particular use is John Evans's list of dissenting congregations (1715), MS 34–4, which gives the numerical strengths of meetings throughout England and Wales. A voluntary General Register of Births for Dissenters was opened on 1 January 1743.

This contains entries from many parts of Britain, but particularly for London, until the introduction of *civil registration in 1837.

wills. The practice of making a will goes back to *Anglo-Saxon times, but was originally restricted to the wealthiest groups. The custom was not widely adopted by farmers and urban craftsmen until the 16th century. Labourers and other poor people rarely made wills, even in later times. The various studies that have compared the numbers of adult males who made a will with those whose deaths are recorded in *parish registers usually show that the figure was about 1 in 3 or 1 in 4.

The ancient responsibility for proving a will lay with the church. Most wills are therefore kept at the *record offices of the ancient dioceses. During the *Commonwealth (1653–60) all wills in England and Wales were proved in the *Prerogative Court of Canterbury and are now kept at the *Public Record Office. On 12 January 1858 the state took over responsibility for proving wills. Since then, they have been kept at the Principal Registry of the Family Division, *Somerset House, The Strand, London.

The ancient Scottish system of proving wills was through one of the 22 *commissary courts, and after 1823 in sheriff's courts. The records are kept at the *Scottish Record Office. In Ireland the system was similar to that in England and Wales, being based on church dioceses until 1858, when responsibility for proving wills passed to a new Principal Registry in Dublin whose records were destroyed by fire in 1922, though the indexes were saved. A miscellaneous collection of wills and will-substitutes, e.g. notebook copies made before the fire, is housed at the National Archives, Dublin. Few wills survive from before 1780.

window tax. Introduced in 1697, after the abolition of the *hearth tax. The occupier of every house was taxed at the rate of two shillings a year, with an additional payment of eight shillings for a house with over 10 windows. In 1709 the rates were increased for larger houses, but those who were too poor to pay church or poor rates were exempt. From the mid-18th century the rates paid by those with over 10 windows were frequently increased. From 1825 occupiers with fewer than eight windows were exempt. The tax was abolished in 1851. Unlike the hearth tax, few returns have survived. They should be sought at county *record offices.

wiseman. A conjuror or wizard who performed 'white' magic which was generally regarded as being beneficial, e.g. the healing of sick people and animals, the recovery of stolen property, and forecasting the weather.

witchcraft. In the Middle Ages prosecutions were few and punishments light. Witchcraft became a felony in 1563. The death penalty was carried out on those who were found guilty of causing death by witchcraft, and lesser offenders were imprisoned. Serious cases were tried at the *assizes, minor offences at the *ecclesiastical courts. Prosecutions rose from 1563 to a peak during the last two decades of the 16th century. They fell away markedly during the 17th century, except for the craze that affected East Anglia and south-eastern England in 1645–7.

woad. The leaves of this plant afforded the essential dye in the colouring of blue, black, and purple cloth until the demand was partially satisfied, from the 16th century onwards, by imports of indigo.

wolves are commemorated in place-names, but were generally extinct by the end of the Middle Ages. The last recorded sighting in the Highlands of Scotland was in 1743 and in Ireland in 1786.

wong. A strip in a shared meadow.

wood-collier. A *charcoal burner. The term often appears simply as 'collier' and is thus sometimes confused with coal miner.

wood pasture. The term used to describe those agricultural districts where the farming economy was significantly different from *champion land which was farmed on the *open-field system. Such districts often had only small areas devoted to open-fields; instead most of the land was in *closes and used for pastoral activities, such as the rearing of cattle or dairying. The neighbouring *woods were often extensive and were a source of grazing rights on the *commons. Settlement was not confined to nucleated villages, but was scattered in hamlets and isolated farmsteads. Wood-pasture districts often had specific social characteristics, notably light manorial control, numerous freeholders, and sometimes a predilection for religious and political dissent, and for rural industry.

woods. The earliest evidence for woodmanship comes from the *Neolithic trackways that have been found in the Somerset Levels. Woodland management was practised by both prehistoric peoples and the Romans. By the time of the Norman Conquest many parts of England were without woods. The interpretation of the woodland entries in the *Domesday Book remains controversial, but it is clear that the surviving woods had to be carefully managed as an economic asset, mostly as *coppice or springwoods, that is, trees which were felled just above ground level, allowing regeneration through young shoots. The alternative method of *pollarding involved the lopping of branches about 7–18 feet above the ground. *Hedges were also a source of wood from early times.

The ancient tradition of coppicing began to decline in the late 19th century, in face of competition from foreign imports, and was largely abandoned after the First World War. Most surviving broad-leaved woodlands have a continuous history from at least the late Middle Ages.

wool. The woollen industry was pre-eminent in the economy of the British Isles during the Middle Ages and the early modern period. The manufacture of cloth was unrivalled as England's principal medieval industry, in both the towns and the countryside. The manufacture of woollen cloth in East Anglia, the Cotswolds, and other regions declined in face of West Riding competition during the 18th and 19th centuries.

workhouse. A few workhouses for the able-bodied poor were founded, from the late 17th century onwards, by local Acts. More were established under the Acts of 1722 and 1782. From 1722 parishes were allowed to farm out their responsibility for the poor to a contractor at a fixed fee. *Gilbert's Act (1782) allowed parishes to join forces in the erection of a workhouse, in an arrangement by which each *parish paid the cost of maintaining its own poor but achieved savings by sharing the premises. The establishment of these 18th-century workhouses is noted in the accounts of the overseers of the *poor, but detailed records usually do not survive, since the operation was often let to contractors.

By the *Poor Law Amendment Act of 1834 the whole of England and Wales was divided into unions of parishes, in each of which a board of guardians was elected to administer poor relief. These unions were often centred on a market town, and they sometimes stretched beyond county boundaries. The new Poor Law met with considerable opposition in the north of England. Each union built a workhouse to house those people who were in receipt of relief. Some unions merely took over existing workhouses, and others were slow to build their own. Contrary to the intention of the Act, the guardians often continued to pay relief to people who lived in their own houses. Workhouses gradually evolved into orphanages and hospitals, especially for the feeble-minded, the aged, and the infirm. In the mid-19th century some workhouses established schools for the children in their care, until local board schools were built in the 1870s. Children were finally removed from the workhouse in 1908. *County and district councils took over responsibility for workhouses from the guardians in 1894. The system was replaced in 1948 upon the creation of the National Health Service.

In Ireland, the same system of Poor Law unions, elected guardians, and union workhouses began in 1838. In Scotland, the *heritors and kirk session of each parish were responsible for the poor until the Poor Law Act (1845) established parochial boards to administer poor relief in each parish. From 1845 poor houses were established more widely than before. Here, too, the old system was replaced in 1894 when responsibility passed to elected parish councils, which were replaced in turn by district councils in 1929, until the reorganization of local government in 1974.

The best-known workhouse records are the master's accounts. Some admission registers survive, together with guardians' minute books and general ledgers. These will be found in local *record offices. *Census returns list the inmates of workhouses on census night.

World Wars, records of. Regimental museums have lists of soldiers who served in the First and Second World Wars, and much background information, including *photographs. Many rolls of honour for the dead in the two World Wars have been published by regiments, schools, and professional bodies. The Commonwealth War Graves Commission, 2 Marlow Road, Maidenhead, Berkshire SL6 7DX, has details of servicemen who died overseas and on ships during the two World Wars.

*The *London Gazette* published despatches, campaign reports, casualty lists, and citations for awards and decorations. The *Public Record Office has First World War records of military tribunals (MH 47), medical and discharge papers (MH 106), and records of pensions and allowances (PIN 15 and 26, PMG 42–47). The PRO's records of the Second World War include the Army Roll of Honour, which lists servicemen and servicewomen who died, noting their rank, regiment, birthplace, residence, and place of death (WO 304), and war pensions paid to widows (PMG 10).

worsted. A type of cloth, using long wools, that was originally made in Worstead, Norfolk, but which became a speciality of the upper Calder and Aire valleys in the West Riding of Yorkshire from the later 17th century onwards.

Wright, Joseph (1855–1930). Known for his work as editor of *The English Dialect Dictionary*, 6 vols. (1898–1905), which despite its title covers Ireland, Scotland, and Wales as well as England.

writ. A written and sealed command from a court, ordering or forbidding an act by the person to whom it is addressed.

Y

yard. A word meaning enclosed ground, as in the sense of back yard, courtyard, farmyard, etc.

yardland. A *virgate, a typical peasant holding in the Middle Ages, often dispersed in *strips in the *open-fields. The acreage of yardlands varied considerably, but as a fiscal unit it often remained consistent over long periods of time.

yeomanry. The local volunteer force of the Victorian and Edwardian era, who were mounted on their own horses and were therefore distinct from the foot soldiers of the *militia.

yeomen. The term has changed its meaning over time. In the 13th–15th centuries it was principally applied to a *knight's servants or retainers, though in the royal household the minor officials under the Chamberlain were known as the Yeomen of the King's Chamber. Under the Tudors the use of the term was gradually widened to include the prosperous working farmers below the rank of the *gentry, the class formerly known as *franklins. They worked their own land, but did not necessarily have to be freeholders. Yeomen increasingly held their land by a variety of tenures: *freehold, *copyhold, and *leasehold. The term had no legal precision, but was used informally to distinguish a farmer who was more prosperous than the average *husbandman.

yoke. A piece of wood curved round the necks of two oxen, or other animals, by which they were harnessed to a plough or vehicle. Yokes were also used by people, e.g. milkmaids carrying pails.

Young, Arthur (1741–1820). Writer on agriculture. His major works include *A Tour through the Southern Counties* (1768), *A Tour through the North of England* (1771), *The Farmer's Tour through the East of England* (1770–1), *Tour in Ireland* (1780), *Travels in France during 1787–88–89–90* (1792–4), *The Farmer's Kalendar* (which went into 215 editions by 1862), and reports on seven counties published in the *General Views of Agriculture* series of the *Board of Agriculture, where he was Secretary from 1793.

Appendix: A Guide To The Records for the Family Historian

Getting Started

The thousands of people who are actively tracing their family tree are probably outnumbered by those who have thought that one day they would get round to doing just that but who never seem to get started. If the plunge is taken the pursuit of one's ancestors quickly gathers its own momentum. The determined decision to make a beginning is often the most important that the family historian will make. Part of the problem is simply finding the time and the energy, but much of the inertia is due to lack of know-how. The beginner who has never heard of the PRO and the IGI can easily be put off by the insider's jargon and may well be daunted by a microfilm reader, the thought of finding and entering a record office, and the need to understand how to interpret the evidence of unrelated sets of archives. It takes time not to be intimidated and to realize that the principal ingredient of success is common sense. The technicalities of the subject can be learned as one goes along.

Most people have at least some knowledge of their family in the past, even if they cannot go back very far. Before visiting the nearest library or record office it is helpful to assemble this information in a notebook or file. The need to record everything that one has learnt and to make a careful note of the source of that information is a lesson that should be borne constantly in mind. Interviewing one's relatives, especially the older ones before it is too late, is clearly an early task. Very often the information is muddled and sometimes downright misleading. It is common to find a belief that the family has had a romantic past, that they are descended from someone important (perhaps in an illegitimate line), or that vast sums of money wait to be inherited if only a firm link could be proved. But amidst all this dross are usually a few nuggets of priceless information about where a family came from, who was related to whom, what they did for a living, why they moved home, and so on. There is often enough to provide a firm lead in the right direction.

The pooled resources of a family usually supply a varied collection of old photographs (nearly always unlabelled), newspaper cuttings, birth, marriage, and death certificates, and other mementoes. These help to stimulate interest and are useful props to take when talking to old people whose memories are often stirred by such things. Write everything down, remain sceptical about claims that the family are descended from King Canute, the Duke of Marlborough, Huguenot refugees, Border cattle-rustlers, or all of these people, and follow the leads that promise to point the way back to the unknown. Do not start with some famous person who had the same surname as yours back in the fifteenth century. The golden rule is to work backwards from the known to the unknown. The records of civil registration (outlined below), the census returns of the nineteenth century, and the parish registers are the basic sources for the beginner. It is very common to find that one can quickly get back to the beginning of Victoria's reign. It is then that the real problems begin.

Seeking the help and company of fellow enthusiasts is a natural step to take as one gets started. Adult education departments often provide courses for the beginner and few parts of Britain are now without a local family history society. The national Federation of Family History Societies keeps them all in contact, publishes cheap and useful guides, and has its own magazine, *Family History News and Digest*. Regular programmes of lectures, conferences, and visits offer instruction and a friendly forum of advice. Most societies produce their own journal and many of them publish editions of local records, such as census returns, hearth tax returns, and indexes of parish registers. Making careful surveys of the tombstones in local churchyards—monumental inscriptions, or MIs, for short—is a particularly useful task that is often carried out by society members.

Armed with all the oral information that can be obtained from relatives, the family historian may usefully decide to try to find his ancestors' gravestones. This is another job that should not be delayed because many tombstones are deteriorating badly and others are being removed. In rural areas the graveyard attached to the ancient parish church may still be in use. The oldest tombstones date from the seventeenth century and are found nearest the church, normally to the south, for the north was once regarded as the devil's side where excommunicates, suicides, and unbaptized parishioners were buried. The memorials of the richer inhabitants will be found inside the church. As churchyards became full and the earlier practice of reusing old graves was prevented by the erection of sturdy tombstones, local authorities had to provide alternative arrangements. The first public cemetery was opened in London at Kensal Green in 1827; soon, other towns and cities followed suit. In 1850 an Act of Parliament authorized the General Board of Health to close old churchyards and establish cemeteries. The records of these cemeteries have sometimes been deposited at the appropriate local record office, but many may still be consulted at the office on the site. They normally record the name, address, age, and occupation of the deceased, the date of death and burial, and the place of the grave. However, this information is filed in chronological order and is not indexed alphabetically, so it helps to have a previous idea of the approximate date of death.

The family historian quickly learns not to take all his evidence at face value. Tombstones may be as inaccurate as any other record, especially if they were erected long after the death of the first person to be named. The recorded age must be regarded with caution. It was common, for instance, to think of someone aged 84 as being in his eighty-fifth year and to note the age as 85. On the other hand, tombstones often convey information, e.g. about a relationship, that the researcher did not know. Write it all down and note the exact position of the tombstone for future reference.

Many of us do not proceed in a systematic way at the beginning, but the sooner the decision is made to organize our material the better. Separate notebooks or files for each branch of the family are obviously desirable, but each individual will develop his own methods to suit his temperament, facilities, and enthusiasm. A computer database helps but is not essential! At all stages of research it will be necessary to construct family trees, however tentative they may be. Do not try to put everybody on the same tree, but use different sheets for each side of the family. Some sheets can be used to include everyone on a particular branch within a particular period, others need to give the barest of outlines so that a clear line of descent can quickly be perceived. It is difficult to give general advice on how to display these trees as the number of children varies so much from one family to another and from generation to generation. Other people's methods may not be suited to your requirements because no two families are alike. It helps to keep people of the same generation at the same level, with husband and wife side by side, and to use the standard genealogical abbreviations:

b.	born	dau.	daughter
bapt.	baptized	s.	son
d.	died	div.	divorced
d.unm.	died unmarried	unm.	unmarried
d.s.p.*	died without children	=	married
		1	left descendants

* From the Latin *decessit sine prole*.

There is no standard or best way of arranging one's material. One learns from experience and adapts as one goes along. The trees need to be updated regularly, so it does not matter too much if early attempts subsequently look amateurish.

It is now time to make one's first visit to a record office. Its whereabouts can be discovered from a telephone directory or from a local library. In most cases admission is free and professional archivists will offer advice. They are more inclined to help those who have already made some progress and have at least some idea of what they are looking for than to assist those who think that others are going to do all the work for them. Most people will start with parish registers, census returns, and the records of civil registration, so it is with these that this guide will begin.

Civil Registration

The national system of registration of births, marriages, and deaths began on 1 July 1837, the year Queen Victoria came to the throne. The indexes of all these registered events are currently available for consultation at the General Register Office, St Catherine's House, 10 Kingsway, London WC2B 6JP, which is open Mondays to Fridays, from 8.30 a.m. to 4.30 p.m. Entry is free and no ticket or prior appointment is required.

The indexes are arranged on shelves, with separate sections for births, marriages, and deaths. Their bulk (especially the earliest ones, which have handwritten entries) makes them heavy and cumbersome to use, particularly as there is rarely sufficient space to open them on the crowded tables, but the effort is often hugely rewarded. The records of civil registration must be counted as the most informative of all the family historian's sources, an indispensable record of events over the last 150 years or so.

Each section of the indexes is arranged chronologically up to the present day. The years are divided into quarters, labelled March, June, September, and December, and the surnames in each quarter are grouped alphabetically. The system is easy to understand and to use. If, to take a fictitious example, a search is being made for the birth of Albert Edward Castle, thought to have been born about February 1878, the first index that should be consulted is the one labelled March 1878. If the relevant entry cannot be found, the next step should be to look at the index marked June 1878; births, in particular, may not have been registered straight away. Often, the searcher will have only a rough idea of the date of birth, based perhaps on an age recorded on a gravestone or a death certificate, in which case a number of indexes around the approximate date will have to be consulted.

In each quarterly index the surnames are listed in alphabetical order, then under each surname the forenames are arranged alphabetically. (From September 1911 onwards the mother's maiden name is also noted.) The next column gives the name of the Superintendent Registrar's District where the birth was registered. These district names may cause some difficulty, for registration districts are much larger than parishes or townships; even people with local knowledge may be unaware of their precise boundaries. Location books are available at the front desk at St Catherine's House, but it is advisable for the family historian to be acquainted with the names of the districts he is likely to be interested in before starting a search of the indexes. Ray Wiggins's booklet *St Catherine's House Districts* (available from the Society of Genealogists, 14 Charterhouse Buildings, London, EC1M 7BA) provides an alphabetical list of the 650 or so original districts, with details of their subdistricts and the adjacent districts, and the Institute of Heraldic and Genealogical Studies, Northgate, Canterbury, has published two small-scale maps that show the approximate positions (but not the precise boundaries) of the registration districts as they were between 1837 and 1851 and between 1852 and 1946.

It is often difficult to be certain that the correct entry has been identified, especially in the early years before the fashion of having a second forename had become widespread. Determining which Mary Turner or William Wright is the ancestor that is being sought will always be problematic. The field of enquiry is narrowed if it is known which registration districts should produce the most likely candidates, but even then one cannot be sure of the identification without confirmatory evidence, perhaps from a census return or a family memory. Most family historians have had the frustrating experience of paying for a certificate which is not the right one.

Once the person who is being sought has been identified (however tentatively), all the details recorded in the index, i.e. surname, forename, registrar's district, volume, and page number, together with the year and quarter recorded on the spine of the index, should be noted for future reference and for filling in an application form for a certificate. The information that has been acquired so far has not cost the searcher anything. A great deal of information can be obtained free; one might be content, for instance, with knowing that the birth of a relative was registered in June 1863, without taking the matter further. With a direct ancestor, however, it is usually desirable to purchase a certificate. Application forms are readily available and, once completed, should be taken to the counter, together with the fee. The certificate may be collected after four working days; otherwise it will be posted in the envelope that you have been given to address, in about 10 days' time. The cost of a postal request for a certificate is far higher than that of a personal application, even if full details are given on an official application form.

The copy of the certificate that is provided upon payment of the fee is usually freshly made, and as with all copying runs the risk of transcription error. If the original certificate is difficult to read, a photocopy may be issued. Birth certificates provide a great deal of genealogical information. They start by giving the birth date (day, month, and year) and the place of birth (a street name in a town, the name of a village, hamlet, or isolated farmstead in the countryside). This is followed by the name and sex of the individual, the father's forename and surname (or a blank space for an illegitimate child), and the mother's forename, surname, and maiden name. Next comes the occupation of the father, then the name of the informant (who was very often the mother) and her place of residence. During the early decades of civil registration, when illiteracy rates were high, the informant's signature was often in the form of a mark. In any case, the signature is not an original one, but a copy made by the registrar.

The information contained in a birth certificate enables the researcher to go back one stage further. An obvious step is to locate the marriage of the parents by working backwards through the indexes, though this will be a laborious job if the birth certificate relates to the twelfth and final child born to the marriage! Armed with the mother's maiden name, which was recorded on the birth certificate, it is sensible to search the marriage indexes for the rarer of the two surnames and to double-check the finding under the names of both husband and wife.

The indexes of marriages provide a separate record of the surnames and forenames of the bride and bridegroom, the registration district where the ceremony was performed, and the volume and page numbers that need to be copied on to an application form for a certificate. From March 1912 onwards the spouse's surname is recorded alongside that of the bride or groom. The procedure for obtaining a certificate is the same as for births. The marriage certificate gives the name and district of the church, chapel, or register office where the ceremony was performed, and the day, month, and year of the ceremony. At first, relatively few weddings took place in register offices, but the proportion grew steadily and now forms a large majority. The certificates go on to record the full names of both partners, their ages, and their 'condition', as bachelor, spinster, widower, or widow. Before 1870 many marriage certificates do not give ages, but simply note that a person was 'of full age'. This does not imply an age of at least 21, as is sometimes suggested, for many examples can be found where the registrar has taken it to mean the age of consent, which until 1929 might have been even lower than 16. The next columns record the 'rank or profession' of each partner, their residences at the time of marriage, and the full names and ranks or professions of their fathers. Even if a father was dead, he might still be recorded by his occupation or rank, rather than be described as 'deceased'. Finally, genealogical clues might be obtained from the names of the witnesses, whose signatures follow those of the bride and groom. Here again, the signatures are copies made by the registrar.

The indexes of deaths are arranged in a similar manner to those of births and marriages. From June 1866 they provide an extra piece of genealogical information, namely the age at death. Of course, this has to be treated cautiously, especially with old people, but it may direct an enquiry to a baptismal register long before the beginnings of civil registration. The certificates start by noting the date and place of death. They then record the forename(s) and surname of the deceased and his or her sex, age, and occupation. The cause of death is given in the next column, followed by the signature, description, and residence of the informant, who was normally the next of kin or another close relative.

St Catherine's House also has a section where indexes are shelved under the heading of 'miscellaneous returns'. These indexes record births, marriages, and deaths which occurred overseas. They include records of the armed forces and registers kept by clergymen abroad. They do not, however, form a complete record of Britons who lived overseas. Valuable advice on the whereabouts of such records can be found in Jane Cox and Timothy Padfield's book *Tracing Your Ancestors in the Public Record Office* (chapter 4).

Local Register Offices can sometimes be used to bypass St Catherine's House, but they do not have the staff or the facilities to deal with many enquiries and indexes are not available for public consultation. A visit to a local register office may reap dividends if fairly precise information about place and date is already known, but sooner or later the search for ancestors is likely to take the family historian beyond the boundaries of a local registration district. A blanket search of all the indexes of civil registration produces a mine of genealogical information. The Society of Genealogists, some public libraries, and Mormon research institutions have microfilms of the St Catherine's House indexes, but these are tedious to use and in order to obtain a certificate the researcher still has to visit London or make an expensive application by post.

In Scotland, civil registration started on 1 January 1855. All the records are kept at the General Register Office, New Register House, Edinburgh EH1 3YT, off Princes Street. Scottish certificates are much fuller than the English and Welsh ones, for they give the date of the marriage on a birth certificate, the names of both parents of each couple on marriage certificates, and the names of both parents of the deceased on death certificates. In Ireland, general registration started on 1 January 1864, though the records of Protestant (and some Catholic) marriages go back to 1845. There is, however, no consolidated index; entries from each county are filed together, but it is difficult to trace a family line, especially as the range of surnames is limited. The registration records up to 1922 are held at the Office of the Registrar General, Joyce House, 8–11 Lombard Street, Dublin 2. The records for Eire since 1922 are held in the same place, but those for Northern Ireland are kept at the General Register Office, Oxford House, 49–55 Chichester Street, Belfast BT1 4HL.

From time to time, a search through the indexes will fail to find a name that ought to be there. The most likely explanation for the failure is that the information upon which one is basing the search is not correct in all its details. For example, family memory may insist that an ancestor came from a certain place, whereas the truth of the matter is that he or she lived at that place as a child but was born somewhere entirely different. Another common mistake is to rely on the age recorded on a gravestone of an elderly person. Confusion may also arise if a birth occurred at a hospital, for then the event would have been recorded under the registration district in which the hospital was situated, not in the district where the family lived.

Even if one's prior information about date and place is correct, the entry may remain elusive because of clerical error. The records of civil registration are as prone to mistakes as are any other written sources. The returns of the local registrars were copied into the indexes by another official, who may have misread the original or have made a slip of the pen. In the early decades of registration, when many informants were illiterate, there was no check on what the registrar had written on the certificate. If the informant was not personally known to the registrar, then confusion over the pronunciation and spelling of the name might easily arise. A searcher must therefore try every variant spelling that springs to mind, adding or subtracting the letter H from the beginning of a name, substituting B for P, M for N, etc., varying the first vowel, and so on.

In some parts of England, notably Surrey, Sussex, Middlesex, Essex, and Shropshire, and also in Wales, about 15 per cent of births were not registered between 1837 and 1860. Parents were not penalized for failing to register births until 1875, and many apparently believed that civil registration was unnecessary if the child had been baptized. We also have to face the fact that some people deliberately avoided their legal responsibilities or gave false information. No system of registration has ever been perfect. Nevertheless, the records of civil registration are the family historian's most productive source. The problems are minor compared with the rewards.

Census Returns

The first census for England and Wales, the Isle of Man, and the Channel Islands was taken in 1801, after half a century or so of debate over whether such a measure would infringe the individual liberties of the king's subjects. Since then, a census has been taken every 10 years, with the exception of the war year of 1941. The first four censuses are of little value to the family historian. In 1840, however, responsibility for collecting the data was transferred to the General Register Office; from then onwards the census returns become a prime source of genealogical information. Separate censuses for Ireland and enumerations in the colonies were taken at the same time as those in England and Wales, but Scotland's different legal, constitutional, and administrative system produced a slightly different form of census-taking. In 1861 a separate Registrar-General for Scotland assumed responsibility for the Scottish census; the enumerators' returns are housed in the same place as the records of civil registration. The early census returns for Ireland were lost when the Public Record Office in Dublin was destroyed by fire in 1922.

The enumerators' districts that were drawn up for the 1841 census were retained, as far as possible, up to 1891, in order that comparisons could be made with previous data. They were supposed to be of a standard size and to consist of units, or parts of units, such as parishes and townships, that had a local meaning. The rapid growth of the population in many parts of Britain meant, however, that some districts had eventually to be altered. Alterations are recorded in the printed summaries of the returns, which are available in good reference libraries and in the volumes of the various Victoria County Histories, which give population statistics derived from the nineteenth-century returns.

The 1841 census was a trial run for the Registrar-General's office. Some significant improvements were made in 1851, in the light of this experience. In 1841 the enumerators were asked to record names according to household or to institution (workhouse, prison, etc.), but the relationship of each member to the head of the household was not noted. Precise ages were recorded for children under 15, but anyone older had his or her age rounded down to the nearest five. The family historian needs to be fully aware that, for example, someone recorded as age 30 in the 1841 census return could have been any age between 30 and 34. The column headed 'profession, trade, employment or of independent means' has fewer pitfalls, except that many Victorian people had more than one occupation; numerous craftsmen, for example, still followed an old way of life by combining their craft with a smallholding. The final column is of little practical use to the family historian; the census merely asked whether or not a person was born in the same county as he or she resided, or whether the birthplace was in Scotland, Ireland, or 'foreign parts'. None of the questions was designed with the needs of future family historians in mind; nevertheless, the improvements made from 1851 onwards may be noted with gratitude.

The 1841 census was taken in June but, as some itinerant workers who were sleeping rough were not recorded, it was decided that any future census should be taken in March or April. Moreover, nightworkers who were absent from home on census night but who returned the following morning were to be enumerated with the other members of their household. The household was retained as the basic institution, and from 1851 onwards the relationship of each member to the head was noted. Another improvement was the decision to record exact ages instead of rounding them down to the nearest five. The most important change of all for the genealogist was the decision that from 1851 onwards the exact place of birth should be given. This information frequently points the researcher in the right direction when an attempt is made to go back beyond the period of civil registration to parish and chapel registers.

Because of the secrecy imposed by the 100-years rule, census records are available for consultation only up to 1891. Although they cover only half a century or so—not even the full length of the reign of Victoria—they are none the less a prime source for the family historian, covering much the same period as the early decades of civil registration. They provide snapshots of all the households of Britain at 10-yearly intervals and offer many a clue for further research.

At the time of writing, the enumerators' returns for 1841–91 may be consulted on microfilm at the old Public Record Office in Chancery Lane, London. The census rooms are open Mondays to Fridays, from 9.30 a.m. to 5.00 p.m. (last orders 4.30 p.m.), except on public holidays and during the annual period of stock-taking in early October. Entry is free, but it is necessary to obtain a reader's ticket at the reception desk (for which proof of identity is needed) and to sign the attendance register. At certain times of year, demand is high and queues may form. Leaflet no. 9, 'How to use the Census Rooms', explains the complicated arrangements for consulting the microfilms. The researcher must allow a lot of time on his or her first visit for the necessary task of learning how to use the indexes in the reference room. The indexes (which are arranged by census year in a distinctive colour) are of places, not of surnames. They provide a reference number for an enumerator's district, which enables the researcher to obtain the relevant microfilm, in the hope that his or her ancestor was residing in that particular district on census night. The search may well be a long one.

In recent years, it has become normal practice for county record offices and the reference libraries of large towns and cities to obtain microfilm copies of the enumerators' returns of all the available censuses of the district that they serve. In some cases, local family history societies have made indexes of at least one of these returns. A major project, organized by the Mormon Church with the co-operation of family history societies and individual volunteers throughout the land, has indexed the whole of the 1881 census.

It does not take long to look at a return for a rural parish, but tracing an ancestor who was living in London or one of the larger provincial cities can be a very time-consuming task. Towns and cities had to be divided into numerous districts, the boundaries of which sometimes ran down the middle of a street. In many cases, the route taken by an enumerator when he collected the returns can be followed street by street. Even in the towns, however, houses were rarely numbered before the 1850s and often a formal system of numbering was not introduced until much later. The rapid expansion of Victorian towns and the subdivision of properties made the address system chaotic. In heavily built-up areas it is often difficult to decide what actually constituted a 'house', as distinct from a 'room', and to compare the information obtained from one census with that of another.

These problems are minor ones compared with those posed by the task of deciding whether or not ages are recorded accurately. Even after the practice of rounding ages down to the nearest five had been abandoned, it is best to treat the recorded ages with suspicion. In many cases people do not appear to have aged 10 years by the time of the next census, and these discrepancies are sometimes too great to be explained by the different month in which the census was taken. Most of the discrepancies are of a year or two, but some 4 or 5 per cent are for longer periods. Some people, of course, had only a rough idea of their age, others may have thought of their age as being the one that would be reached next birthday, but some deliberately misled the enumerator. The recorded age does not always lead to a precise year in a baptism register; the searcher who is looking for the baptism of, for example, someone aged 46 in 1851 should therefore consult the baptism registers for the years 1803–7.

The information about the place of birth should be treated with similar caution. Sometimes the nearest town, rather than the actual village or hamlet, is given, especially if a family had moved far from the birthplace by the time of the census return. People may have said that they came from a certain place because that is where they spent most of their childhood or youth, yet they may have been born elsewhere. Generally speaking, the information is more likely to be accurate the younger the person to whom it relates. It is a common experience to find that an ancestor's place of birth was recorded differently in two succeeding census returns. Professor Michael Anderson found that in mid-nineteenth-century Preston, 14 per cent of a sample of 475 persons whom he traced in successive censuses had a discrepancy in their birthplace; some of these discrepancies were unimportant, but some involved considerable distances. Sometimes, parents may have forgotten which child was born where, sometimes they may have deliberately falsified their entry. On other occasions, an enumerator may have recorded the parish where the birth occurred rather than the smaller unit within the parish that was noted earlier. Nevertheless, these problems should not be overstated. In general, the census returns are an invaluable guide to birthplaces, and although they do not set out to record movement between census nights, the birthplaces of successive children often indicate the approximate dates when a family moved home and the routes by which they came to settle in a particular place.

The occupations that are recorded seem, on the whole, to be accurate and to conform with descriptions derived from other sources such as trade and commercial directories. They rarely take account of dual occupations or casual employment, however. In the Victorian period many people worked at different jobs at different times of the year. A man who appears in the returns under the description 'labourer' may have performed a variety of tasks, some of them skilled. The contribution of women and children to the household economy is also understated; many of the 'scholars' may have been casually employed.

The information derived from the census returns can often be linked with that obtained from other sources. It may help, for example, in the search for a death certificate, for if a person appeared in the 1861 census but not in the one taken 10 years later, the civil registration indexes of deaths should be consulted from June 1861 onwards. St Catherine's House is within easy walking-distance of the old Public Record Office in Chancery Lane, where the census returns are currently held on microfilm, so such clues can be followed up immediately. Likewise, the age of the eldest child in an enumerator's return will suggest a starting-date for a search of the marriage indexes, though of course older children may have died or have left home. The ages and birthplaces recorded in the census returns are valuable pointers in the right direction for further genealogical evidence, provided they are treated cautiously and not regarded as concrete evidence that should never be challenged.

Trade and Commercial Directories

A good reference library will normally have a collection of trade and commercial directories stretching back well into the nineteenth century and sometimes into the eighteenth. In London, the earliest was Samuel Lee's list of the City merchants in 1677, but this example was not followed for another half-century. Brown and Kent's London directory of 1734 was revised each year by Kent up to 1771, and then by others until 1826. In the provinces, the people who ran the registry offices of the growing industrial towns took the lead. James Sketchley published an alphabetical list of the names and addresses of the merchants and tradesmen of Birmingham in 1763, and Elizabeth Raffald published similar information for Manchester in 1772. Many of the early compilers of directories came from a printing and publishing background, but firms were often small and ephemeral. The information in the early directories is of limited value to the family historian, but by Victoria's reign much fuller directories were published on a regular basis. These must certainly be consulted.

The two essential works of reference are J. E. Norton's *Guide to the National and Provincial Directories of England and Wales, Excluding London, Published before 1856* and G. Shaw and A. Tipper, *British Directories: A Bibliography and Guide to Directories Published in England and Wales (1850–1950) and Scotland (1773–1950)*. These list the holdings of each major library and indicate where directories may be found.

In the late eighteenth century it was thought worth while to publish directories that covered wide geographical areas. William Bailey's *Northern Directory* appeared in 1781 and continued to be published until 1787. *The*

Universal British Directory, compiled largely by John Wilkes, was issued in five main volumes and 69 parts between 1790 and 1799. These soon gave way to the more detailed (and cheaper) directories that were produced by local publishers or printed as part of a national series such as that of James Pigot, whose first provincial directory was published in 1814, and who continued to publish until 1853, when the firm was taken over by Kelly's. Francis Kelly established his business in London and began to produce provincial directories in 1845. By the following decade, he had become the major publisher of directories over the south of England. Kelly's remained the best-known name in the business up to the middle years of the twentieth century.

Many of the medium-sized publishers were not active very long. Some catered for a particular market by printing specialized trade directories. The general trade directories conformed to a common style. The earliest arranged the names of local inhabitants in alphabetical order and gave their addresses. The later ones provided separate street sections with the names and occupations of the residents and classified entries of the various trades. Such directories provide an enormous amount of information, but even the best were far from comprehensive. The biggest firms employed full-time agents who visited houses to obtain information. Suspicion of the motives of the agents, simple annoyance at being pestered once a year for personal details, and absence from home account for the number of unrecorded householders in the street sections.

Directories did not claim to provide complete coverage like a census. Gore's Liverpool directory of 1851, for example, listed only 65 per cent of the householders that were recorded in the census of that year in those parts of the city which were dominated by court dwellings and multi-occupied houses. Even in smaller places, directories concentrated on the craftsmen and tradesmen and the professional inhabitants and neglected the labourers and servants. A study of Ashby de la Zouch, as revealed by White's directory of 1862 and the 1861 census returns, showed that tradesmen accounted for 33 per cent of the names listed in the directory but only 18 per cent of the householders in the census; no labourers or domestic servants were listed.

The addresses recorded in directories can often be used to quicken a search of a contemporary census return. With this in mind, it is useful to remember that the information collected for a directory was slightly out of date by the time it appeared in print. The maps and town plans that are contained in the best directories may also be used profitably alongside a census return. Of special value to the historian are the introductory sections on the history and topography of each settlement, for they provide details of land ownership and tenures and of townships, parishes, and manors at a time of considerable change. Some of the statements about the history of the place should be treated warily, but directories are a rich and accessible source which the family historian will often find rewarding.

Parish Registers

The most important source of genealogical information prior to the beginning of civil registration in 1837 and the census returns of 1841–91 is undoubtedly the parish register. Nor does this source cease to be useful during the reign of Victoria, particularly if a family remained in the same district for a long period of time; in such cases, it is possible to bypass the records of civil registration altogether, and often cheaper to do so. From 1 January 1813 the registers of the Church of England follow a standard format and are easy to use. In earlier times, they are far from straightforward. Considerable background knowledge is needed to use them effectively.

The system of parish registration of baptisms, marriages, and burials began in 1538, but only a minority of parishes have registers that go back that far. It seems that the normal practice at first was to record events on loose sheets, many of which were lost or destroyed in the course of time. In 1597 it was ordered that henceforth a special register should be kept and that previous records, where they survived, should be entered into this book. The minister and churchwardens were charged with signing each page as a true transcript. In many cases, ministers interpreted the instruction to mean that records should be copied only as far back as the beginning of the reign of Queen Elizabeth. It is common to find, therefore, that surviving registers begin in 1558 rather than 20 years earlier. The same Act, in 1597, ordered that in future a copy of the events registered during the past year should be sent to the bishop's office. These bishop's transcripts, as they are called, are kept at the archive offices which house the records of the ancient dioceses, e.g. Lichfield, Lincoln, or York, as distinct from the new dioceses which were created in the late nineteenth or twentieth centuries. They are invaluable where an original register has been lost or is inaccessible or difficult to read. On the whole, however, the original registers have been preserved better than the bishop's transcripts, especially in the earlier period of registration.

England and Wales had some 11,000 ancient parishes. These varied considerably in size, ranging from a few hundred acres to tens of thousands of acres. The largest ones were subdivided into chapelries, or chapels-of-ease, many of which acquired rights to conduct their own baptism, marriage, and burial services. Sometimes, these chapelries kept separate registers, but in other cases their records were copied each year into the parish register, usually in a separate section. This can cause a great deal of confusion when a search is made in a register. The family historian needs to become familiar with the administrative arrangements in the district that he is researching. Maps showing the ancient parish system are commonly available at record offices, and a series covering each county and giving the starting-date of every surviving register has been published by the Institute of Heraldic and Genealogical Studies, Canterbury.

Some important places today were small or non-existent at the time when parishes were created and may have formed part of a parish named after a place that is now insignificant. Indeed, new and growing towns may have spread over the borders of more than one parish. During the nineteenth century, many new parishes were created in the expanding towns and cities. The researcher who is working backwards in time and has become familiar with the structure of local parishes in the Victorian age therefore needs to adapt his searches to a different administrative framework in earlier periods. The standard reference work is F. A. Youngs, Jr., *Guide to the Local Administrative Units of England*. London and the major provincial cities such as Norwich and York had long been divided into numerous parishes, some of which disappeared when the population moved out of the ancient central areas and churches were closed. Tracing an ancestor in the capital city or in a great provincial centre can be a time-consuming business involving the search of numerous registers.

Locating the present whereabouts of a parish register is not a straightforward task, though a local record office will usually be able to advise. Some parishes deposited their registers for safe-keeping with record offices long before the measure of 1979 which insisted that this should be done unless a parish could prove that it had adequate facilities for storing and preserving such records. Only a minority of registers are still kept in parish churches; most are now deposited with the county or city record offices that are used by the modern dioceses. Before searching for an original register, however, it is worth consulting all the indexes at a reference library to see what is in print. Many parish registers have been published, at least in part, either privately or by a parish register society. Some of these societies are now more than a hundred years old and have an extensive series in print.

It is common policy in record offices for registers to be made available for study only on microfilm. A prior appointment has usually to be made in order to reserve a microfilm reader. The bishop's transcripts at the ancient diocesan record offices have also been placed on microfilm in many cases. This policy has become necessary because of the deteriorating condition of the documents through their unprecedentedly heavy use. One benefit arising from this policy has been that local record offices or libraries have sometimes obtained microfilm copies of bishop's transcripts that are held at other places, often far away.

The Church of Jesus Christ of Latter-Day Saints, commonly known as the Mormon Church, requires its members to trace their ancestors in order to baptize them by proxy. The Mormon Church has made a huge investment in transcribing records and in reproducing them on microfilm or microfiche. These records have been computerized as the International Genealogical Index, which is updated regularly and is available on microfilm. (The next updating will also be on disc.) The IGI, as it is universally known amongst genealogists, can be consulted by anyone, regardless of whether or not he or she is a member of the Mormon Church. The Mormons have constructed special buildings in various parts of Britain which are open to the public for the purpose of genealogical research. The IGI and other records on microfilm may be consulted free of charge, or for a voluntary donation. Otherwise, microfilm copies of the IGI are available at public reference libraries and record offices and at the meeting-places of many of the various family history societies. The index is far from complete, partly because such an extensive programme takes time, but also because some bishops or parish priests have theological objections to baptism by proxy of people whose parents chose to baptize them according to the rites of the Anglican Church. It is important to remember that the information in the IGI must always be checked, for much of it has been gathered by untrained amateurs who may have made mistakes. Nevertheless, the IGI has been a fruitful source for many a family historian; it can save a lot of time and point one in the right direction.

The entries in the early parish registers are often disappointingly sparse. A record of baptism may simply give the date of the event, the name of the child, and the name of the father. The style of entries varies from register to register and over time in the same place. Nor should we expect improvements as time goes on; even if the form of entry improves for a short period, it usually lapses back into the meagre standards of an earlier age. Some registers were very well kept from the sixteenth century onwards; others have numerous gaps. If entries were made at the end of a week or a month, then names may have been misremembered or a space left blank. William Holland, the parson of Over Stowey, Somerset, in the early nineteenth century, appears to have written the entries in his register on Fridays or Sundays, and to have dated them according to the date of the writing, not that of the actual events. If a clerk was responsible for keeping the register, he may not have written it up until the end of the year. The register of St Peter's, Dorchester, for 1645 notes that: 'In twelve months there died 52 persons whose names are not inserted, the old clerk being dead who had the notes.'

A great deal of confusion is caused by the old custom of starting the official year not on 1 January but on 25 March (Lady Day). The entries for each year do not stop on 31 December but continue to the following Lady Day. All the dates between 1 January and 25 March therefore need to have another year added to them to convert them to modern reckoning. For example, a baptism recorded as taking place on 24 January 1694 needs to be noted as 24 January 1694/5, a method of notation that was occasionally used at the time. Such dates must be recorded carefully, for it may be assumed falsely that a baptism recorded on 21 February 1708 occurred before the marriage of the parents on 11 April 1708, whereas in fact the baptism was 10 months later. This method of recording was abandoned on 1 January 1752, and in the same year Britain fell into line with the rest of Europe by adopting the Gregorian calendar in place of the Julian. The old calendar, which did not have a leap year, was 11 days out by this time, so 14 September was decreed to follow 3 September. Minor genealogical problems are caused by the adjustment of birthdays to the new calendar, but they need not concern us seriously. It took a while for people to adjust their thinking to the new style. For years afterwards some fairs were held on the traditional days; in 1760, for example, a fair at Chapel-en-le-Frith was advertised for the Thursday before Old Candlemas and one at Belper for Old May Day. If the government's financial year still ends on 6 April, 11 days after Lady Day, it is not surprising that even after 1752 some parish registers continued to be written in the old manner until a new man took over or the clerk got in a hopeless muddle.

Such problems are minor compared with the difficulty of reading sixteenth- and seventeenth-century registers. There is no easy way round this; anyone seriously interested in searching the records of this period must acquire some competence in palaeography. Knowing the format of a document is half the battle. The early registers are simple in form and give only the barest of details. Although Latin was commonly used, this does not present much difficulty. Robertus and Henricus are readily identifiable as Robert and Henry, though Guillelmus may not be an obvious William. Fortunately, the surnames are given in their English form. The searcher quickly learns the few common phrases, e.g. *baptizatus erat*, *nupti erat*, *sepultus erat*, that were used to record baptisms, marriages, and burials. (Many English words are based on Latin originals, and so the meaning of *nupti* and *sepultus* may be guessed from 'nuptials' and 'sepulchre'.) A variety of Latin terms, e.g. *filius populi*, or the English 'base', 'bastard', etc., were used to record illegitimacies. Abbreviations may cause other difficulties and spellings reflect the way that the writer spoke. These difficulties must be faced, but they are not insurmountable.

Anyone addressed in the register as Mr or Mrs was of gentry rank; sometimes their entries are written in larger and bolder letters. Before the eighteenth century a clergyman was not normally styled Reverend, but noted as clerk, meaning cleric. Most entries record a person simply by his or her Christian name and surname. Sometimes, however, a great deal of extra information is provided, either on the whim of the person doing the recording or in response to some directive from the government or a bishop. Some parish registers are a valuable source of information about occupations, noting these when a man was married or buried or when he baptized a child. If such information is provided consistently over a period of years, it can be used to reconstruct the occupational structure of the entire parish in a way that is normally possible only with nineteenth-century census returns.

The baptism registers are not a record of actual births, but of the church ceremonies that followed. It has been commonly stated that baptism took place three days after a birth. William Shakespeare's baptism on 26 April 1564 has been widely accepted to mean that he was born (appropriately for the national bard) on 23 April, St George's Day, but in fact the interval between birth and baptism varied from time to time and from place to place. William Camden, Shakespeare's contemporary, wrote in *Remaines Concerning Britain* that 'our Ancestors in this Realm until later time baptized and gave names the very birth day or next day after'. In later times, it is safe to assume that the majority of baptisms took place within two or three weeks of the birth, though many examples can be quoted of even longer delays. The custom of private baptism at home was fashionable in the late seventeenth and eighteenth centuries, particularly in London. These private events were normally entered as such in the parish register. It cannot be assumed that the lack of an entry means that a child was not baptized. Carelessness on the part of whoever was responsible for the register is a more likely explanation. Such carelessness may mean that we can now proceed no further with a particular line.

Most marriages were performed in a parish church after the calling of banns, but even people of modest incomes sometimes preferred to marry by licence. The normal practice was for the bridegroom to apply to the chancellor or surrogate of the diocese in which he or his prospective wife lived and in which the marriage was to be celebrated and to make a formal statement, or 'allegation', upon oath, that there was no lawful impediment to the marriage. Licences were normally issued through diocesan consistory courts and were recorded in the bishop's register, though they can also be found in the records of certain peculiar jurisdictions. When the bride and groom lived in different dioceses, however, they had to apply to the Vicar-General of the Archbishop of the province, either Canterbury or York. If a parish register has subsequently been destroyed, the record of such a licence may be the only surviving evidence that a wedding took place. The marriage of William Shakespeare and Ann Hathaway, to quote a famous example, is proved by the licences issued by the consistory court of the Bishop of Worcester, but cannot be found in the parish registers of Stratford and the surrounding countryside. In Shakespeare's case, his bride was pregnant and the close season of Advent prevented the calling of banns on three successive Sundays.

Burial registers provide a fuller record of events than do those which record baptisms and marriages, but even they are incomplete. A family historian may occasionally find a tombstone in the churchyard but no equivalent entry in the burial register. Such omissions can have resulted only from the carelessness or oversight of the keeper of the register. Excommunicates and suicides were forbidden burial with Christian rites, though some were buried surreptitiously in a corner of the churchyard. The use of the word 'interred' in a burial register may suggest such an event, but usually indicates that the deceased was a Roman Catholic who did not wish to be buried according to the Anglican form of service. Most entries are straightforward, though modern readers may find curious the provision of the Acts of 1666 and 1678 that shrouds should be woollen and that the register should confirm that a person was buried 'in wool'.

Important changes in registration procedure took place during the Commonwealth. The Act which came into force on 29 September 1653 transferred responsibility to an elected officer, known as the Parish Register (*sic*). In practice, either the minister or the parish clerk was often elected as register, and some parishes simply ignored the legislation. The overall quality of parish registers during the Interregnum is poor, but in some parishes a new volume was purchased and the entries became fuller. The Act stipulated that births rather than baptisms should be recorded, but local practice varied substantially; some registers noted both events. The greatest change involved the marriage ceremony, which until 1657–8 could be solemnized by a JP after the reading of banns on three successive weeks in church, chapel, or market-place. Upon the Restoration of King Charles II in 1660, the Act was repealed and registration procedure reverted to the previous local practice.

In the later seventeenth and eighteenth centuries various attempts to improve the quality of registration were made by the central government or by the bishops of certain dioceses. In some parishes fuller information was provided after 1694, following the decision to tax entries, but elsewhere the form of entries did not improve. In the diocese of York, for a few years after 1777, some registers give remarkably full details. Thus, an entry in the Kirkburton register for 11 October 1777 records the baptism of Robert Hey, son of Abraham Hey of Thorncliff, clothier (the son of George Hey), and his wife Sarah, the daughter of John Sikes of Lepton, by Esther, the daughter of Abraham Hey of Thorncliff. Unfortunately, ministers and clerks soon got tired of providing such detailed genealogical information.

Lord Hardwicke's Marriage Act of 1753 brought about a standard form of entry for marriages. In order to prevent the laxity of clandestine marriages, the Act stated that every marriage must be preceded by the issue of a licence or the calling of banns, that the ceremony must be performed in the parish where at least one of the parties resided, and that a record must be made in a proper book kept for that purpose. The entries henceforth had to be signed by the parties and by witnesses, in a bound volume of printed forms. The insistence on a licence or banns remained in force until 1836, when civil ceremonies conducted by a registrar were allowed.

Entries in the Church of England registers were finally standardized by an Act of 1812, which came into effect on 1 January 1813. From that time onwards, Anglican registers consist of bound volumes of printed forms; they are easy to use and much more informative than previous registers. A baptismal entry gives the name of the baptized child, the date of the baptism, the Christian names and surnames of the parents, their abode, and the occupation of the father. The burial register records the name of the deceased, his or her abode, the date of the burial, and his or her age. A marriage record notes the names of both partners, their parishes, the date of the wedding, and the names of the witnesses. If a family lived in a restricted area for a long period in the nineteenth century, and attended church rather than chapel, the family historian may well find all the genealogical details that he requires from a parish register without searching the records of civil registration. In the three centuries that preceded civil registration, parish registers are an essential source that cannot be bypassed.

Records of Protestant Nonconformity

On Sunday, 29 March 1851 a national census was taken of those who attended religious services that day. It revealed that in the country as a whole less than half the population went to any form of service and that in the great industrial cities the proportion fell to as low as 1 in 10. A further blow to the Established Church was the finding that about half of those who did meet for worship preferred a Nonconformist chapel. In some parts of Britain the proportion of Nonconformists to Anglicans was even higher, and nowhere in the country did it fall to below 1 in 3. The family historian clearly needs to be aware of the strength of the various Nonconformist sects in the nineteenth century and to consider whether a vital piece of information about an ancestor which does not appear in a parish register might be contained in the records of a chapel or meeting-house.

The term 'Nonconformist' was applied originally to those who refused to subscribe to the Act of Uniformity of 1662 and the other provisions of the 'Clarendon Code', after the Restoration of Charles II. The Old Dissenting sects of the later seventeenth century consisted of the Presbyterians, Independents (or Congregationalists), Baptists, and Quakers. Some of these terms were used loosely and, of course, congregations may have modified their beliefs over time. Thus, the Sheffield Dissenters were described either as Presbyterians or Independents in the late seventeenth century, but a split in 1715 led one group on to the road to Unitarianism, while the others remained fast in their beliefs but became known as Congregationalists.

Enquiries made by Bishop Compton in 1676 suggest that in Charles II's reign Protestant Dissenters formed only 4 per cent of the national population, though in some parishes the proportion was considerably higher. Even if this figure underestimates the true strength of Nonconformity, it shows that Dissenters were far fewer in number than in Victorian times. These early Dissenters often used the Church of England for their baptism, marriage, and burial services, so these events were recorded in the parish registers of the Anglican Church (with no mention of the fact that the participants were Dissenters). The separate registers that were kept by some seventeenth-century Nonconformist congregations were often a record of baptisms only. Unless an ancestor was a Quaker, the family historian is not often faced with the problem of finding alternative registration during the seventeenth century and much of the eighteenth.

The Old Dissenting sects continued to use the Established Church for services that involved registration long after Nonconformists had achieved freedom of worship in 1689. If a baptism of a child of a known Dissenting family cannot be found in an Anglican register, however, it is worth visiting Doctor Williams' Library, London, where a voluntary General Register of Births was opened for Dissenters on 1 January 1743. Births were registered from many parts of Britain, though clearly the register was most commonly used by Londoners. It was closed in 1837 upon the commencement of civil registration.

The Society of Friends were the first Dissenters to keep registers systematically. George Fox's earliest converts were particularly numerous in Westmorland, Lancashire, and Yorkshire, but the movement soon expanded rapidly in London and the south-west, in Bristol and Norwich, and then in Scotland and Ireland. It achieved considerable success in America, where in 1681 William Penn founded the state of Pennsylvania. In England, the Quakers became the most numerous of all the Nonconformist sects in the late seventeenth century, but after Toleration in 1689 their membership gradually dwindled.

From their earliest days the Friends adopted a structure of monthly and quarterly meetings. Records of births, marriages, and burials were sometimes kept by particular meetings, but more often this task was the responsibility of the monthly meetings which may have been held at some distance from the local meeting-house. Most registers were started before 1670, though some entries are retrospective. The Society of Friends rejected the names of the days and months because these were derived from heathen gods. Sunday was referred to as the First Day, January as the First Month, and so on. This practice does not present undue difficulty to the genealogist, except that up to the change of calendar in 1752 March was the First Month, April the Second Month, etc. The form of entry in Quaker registers was not standardized until 1776, from which time duplicate entries were sent to the quarterly meetings. Membership lists are uncommon before the late eighteenth century; indeed, many meetings did not keep them until 1836.

Even the Quakers were sometimes prepared to use the Church of England for some of their vital events. Few Quaker marriages, but some births and many more burials, are recorded in parish registers. The first Quakers were often buried in gardens or orchards rather than the parish churchyard, but by the end of the seventeenth century most meeting-houses had a burial ground. The earliest graves were unmarked. It is rare to find headstones before 1850, when they were permitted by the Yearly Meeting, provided there was 'such an entire uniformity . . . as may effectually guard against any distinctions being made in that place between the rich and the poor'.

The best Nonconformist registers after those of the Quakers are the ones kept by the Moravians. Their earliest register is that of the Fetter Lane congregation, London, which was begun in 1741, 13 years after three brethren had been sent to London and Oxford from Saxony by Count Zinzendorf. Moravian settlements at Fulneck, Yorkshire, Ockbrook, Derbyshire, etc. still survive, but the sect was always overshadowed by the Methodist denomination, with which it had many affinities.

Until 1742 John Wesley's preaching was largely confined to London and Bristol, but for the rest of his life he travelled incessantly over the whole of Britain. In 1744 circuits for Wesleyan preachers were established and the first national conference was held. The followers of George Whitefield had already broken away and had founded 31 societies by 1747. When Whitefield died in 1770 the leadership of his Calvinistic Methodists passed to the Countess of Huntingdon, but many of the societies drifted into Congregationalism. The break between the Wesleyan Methodists and the Church of England did not come until 1784. Further splits occurred when the Methodist New Connexion was founded in 1797, when the Primitive Methodists broke away in 1812, and when the Wesleyan Reform Union was established in 1849. At first, the rise of Methodism had little effect on parish registration, for like the older Dissenters most Methodists attended the local Anglican church for their baptism, marriage, and burial services. Very few Methodist registers date from before the 1790s and most begin in the second decade of the nineteenth century; even then, the majority are merely records of baptisms.

Lord Hardwicke's Marriage Act of 1753 brought to an end the practice of marrying simply by making a declaration before witnesses. This practice had allowed Nonconformists to celebrate marriages in their own chapels and meeting-houses. After 1753 all Nonconformists, except the

Quakers, were expected to marry in the Church of England. Although many Roman Catholics defied the Act, the Protestant Dissenters seem to have complied with its terms.

The Nonconformists had a long battle to get their baptism or birth registers recognized by the State. Before the reign of Victoria no one could obtain a government post without producing proof of baptism in the Established Church. The beginning of civil registration changed the situation. In 1836, following the General Registration Act, a commission was set up to enquire into the 'State, Custody and Authenticity of Non-parochial registers'. The Commissioners approached the various dissenting bodies, asking them to send in their registers to the Registrar-General where they would be examined and, if approved, authenticated. Their suggestion that the registers should be deposited with the Registrar-General and made legal evidence was embodied in the Non-Parochial Registers Act of 1840. Some 856 volumes of Nonconformist registers were surrendered to the state for authentication. A second deposit of 'non-parochial' registers was catalogued in 1859. In all, some 7,000 volumes and files are now stored in the Public Record Office, where they may be consulted free of charge, under the reference RG. 4 to RG. 8. No indexes are provided, so it is helpful to have some idea of the locality (and preferably the particular denomination) in which a birth, marriage, or death occurred. Most early registers were surrendered; many later ones have since been deposited in record offices; but others were lost when chapels closed.

Records of Roman Catholicism

Very few Catholic families can trace their descent in the male line from English Catholics who were living in the eighteenth century. Most are descended either from nineteenth-century immigrants from Ireland or continental Europe or from converts and those who married into Catholic families. During the later sixteenth, seventeenth, and eighteenth centuries English Catholics formed only a small, persecuted minority, though in certain rural areas, under the leadership of gentry families, they were much stronger than national figures imply.

Some of the earliest parish registers date from a time when England was still a Catholic country, but after the accession of Elizabeth in 1558 Roman Catholics were faced with the problem of complying with the law whilst at the same time worshipping as their consciences dictated. Most Catholics in the sixteenth, seventeenth, and eighteenth centuries opted for an Anglican burial service but private baptism and marriage services. The fear of persecution meant that registers were rarely kept before the middle of the eighteenth century. When a register was started, retrospective entries were sometimes made. More registers were kept after 1791, but many do not begin until the early nineteenth century. At first, priests seem to have regarded these registers as their personal responsibility and took the registers with them when they moved. The areas that they served were in any case often large and bore no relationship to the Anglican parishes.

'Popish Recusants' were frequently presented before the ecclesiastical and civil authorities. Their names therefore appear in the records of archdeacons' courts and quarter sessions. These records are far from being comprehensive, for many an incumbent was prepared to turn a blind eye to Catholic practices. Two sets of returns for the years 1705 and 1706 for Derbyshire illustrate the difficulties. The earlier set is kept in the House of Lords, for that is where concern about the strength of Catholicism was expressed, leading to the decision to hold a national enquiry. The second set is housed at the Lichfield Joint Record Office, which holds the records of the diocese of Coventry and Lichfield. The differences between the two accounts are considerable and in some parishes the incumbents refused or neglected to provide the information. As no guide-lines were issued, the returns took a variety of forms. Some incumbents listed whole families, some husbands and wives only, and others just the heads of households.

By 1811 the total of English Catholics was somewhere in the region of 250,000. Already the greater part consisted of Irish immigrants, together with French *émigrés* and refugees. Between 1791 and 1814 large numbers of Catholic chapels were opened, mainly in the north. The Catholic Emancipation Act of 1829 allowed Catholics to worship as they pleased and led to the building of more churches and some new cathedrals.

Catholic Irish people began to emigrate to England in significant numbers during the first half of the eighteenth century, when they settled in certain parts of London and Liverpool. By the beginning of the nineteenth century Liverpool was the most favoured destination. The Catholic population of the city numbered 12,000 by 1821, 60,000 by 1832, and 80,000 by 1840. Some Catholic immigrants came from other parts of Lancashire, but the great majority were Irish. From Liverpool they soon spread to the industrial towns of south Lancashire, across the Pennines to Leeds, and south to the Potteries, the Staffordshire coalfield, and Birmingham. Irish navvies who worked on the railways in the boom years of the 1830s and 1840s sometimes settled far from their original bases. Meanwhile, the Irish colonies in London were growing rapidly. The great famine of 1845 forced many more Catholic Irish to emigrate. It has been estimated that three-quarters of the Catholic population in England by the middle of the nineteenth century was of Irish origin.

Catholic authorities were reluctant to deposit their registers alongside those of the Protestant Nonconformists, upon the start of civil registration, on the grounds that they were required for religious purposes and that extracts had to be certified by a priest. The northern registers were deposited, however, and these can now be consulted in the Public Record Office. In recent years, many Catholic registers and other records have been deposited in local archive repositories, such as the Lancashire Record Office.

Records of Jewish Congregations

European Jews belong to one of two main groups. Those whose ancestors lived in Spain are called Sephardim, from a medieval Hebrew word meaning Spaniards. Those whose ancestors inhabited the Rhine valley during the Middle Ages and later moved across Germany and into Poland and Russia are called Ashkenazim, from a medieval Hebrew word meaning Germans. Both communities belong to the main stream of Rabbinic Judaism and the differences between them are of Hebrew pronunciation, liturgical tradition, custom, temperament, and some minor points of religious practice rather than of belief.

The first Jewish immigrants were brought from Rouen by King William I, shortly after the Norman Conquest. By 1290, when they were expelled from England by Edward I, their estimated numbers were not more than 3,000, nearly all of whom were based in London or a few of the great provincial cities such as Lincoln or York. A small colony of Sephardic Jews eventually resettled in the capital from 1541 onwards, but it was not until the middle of the seventeenth century that Jews were formally readmitted into the country. By 1734 the total number of Jews in England was estimated at 6,000.

Most of the sixteenth- and seventeenth-century Jewish immigrants were Sephardic Jews, who came principally from Portugal. Many of them were wealthy merchants. During the eighteenth century other Sephardic Jews, from Italy, Morocco, Turkey, etc., settled in London and joined the Portuguese synagogue. Some eventually moved on to India, the West Indies, and the American colonies. The majority of English Jews, however, are of Ashkenazic origin, their ancestors coming from Poland, Germany, or Central Europe. Their native language was Yiddish, an offshoot of German written in Hebrew characters. Many of these were poor men who earned a living by travelling around the countryside, hawking jewellery and haberdashery, hoping to save enough to open a shop in a provincial town. Others practised skilled crafts, such as engraving. Perhaps half of the 6,000 English Jews in 1734 were Ashkenazim. Immigration in the nineteenth century altered this proportion considerably. By 1882 the Sephardic Jews of London were estimated at about 3,500 and the Ashkenazic at about 15,000, half the latter being immigrants or descendants of immigrants who came after 1800. Thousands of Ashkenazic Jews entered England to escape persecution in Central and Eastern

Europe in 1848–50, 1863, and from the 1880s onwards, until an Act of 1905 restricted the scale of immigration. Many of these poor immigrants flocked to the East End of London or to some of the burgeoning industrial cities, notably Leeds.

In his chapter on 'The Jews' in *Sources for Roman Catholic and Jewish Genealogy and Family History*, edited by D. J. Steel, Edgar R. Samuel makes the point that one of the principal difficulties in tracing an Ashkenazic Jewish ancestry is the variable nature of the surnames, which developed both through Anglicization and translation. For example, a Bristol Jew, Eliezer, the son of Jacob, who built a synagogue there in 1786, was known to the townsmen as Lazarus Jacobs. His descendants all called themselves Lazarus. Similarly, the descendants of David might be called Davis, and those of Moses, Moss. The Hebrew Zevi (a stag) was Germanized into Hirsch or Hirschel, then Anglicized into Hart, only to emerge finally as Harris.

Synagogue records have often been deposited in local record offices. Most early synagogues kept an accurate record of marriages and burials, but were less careful with births. The records of Ashkenazic synagogues are particularly difficult to use because they are written in Hebrew or Yiddish in a cursive script and because they record Hebrew or synagogical names, which do not always correspond with the English names that were used every day; nor do they note surnames. Specialist guidance is clearly needed here. Of course, many Jews appear in the ordinary parish registers of the Church of England, just like Protestant Nonconformists or Roman Catholics.

Probate Records

The numerous wills that survive from the Middle Ages were made mostly by members of aristocratic and gentry families or by rich town merchants. In some dioceses the wills of large numbers of middle-income and even quite poor testators were being registered in the late Middle Ages, but in general the practice of making a will did not become common amongst farmers and craftsmen until the sixteenth century. At all times, the poorer sections of society remained largely unrepresented. Even among the social groups that were most likely to make a will, however, many did not bother. Studies of the number of wills made in a parish compared with the number of entries for adult males in the burial register always demonstrate that making a will was a minority concern, usually in the order of 1 in 3 or 1 in 4. Very few wives made wills (for, according to the law, a married woman could do nothing without the consent of her husband), but many widows and spinsters did.

Families had other methods of transferring property, for example, helping sons to obtain a suitable property at the time of marriage and

248

providing daughters with marriage portions. If the children were still minors a man might make provision for them in the event of his wife re-marrying, otherwise the property would pass to her new husband during her lifetime and the children might be disadvantaged. If the children had already left home and everyone in the family knew what was to happen to the remainder of the patrimony then a will was unnecessary.

Until 1858 the responsibility for proving a will lay with the Church. Probate records before this date are therefore held at the ancient diocesan record offices, with the exception of those proved between 1653 and 1660, when the Prerogative Court of Canterbury (the PCC) was given sole jurisdiction throughout England and Wales. The probate records for these seven years are now housed at the Public Record Office, as are all those proved through the PCC between 1383 and 1858. Indexes of all PCC wills before 1700 have been published by the British Record Society and indexes of later material are being prepared. Elsewhere, the provision of indexes varies considerably in quality from one record office to an-other and from period to period. Thus, the indexes of wills proved through the diocese of York from 1389 to 1688 have been printed in sev-eral volumes of the Yorkshire Archaeological Society Record Series, but after 1688 one has to consult the typed index at the Borthwick Institute of Historical Research, York. Some other record offices still rely on hand-written indexes compiled a long time ago.

The family historian has to familiarize himself with another set of administrative units before he can find the probate records for his parish. Archivists will advise and maps may be available at record offices. The standard guidebooks are A. J. Camp's *Wills and Their Whereabouts* and J. S. W. Gibson's, *Wills and Where to Find Them*. The structure of the pro-bate courts in the province of Canterbury was different in some respects from that of the province of York. In both provinces, however, the prin-ciple was that a higher court had to be used if a testator held property in more than one lower jurisdiction. Those with land or other goods in only one archdeaconry used the archdeacon's court, those with property in two archdeaconries went to the episcopal courts, those with possessions in two bishoprics had to go to the Archbishop's Prerogative Court, and finally those with property in the two provinces went to the senior court at Canterbury.

Many parishes (and sometimes scattered properties within a parish) belonged to peculiar jurisdictions, whose records are kept separately. These peculiars were often parishes whose tithes went to support a prebend at the cathedral and whose records were therefore proved by the Dean and Chapter. Other peculiars included parishes whose tithes had once belonged to the Knights Templar or the Knights Hospitaller and others which had been special liberties, e.g. a royal castle or a possession of an archbishop. Fortunately, nearly all these collections are housed alongside the main body of probate records in the archives of the ancient dioceses. Sometimes they may turn up elsewhere, e.g. in a solicitor's deposit at a local record office, when the rights of a peculiar had been purchased upon the dissolution of the original owning body.

Wills were originally proved by the Church. They usually began by committing the testator's soul to Almighty God and his or her body to burial in a church or churchyard. Only the richer members of a local society could expect to be buried within the church. Most wills have a long preamble which follows one of the standard forms taken from books of advice on how to draw up a will. Before the Reformation a typical Catholic formula might read: 'I bequeath my soul to Almighty God, our Lady Saint Mary and all the Holy Company of Heaven . . .'. Later preambles express a belief in salvation and redemption through Christ, e.g. 'I commend my soul unto Almighty God my Maker and Redeemer by whose precious blood shedding I trust to be saved.'

After making provision for the payment of all debts and the funeral expenses, the testator proceeded to dispose of his or her worldly goods. Last wills were normally made shortly before death (as is evident from shaky signatures) and so a clause was often inserted to say that all previous wills were thereby annulled. If a dying person was too ill to make a will, then a nuncupative will, i.e. an oral statement attested by sworn witnesses, was accepted by the church court. If a person died intestate, the court had the power to grant letters of administration of the estate to those whom it considered legitimate administrators.

The will of John Burton of Totley, Derbyshire, made in 1571/2, illustrates many of the typical forms of the wills of that period:

In the name of god amen. In the year of our lord god 1571 and the xxviith day of februarie I John Burtone of totley in the p[ar]yshe of Dronfield Sycke of body and houlle of mynd and good of Remembrance macke my Testament and last will In this maner fowlowynge fyrst I geve my soule unto god almyghty my maker and Redymer and my body to by buryed In the parishe chyrchyarde of Saynt John Baptys at Drounfeld Ite[m] I geve and by queath my farme unto Joanne my wife to have enjoy and Occupy at the pleasur of Mr John Barcar to brynge up my chyldren so lonnge as she keepth heere weadow and if it forton Joane my wife mary that then hear tearme of years to seace and then all the sayd tearm that I have to by to the bryngyne up of all my chyldren untyll my s[o]n andrew by at his age and able to occupy it him selfe and if she mary my son andrew to have all my tearme of years Item I geve and by queath unto my s[o]n andrew an Irne bund wayne and a plough youcke and all such thynges belonngynge unto husbandry also a great arcke a basket an ambry and a long boord also I geve and by queath unto my good measter Mr John Barcar xiiis iiiid desyryng hym to by good Measter unto my wife and Chyldren as I tryst he will also my mind and will is my wife to have the third part of al my goodes after the maner and custom and all the Residu of my goodes to by Equally divided Amonnge my Chyldren Also I macke Joane my wife my full exec[u]tor to Dyspose for the health of my soule as she thought best and p[ro]vide and sy that this my p[re]sent will by fully contented and fullfylled and also my will is that my uncle Thomas Burton Thomas Calton John owtrym and Robert Poynton by over syers of my Chyldren Thes by me Deats owynge unto my John Burton Willm Robynson xls Thomas Sayles xvs iiiid.

Great care has to be taken in interpreting words whose meaning seems obvious but which might have been used differently in the past. Cousin was used to denote a wide range of kinsmen, and even father, son, daughter, and brother may have been used for in-laws. Children who had already been provided for may not be mentioned in a will. Conversely, people who are mentioned may not have been alive by the time that a will was proved.

From the reign of Henry VIII onwards it was the practice of the church courts to insist that the executors appointed three or four local men to make 'a true and perfect inventory' of the personal estate of the deceased. This practice continued well into the eighteenth century, varying from one locality to another. Tens of thousands of inventories survive, covering most parts of the country. They are normally attached to the will or to the letters of administration where no will had been made. The appraisers, as the valuers were normally called, listed every piece of household furniture, room by room, and then perhaps the livestock and crops, the contents of a workshop, and all the bits and pieces that were valued together as 'huslement'. A family historian who finds an inventory of the possessions of a forebear gets a marvellous insight into the way of life and standard of living of his sixteenth-, seventeenth-, or eighteenth-century ancestor. Inventories have been widely used by social and economic historians and there is a vast literature concerning them, including numerous glossaries of the archaic and dialect words that were used.

On 12 January 1858 the State took over responsibility for proving wills through either the Principal Registry in London or the district offices in the rest of the country. Since 1874 the Principal Registry (Family Division) has been at Somerset House in the Strand, which is open to the public (free of charge and without the necessity of obtaining a ticket) between 10 a.m. and 4.30 p.m., Monday to Friday. This registry also receives copies of the wills proved in the district offices. The annual indexes of probates and of letters of administration (known as admons) for the whole of the country may be consulted here or in some of the larger municipal libraries which have printed copies. The indexes record the name of the testator, his or her address, the date and sometimes the place of death, the date of probate, the names of the executors or administrators, the value of the estate, and the name of the office in which the will was proved. A small charge is made for a registered copy of a will.

Manorial and Estate Records

The family historian will normally turn to manorial records only after he has made a thorough search of parish registers and wills. The chances of finding genealogical information in this source depend not only upon the survival of archives but on the size, the importance, and the length of life of the manor concerned. It is a common experience to find nothing of value, but sometimes manorial records will not only fill out the picture for the early modern period but will take the searcher back well into the Middle Ages. The records of the manor of Wakefield, to quote one outstanding example, provide continuous information from the thirteenth to the twentieth century.

A manor was sometimes coterminous with a parish, but very often it bore no relationship to the other unit. Manors varied in size from a few hundred to many thousands of acres. Some parishes contained two or three manors within their bounds, and some of these manors stretched over parts of neighbouring parishes as well. It is often difficult to establish the precise boundaries of a manor, many of which had numerous detached portions. Moreover, many manors contained large parcels of freehold land, whose owners made only a token recognition of the lord. Ownership of a manor did not necessarily mean that the lord owned most of the land, but only that he had certain customary rights, which varied from place to place.

Some manor courts ceased to function during the sixteenth and seventeenth centuries, but others continued to meet at regular intervals even into the nineteenth century. A handful, most famously that at the surviving open-field village of Laxton, meet at the present day. Manorial records are not always easy to trace, for if the ownership of a manor passed to someone who lived away then the records might have been moved out of the district. Many have been deposited at county and city record offices, while those of the numerous manors which belonged to the Crown or to the Duchy of Lancaster etc. will be found in the Public Record Office. Other manorial and estate records are kept in the British Library Department of Manuscripts. An archivist at the local record office will be the best person to give advice on the whereabouts of the records of individual manors.

Post-medieval manorial records are commonly listed in catalogues of archives under the heading 'estate papers'. The manor was indeed a unit of estate management and with the decline of manorial courts the records take the form of rentals, leases, surveys, and accounts. Even where courts continued to function, the term 'manorial court rolls' is rather misleading for the post-medieval period when stewards preferred to use bound volumes or sheets of paper.

Manorial courts were of two kinds. The court baron registered transfers of copyhold lands and the court leet saw to such day-to-day matters as the repair of hedges, the scouring of ditches, the rounding up of stray cattle, and the punishment of petty crime. A record of a meeting of a court leet commonly starts with a list of the ordinary members of the community who formed the jury, or 'homage', of the manor. Sometimes, all those freeholders who owed some form of allegiance to the manor are listed; many of them were absentee owners who never set foot in the district. The 'homagers' or 'jurymen' were the local inhabitants. After electing various officials, the jury agreed by-laws, known as 'paines' from the penalties which were imposed for their non-observance. Offenders against previous laws were fined and their names recorded.

A family historian may well find his ancestor serving on the manorial jury or being brought before the court for a specified offence. The records of the court baron will be of more use than those of the court leet in searching for genealogical information and for noting the transfer of copyhold property. The descent of a family holding can sometimes be traced over several generations. Dates of death are often given or can be inferred and family relationships are sometimes stated or can be deduced. The term 'copyhold tenure' is derived from the custom whereby a tenant held a copy of the entry in the manorial court rolls which recognized his possession of a holding according to agreed terms. Each manor had its own customs regarding the ways that holdings could be transferred. Copyhold tenure began to give way to leaseholding during the sixteenth century, but it was not legally abolished until 1922.

The records of manorial courts baron are often difficult to interpret. Even scholars who have considerable experience may be misled by forms which are frequently complicated and sometimes downright ambiguous. The indispensable guide is P. D. A. Harvey's *Manorial Records*. The transfers or conveyances recorded by a court may represent either sales, mortgages, or inheritance through entails, endowments, or trusts. These observations apply equally to the deeds that are kept in family or solicitors' collections in local record offices or registries of deeds. Such deeds are usually even more difficult to understand because of the long-winded forms of expression that were used from the sixteenth to the nineteenth centuries. Nevertheless, the difficulties should not be overstated. Manorial records can be a mine of genealogical information, going back well before the beginning of parish registration of baptisms, weddings, and burials.

A survey of a manor is of special value, particularly if it is accompanied by a map. Surveys become more common in the post-medieval period and often signify a change of ownership; a new lord was understandably keen to know exactly what he had purchased or inherited, often with a view to increasing the entry fines and rents. A survey might name each tenant, describe his buildings, give the acreage and use of every part of the holding, and record the conditions of tenure. In most cases, surveys will give a good indication of who was living in a particular place at a certain point in time, but they must not be regarded as comprehensive lists of the inhabitants of a particular community. As we have already noted, a manor was not necessarily the same unit as a parish; householders who were tenants of another manor will not be listed alongside their neighbours. Moreover, a farmer might have held only part of his land from a particular manor; the acreage that is recorded may not have been the only land that he farmed. A more serious problem is that tenants may have sublet their land to others who were not recorded. The family historian can therefore be easily misled. He will usually be grateful for getting at least part of the picture.

Rentals are less informative than surveys and their survival is often patchy. They give the names of the tenants of the estate and the rents that were due each year, at Lady Day and Michaelmas, or Christmas and Midsummer. However, they too may record the names of absentee tenants rather than the subtenants who actually lived there and farmed the land. Leases may be found amongst manorial and estate records or amongst solicitors' collections and private deposits. Those which were granted for three lives (the common method in western parts of England) are particularly useful to the family historian, for the lives that were entered were commonly those of the parents and the eldest son. A good run of leases will help the searcher to trace the descent of a property.

Manors were not just rural institutions. In many towns, they existed alongside the borough; elsewhere, corporations had acquired the manorial rights. In Sheffield, the Dukes of Norfolk continued to hold manorial courts well into the nineteenth century, though many aspects of local government were the responsibility of an independent Town Trust, while in neighbouring Doncaster the mayor and corporation had acted as lords of the manor since the Middle Ages. The records of Doncaster corporation therefore include numerous rentals and leases.

Enclosure Awards, Tithe Awards, and Land Tax Assessments

In many parts of the country the family historian may find rich information about an ancestor amongst the records of parliamentary enclosure, but this is not a source that is available everywhere, nor is it one where the information is set down in a consistent manner. About 6 million acres of open fields, commons, and wastes were enclosed by some 4,000 private Acts of Parliament, the great majority between 1750 and 1850. The many other manors and parishes which had been enclosed privately by agreement in earlier times have no such records. An Act of Parliament was necessary only when agreement could not be reached amicably. W. E. Tate's *Domesday of English Enclosure Acts* gives a list of the places that were enclosed by the parliamentary process and some record offices have published catalogues of the awards that are available for particular counties.

Whereas a local historian will be interested in the whole process of enclosure and the effects that it had on his particular community, the initial interest of the family historian will be concentrated on the legal document known as the award, which was drawn up after all claims had been considered and a thorough survey had been made. In many places, only the commons and wastes were enclosed; in such cases the award will specify only the allotments of former common land that were distributed amongst those who had previously enjoyed common rights. In those parts of England, notably much of the Midland Plain, where the arable land was still farmed on a communal system in open fields, an award will cover all the land in the parish. Similar comprehensive awards are found in cases where only the commons and wastes were enclosed but where the opportunity was taken at the same time to convert tithe payments to a fixed sum. A schedule lists the owners and tenants of every piece of property that is covered by the award. These properties are shown on an accompanying map.

If tithe payments were not altered at the time of enclosure the family historian whose ancestors were country-folk at the beginning of Victoria's reign should look for a tithe award. These were made in the years following the Tithe Commutation Act of 1836. Three copies of each award were made; one was deposited in the parish chest and should now be in a local record office, a second went to the bishop and should be kept in the archives of the ancient diocese, and a third went to the central government and should now be in the Public Record Office's store at Ashridge. The national reference work is R. J. P. Kain and H. C. Prince, *Tithe Surveys of England and Wales*, but catalogues for some counties are available at local record offices. About 2 out of every 3 parishes or townships have a tithe award. Most were drawn up by 1841 and all were completed by 1860. There is nothing comparable until the Inland Revenue house surveys of 1910–13, when detailed descriptions and valuations of each house in the country were made and the names of owners and tenants (but not necessarily occupants) were recorded. These are kept in the Public Record Office at Kew under IR.58 and IR.121–35.

Tithe awards list the owners and each of the occupiers of every piece of property. The properties are described as house, cottage, garden, orchard, field, etc. and their size is recorded. Tithe awards are a valuable source of information about field names; some even say what crop was being grown at the time of the survey. The large-scale maps which accompany the awards are often the earliest detailed maps available for a particular parish. They can be used with the 1841 and 1851 census returns to build an accurate picture of a place in the middle years of the nineteenth century. Six-inch ordnance survey maps are not usually available until the 1870s, though a pilot survey was carried out in Yorkshire 20 years earlier.

The family historian who becomes deeply interested in the history of the places where his ancestors lived will need to examine the enclosure and tithe awards in much greater detail than the researcher who at this stage is merely trying to find out where exactly his ancestor resided. Part of this deeper interest will lead the historian to the land tax assessments of that period. Here again, however, the beginner will find much that is immediately useful.

The land tax was introduced in the late seventeenth century, but the chances of assessments surviving before 1780 are very hit and miss. These assessments take the form of annual lists of the names of the proprietors of land in each parish and (at least in theory) the names of the actual occupiers. Assessments were organized on a county, hundred, and parish basis, so the returns may be found amongst quarter sessions records, in estate and family archives, or in parish collections. The duplicate returns that were made each year between 1780 and 1832 and deposited amongst quarter sessions records have the best chance of survival. The only record that covers almost the whole of England and Wales in a uniform way is that for the year 1798, which is contained in 121 volumes in class IR.23 at the Public Record Office, Kew. After 1798 standard printed forms were used. The reliability of land tax assessments has been hotly debated, but the family historian will find them a useful source for the period immediately before civil registration and the census returns, when parish registers are at their least reliable. By using a series of assessments a family historian can see who occupied a property over time and he can identify the year when the name of a head of household was replaced by a different one.

Poor Law Records

The Tudor monarchs made the ecclesiastical parishes (or their subdivisions, known as townships) responsible for certain civil functions, notably the relief of the poor. The Elizabethan Acts of 1598–1601 formed the basis of the Poor Law until the 1834 Poor Law Amendment Act created unions of parishes to serve in their place. Unpaid Overseers of the Poor were chosen at a yearly meeting of parishioners about Easter. They normally served for one year and were responsible for raising taxes (the 'poor rates' or 'assessments'), relieving the poor, and keeping accounts which had to be presented at the end of their period of office. Men were expected to serve without payment for loss of earnings, and they were responsible for their conduct to the Justices of the Peace. Records concerning the operation of the Poor Law are therefore normally found at county record offices, either amongst the deposited parish records or amongst the records of the quarter sessions.

The Elizabethan Poor Law aimed to relieve the 'deserving poor', to provide work, and to discipline the idle. Begging was punished by whipping, unless the JPs granted a special dispensation. The problem for the Overseer was how to define the 'deserving poor'. Overseers were responsible to the local rate-payers, who were anxious to keep the rates low, but they were the ones who had face-to-face contact with the poor who were requesting relief. The Overseer knew full well that if he turned down a request the person seeking relief might appeal to the nearest JP. He was therefore frequently faced with a dilemma. Some quarter sessions records include petitions, such as that of Elizabeth Hepworth of Owlerton in the parish of Sheffield, a widow for 11 years, who claimed that she 'has had no relief all that time but what she earned by her hard labour without being chargeable to her neighbours . . . now of great age being 69 years old and much weakened with bodily infirmities being disenabled to work for a livelihood is driven into great distress and want'. The JPs ordered the parish overseers to pay her 6*d.* a week maintenance. Overseers were not always as tight-fisted as they appear to have been in this case and often showed compassion for the poor. For example, many parishes did not take up the 'badging' powers of 1697, which allowed these local authorities to insist that poor people in receipt of charity should wear a letter P, or some similar distinguishing mark, on their apparel. Generally speaking, most parishes looked after those whom they considered their own 'deserving poor'.

All parishes had the problem of finding homes for poor orphans and finding employment for the children of parents who were in receipt of poor relief. The Acts of 1598–1601 empowered overseers to bind such children as apprentices and to pay their premiums from the parish rates. The Overseer had the often difficult task of finding a master. The 1697 Act imposed a £10 penalty on anyone who refused, without good reason, to accept a pauper child into his home and workplace, though anyone who felt aggrieved could petition the JPs. Quarter sessions depositions, where they survive, record many distressing cases.

The Act of Settlement of 1662 gave statutory authority to the previous practice of many parishes throughout England in stating that poor people were the responsibility of the parish where they were last legally settled. In the first place, a person was legally settled in the parish where he or she was born. However, if work was obtained in another parish for more than a year, or if an apprenticeship was served elsewhere, or if a family moved to a new parish and resided there unchallenged by the Overseer for more than a year, then the new place of residence became the legal settlement. When a woman married, she became the responsibility of her husband's parish. A parish would often allow newcomers within their boundaries only if the parish where the immigrants were legally settled would issue a certificate to this effect. An Act of 1691 defined the various ways in which a certificate could be obtained. Such settlement certificates may survive among the parish records that have been deposited at a local record office.

Settlement disputes formed a major part of the business at meetings of the quarter sessions. Both sides in a dispute employed learned counsel to argue their case. Parishes thought it was worth their while to do so, for losing a case might mean that they were saddled with maintaining a poor family for ever. In 1701 Richard Gough remembered the salutary experience of the case of Humphrey Beddows, a lame man who was born in the parish of Cardington and who settled in Myddle upon his marriage to Mary Davis. The parish officers complained to the local JP, who issued a 'warrant of disturbance'. Sometime later, Beddows fell ill and was removed to Cardington, but the officers there claimed that he was legally settled in Myddle. By this time, the warrant had been lost, so the removal order by which Beddows was sent back to Myddle was confirmed. 'This was the first contest that we had and thus we lost it,' commented Gough, 'but thanks be to God we never lost any afterwards.' The consequences for the parish of Myddle were considerable. Beddows's daughter Elizabeth, 'an idle, wanton wench', gave birth to a child and claimed that she was married to a soldier. The father was apprehended, escaped, and was recaptured, and after two cases argued by learned counsel before the JPs, the family was removed to Condover, where the husband was legally settled. Beddows's son was another cause of trouble. He was twice set apprentice, but each time ran away; he ended up in the House of Correction. Beddows's mother-in-law, Sina Davis, 'a crafty, idle, disembleing woman', who pretended to be lame and who 'went hopping with a staffe when men saw her, butt att other tymes could goe with it under her arme', had maintenance from the parish for many years, and her blind son Andrew received from the parish £3 per annum for 40 years or more. It was clearly worth while for a parish to try to persuade the JPs to take a poor family off their hands and pass them on to others.

Quarter sessions records are kept in county record offices. Some of the earliest ones have been published by the relevant county record society. The formal business of the courts is recorded in the indictment and order books, but these are in the form of brief minutes. Where depositions and petitions survive, the detail is much more human and vivid. Few counties have quarter sessions records from the sixteenth century—Essex is exceptional in having rich material—but most have records dating at least from the second half of the seventeenth century. The JPs had a lot of other business to see to, of course, including disputes concerning highways and bridges, licensing alehouses, regulating inland trade, punishing those who broke the law, and so on. An ancestor might appear in the quarter sessions records under any of these headings.

Those records which deal with the poor are the ones which provide the greatest amount of genealogical material. When a poor person was examined by a JP, a careful note was kept of his or her movements over the previous years, in order to establish where responsibility for maintenance lay. These settlement depositions may survive either amongst quarter sessions records or amongst the collections of individual parishes. An example from Yorkshire at the end of the eighteenth century reads as follows:

West Riding of Yorkshire. The Voluntary Examination of Robert Townsend of Sheffield in the said Riding taken on Oath this 3 Day of December in the Year of our Lord 1798 before us two of his Majesty's Justices of the Peace in and for the said Riding, as touching his last Place of legal Settlement.

This Examinant saith and deposeth, that he is about Forty nine Years of Age, was born in the Army when his father then served as he has been informed and believes the same to be true, but both his Father and Mother died before this Examinant had any knowledge of them, that when he was about Fifteen years of age he was sent to sea but in what capacity he does not know previous to which Time he traveled up and down the Country wit, Hawker and Pedlar this Examinant says that he was about Four or five years upon the seas that the Ship in which he went out in was lost and that this Examinant and some other of the Ship Crew was taken up and Landed at Park Gate [near Liverpool] he then went to Manchester and worked as a Day Labourer there and in the Neighbourhood for about four years he then went to Hoyland in the County of York and worked with several People as a Day Labourer for about Five years he then went to Sheffield and worked in different branches of business till the year 1791 when he went to Bolton upon Dearne in the said Riding when he served with different Masters for about half a year when he intermarried with Rachael Hague whose legal settlement was at Bolton aforesaid soon after this Examinant returned to Sheffield where he has resided ever since.
(Sheffield Archives, PR9/93/32)

Information obtained from quarter sessions and parish records can sometimes be pieced together to reconstruct events in the history of a pauper family over a long period of time. William Peace of Hunshelf, Yorkshire, was described as a labourer when he appeared before the magistrates at Pontefract quarter sessions in 1752 for stealing beef, as a result of which he was whipped. On 8 June 1752 an order was issued by the JPs for his removal from the township of Penistone to the township of Hunshelf, with his wife, Ann, and daughter Jemmy. Penistone and Hunshelf were in the same ecclesiastical parish, but were separate townships, or civil parishes. William Peace remained the responsibility of Hunshelf township until he died in 1768, though he normally managed to maintain himself. Ann received a total of £192. 16s. 0d. in relief from 1783 until her death in 1812, when her funeral expenses were met by the township. Their daughter Jemmy married M. Walker and had 10 children. In 1794 Walker was charged at the quarter sessions meeting held at Sheffield with stealing three-pennyworth of goods from Joseph Wood's warehouse. He was ordered to be transported to Botany Bay, but never reached there and probably died in the bulks.

Dr Keith Snell has emphasized the significance of settlement from the point of view of poor families, who treated proof of a claim on 'their' parish much as a family heirloom. Details of the family's settlement were carefully preserved and repeated to children from an early age. Certificates acknowledging settlement (or apprenticeship indentures) were passed from father to son; receipts of rent paid in excess of £10 per annum were produced decades later in evidence; and details of old removal cases affecting the family were told during examinations. The knowledge of the law possessed by some pauper families rivalled that of the lawyers who were consulted in parochial settlement disputes. The law was seen by the poor as a guarantee of parish relief during a period of poverty; this was some compensation for the restrictions imposed on their freedom of movement.

Military Records

A great deal of information about men who served in the armed forces can be obtained from the General Register Office at St Catherine's House, London, and the Public Record Office at Kew. The regimental registers that are kept at St Catherine's House record the births, marriages, and deaths of soldiers who were stationed in the United Kingdom upon the occasion of these events during the period 1761–1924; the marriage records also note the names, births, and baptisms of any children who were born to the marriage. For those who were serving overseas at the time of births, marriages, and deaths, the searcher has to turn instead to the Army Register Book (1881–1959) or to similar books for the Royal Navy (1837–1959) and the Royal Air Force (1918–59). Since 1959 the entries for all three forces are recorded together. Certified copies of these entries may be obtained at the same cost as the ordinary birth, marriage, and death certificates.

The Public Record Office issues a number of useful leaflets on the military and naval records in its custody at Kew. If the name of the regiment in which an ancestor served is known, a great deal of time is saved in searching a mass of material. The Army and Navy records which provide genealogical information are many and varied. They include the muster rolls of each regiment, which give place of birth, age on enlistment, and often the trade of the recruit. The earliest rolls are those of the Royal Artillery, which start in 1719. Certificates of baptism survive for officers from 1755. For all ranks, there are the chaplains' returns of 1796–1800, which register births, baptisms, marriages, and deaths abroad; these returns have a comprehensive index. The original registers of births, baptisms, marriages, and deaths, which were kept by regiments both at home and abroad between 1790 and 1924, are also housed at Kew. The records of service in the Royal Artillery between 1756 and 1917 give the places of birth, marriage, discharge, or death. Records pertaining to widows' pensions, 1735–1912, include proof of marriage and often sworn statements regarding the date and place of birth. The Chelsea Hospital registers record baptisms (1691–1812), marriages (1691–1765), and burials (1692–1856). Other records include casualty returns (1809–57), which give name, rank, place of birth, trade on enlistment, details of the casualty, and the next of kin.

The naval records that are held at Kew begin with the ships' musters, which start in 1680, become fuller from 1696, and are more or less complete from 1740 onwards. These list everyone who was serving on board, and give the ages and places of birth of the ratings. Dates and places of birth of seamen are also given in the Description books from the 1790s. Other useful records may be listed briefly. Lieutenants' passing certificates, which were issued from 1789 onwards, are accompanied by certificates of baptism. Certificates of service survive for ratings from 1802 to 1894. Bounty papers from 1675 to 1822 give the names and addresses of recipients of bounty. Pensions records include details of service and place of birth, and the marriage certificates of widows. The Greenwich Hospital records include registers of baptisms (1720–1856), marriages (1724–54), and burials (1705–1857), and the entry book of pensioners who resided there at some time between 1704 and 1869.

If the name of the regiment in which an ancestor served is known, it may be worth while to contact the appropriate regimental museum. Even if no further genealogical information is forthcoming, the museum will be able to provide a great deal of background information about the life of a soldier and the campaigns in which an ancestor might have been involved.

Adult males throughout Britain were liable for service in the local defence force, or militia, when occasion arose. Lists of names, known as muster rolls or militia returns, were drawn up from time to time, from the sixteenth to the nineteenth centuries. Most of the Tudor and Stuart ones are kept in the old Public Record Office at Chancery Lane, London, though some are found in local record offices. The indispensable guides are Jeremy Gibson and Alan Dell, *Tudor and Stuart Muster Rolls: A Directory of Holdings in the British Isles* and Jeremy Gibson and Mervyn Medlycot, *Militia Lists and Musters, 1757–1876: A Directory of Holdings in the British Isles*.

The early Tudor rolls are valuable in proving the existence of a surname within a particular locality before the beginning of parish registration. A number of muster rolls have been printed by county record societies. The most famous is that for Gloucestershire in 1608, which has been published as *Men and Armour for Gloucestershire in 1608*. This is arranged on a parish basis and records 19,402 individuals by name, approximate age, and occupation. The occupations have been analysed by A. J. and R. H. Tawney in their article 'An Occupational Census of the Seventeenth Century'. The surnames (which are indexed alphabetically) can be analysed in the same way as those in the printed hearth tax returns for various other counties. The pattern of migration into Gloucestershire is clear from the numerous surnames of Welsh or Welsh Border origin, compared with the insignificant number of northern locative names. The large number of distinctive regional surnames that appear in the list include Aly (6), Baddam (14), Berrowe (11), Cloterbrooke (28), Eddon (12), Millard (25), Nelme (36), Pegler (35), Sly (12), Tylladam (12), and Wollams (8). Their original homes may well be found in or close to Gloucestershire.

The militia was re-established in 1757, when it was ordered that each parish should provide for training a number of able-bodied men aged 18 to 50. Lists of all men within this age-range (which was lowered to 45 in 1762) were therefore drawn up from time to time, so that ballots could be held. From 1806 onwards the age of each man in the lists was recorded. As the militia was the responsibility of the Lord-Lieutenants of the counties, these records tend to be found in local rather than central record offices. The muster rolls or enrolment books are of limited use as they only give the names of those who were balloted for service. In many parts of the country, however, there are complete lists of all those who were balloted. Good collections survive for Cumberland, Dorset, Hertfordshire, Kent, Lincolnshire, Northamptonshire, and the city of Bristol, and elsewhere for various hundreds or wapentakes and for individual parishes. The best lists are both thorough and informative. Those for Dorset in the 1790s, for example, record not only a man's name, but also his occupation, any infirmity, height, marital status, and number of children aged under 10, and they distinguish the 'young men' of the parish from the rest. On the other hand, although the various Militia Acts from 1758 onwards always stipulated that the lists must record the names of all men in the appropriate age-range, it is clear that this did not always happen. Those who were exempted on account of their occupation, infirmity, etc. were sometimes not included and others may have been left off through carelessness or perhaps bribery.

The best of the eighteenth-century militia lists, compiled under the Act of 1757, are those for Hertfordshire (1758–65), which are gradually being published by the Hertfordshire Family and Population History Society, and a series of six for Northamptonshire, covering the period 1762–86, the fullest of which has been published under the title *Northamptonshire Militia Lists, 1777*. This has an analysis of the recorded occupations and an alphabetical index of surnames. The index notes numerous names that were common in the county but rare or absent beyond, names such as Ager (12), Allibone (5), Beeby (14), Blencowe (20), Buswell (26), Chater (9), Clever (21), Cunnington (14), Dunkley (60), Essam (8), Henson or Hemsman (39), Iliff (10), Judkins (14), Labram (9), Linnell (31), Mobbs (12), Peach (18), Pettifer (20), Pratt (22), Satchel (20), Tarry (25), Treadgold (7), Vann (18), and Wooding (19), many of them with alternative spellings. The list provides a springboard for further research into the homes of these family names.

The 'Defence Lists' of 1798 and 1803–4, i.e. the *Posse Comitatus* lists of 1798 and the *Levée en Masse* lists of 1803–4, are similar in appearance to the militia ballot lists. Their purpose was to organize a reserve defence force at the time of war with revolutionary France. Parish constables were ordered to record the names of all able-bodied men aged 15–60, who were not already serving with the yeomanry, volunteers, or the militia. In 1803 the instructions were to list all men aged 17–55. Buckinghamshire is the only county with a complete return. This valuable document has been edited by F. W. Beckett and published as *The Buckinghamshire* Posse Comitatus, *1798*. The editor has analysed the occupations of the 23,500 or so men who are listed, and the surnames are indexed alphabetically. They too are a rich source for discovering the distinctive local names of the county. These include Allnutt (16), Anstee or Anstiss (31), Badrick (20), Boddy or Bodily (40), Cooling (14), Dancer (21), Deeley (19), Dormer (20), Ginger (34), Gomme (29), Grace (61), Grimsdale (18), Gurney (80), Illing (13), Munday (46), Neighbour (21), Oxlade (16), Peppitt (12), Plumridge (28), Puddifoot (15), Seabrook (18), Showler (27), Shrimpton (33), Stallwood (23), Stuchbury (13), Syred (35), Tappin (22), Theed (9), Verney or Varney (39), and Wooster (20). In all, 771 Buckinghamshire men who appear in the list of 1798 possessed one or other of these 30 names, whereas in neighbouring Northamptonshire 21 years earlier only 7 of these surnames were recorded, and even they were shared by only 14 men.

Apprenticeship and Freemen Records

Individual apprenticeship indentures survive in their thousands in miscellaneous collections all over the country, but there is no national collection except Crisp's Bonds at the library of the Society of Genealogists, which lists about 18,000 apprentices between 1641 and 1888. The Inland Revenue records at the Public Record Office for the period 1710–1811 are worth consulting for various trades. For example, anyone who has an ancestor who was a framework knitter in Nottinghamshire, Leicestershire, or Derbyshire might find this source rewarding, but those with an ancestor who was a Hallamshire cutler will find nothing of value here.

The records provide the name, place of residence, and trade of the master, the name of the apprentice, and, until 1752, the name of the apprentice's father. Indexes compiled for the Society of Genealogists cover apprentices up to 1774 and masters up to 1762. Some local indexes have been published by record societies, e.g. in Surrey, Sussex, and Wiltshire.

In those parts of the country where a particular group of trades was dominant a record of all apprentices and freemen of a trade company might be preserved. The records of the Cutlers' Company of Hallamshire from the incorporation of the company in 1624 have been printed. They note the name of the apprentice, his father's name, occupation, and residence, the master's name, trade, and residence, the year when the apprenticeship began, its length, and the date of entry into the freedom of the company. Sons of freemen of the company had an automatic right of entry without the necessity of a formal apprenticeship. Anyone with an ancestor in this district should certainly consult this source, for even in the seventeenth century over half the local work-force were employed in the cutlery and allied trades.

Another type of freedom allowed a man to enjoy the privileges of one or other of the major cities and corporate towns. These included the right to practise a trade and the right to vote. The sons of other freemen and those who had completed an indentured apprenticeship in one of the recognized local trades formed the main body of the freemen, but others had purchased their freedom or had been honoured by such an award. The municipal authorities kept a register (or a series of rolls) of those who had been admitted into freedom. These records are normally kept in local record offices, but many have appeared in print. Some cover a long period from the Middle Ages to modern times. A good example is M. M. Rowe and A. M. Jackson's *Exeter Freemen, 1266–1967*. By the eighteenth century such records are far less valuable to the historian.

At their most complete, the rolls record the date of· admission, the name of the freeman, the name and residence of his father, and (where an apprenticeship had been served) the name and trade of the master. The evidence provided by the rolls has been used to study urban occupations and the social and geographical background of freemen, but the reliability of freemen's rolls has been questioned by historians and it should be borne in mind that they cover only a proportion of the local population. Nevertheless, a family historian might strike lucky and the source should certainly be consulted.

Hearth Tax and Protestation Returns

The various hearth tax returns of the 1660s and 1670s and the protestation returns of 1641–2 can be of great value to the family historian who is having difficulty in tracing his ancestors in the seventeenth century.

They locate certain people at particular points in time, and by demonstrating the distribution patterns of surnames within a county they suggest which parish registers might be profitably consulted in the search for an individual event. The family historian who does not know where to search for an ancestor in the late seventeenth or early eighteenth century might well find a lead from these sources. Thus, an eighteenth-century Lincolnshire family whose surname was recorded in such forms as Edenborough or Eddingborrow (which appear to have been derived from Edinburgh) can be traced back to Thomas Edenborough, who married Frances Thorp at Heckington in 1701. A possible line of enquiry to an earlier generation is suggested by the appearance of the name James Edenborow in the hearth tax return for Orston, Nottinghamshire, in 1664. Orston lies on the road from Nottingham to Grantham, near the Lincolnshire border. The Jacob Ettenborow who paid tax on one hearth at nearby Scarrington in 1674 may have been the same person. An obvious task is to search the parish registers of Orston and Scarrington to see whether James was Thomas's father.

The hearth tax was payable on the number of chimneys possessed by each house in England and Wales during the years 1662–88. It formed a major part of the government's revenue during the reigns of Charles II and James II, but was abolished after the Glorious Revolution deposed King James. The tax was collected at a county level, so occasionally a return may survive at a local record office. Thus, the original return for the West Riding of Yorkshire for Lady Day 1672 is kept at Wakefield Library, but the edited version which was forwarded to London is housed at the Public Record Office. Selected returns for various counties have appeared in print, with full indexes. Family history societies are conscious of the need to publish the best returns for their area, but at the moment only a minority of counties have anything in print.

The returns that were made to central government are kept in the Public Record Office, Kew, London, in the Exchequer division, under the call number E.179. No county has a complete set of returns for the whole period; indeed, in some counties, such as Wiltshire, the searcher is likely to be disappointed. The indexes note the length of each return, and this information is usually a good guide to which list is the fullest. A dedicated researcher will consult each of the returns that is available.

The collectors of the tax divided each county into its respective hundreds or wapentakes. These were then arranged by township, sometimes in alphabetical order. The family historian's task is eased if he has some grasp of the administrative structure of the county that he is interested in. Townships were the smallest units of local government from the Middle Ages until the nineteenth century. They were often identical with the ecclesiastical parishes, but in those parts of the country where parishes were large they formed subdivisions of the ecclesiastical units.

The entries for each township reflect the way in which the collector (assisted by the constable) toured the township to inspect each property. In estate villages, the name of the squire heads the list. Such men were given their titles or were addressed as 'Mr'. Here, as elsewhere, 'Mr' and 'Mrs' signified gentry status; the majority of people were recorded simply by their Christian name and their surname. Only the head of household was recorded; if this was a woman she was often named as Widow instead of by her first name. The number of hearths in the house was noted alongside the name. Those who were exempted from payment of the tax were recorded as 'poor' in the margin or were listed together at the end of each township's return. Unfortunately, in many cases the exempted poor were numbered but not named, or were simply not recorded.

Even though no single return is likely to be complete, collectively the records of the hearth tax are a major source of genealogical information for the third quarter of the seventeenth century. The protestation returns of 1641–2 can also yield rich pickings, where they survive in the library of the House of Lords. They list all males aged 18 and over who were called upon to subscribe to an Oath of Protestation of loyalty to king, Church, and Parliament shortly before the Civil War. The surviving lists appear to be remarkably comprehensive and include the names of the few individuals (determined recusants) who refused to take the oath. As they do not give the names of widows, they do not provide as full a record of local surnames as do the later hearth tax returns; such surnames might well be continued by males who at that time were under the age of 18 but whose fathers had died.

The returns for some counties or hundreds are missing. There is nothing for the counties of Leicestershire and Norfolk, or for the Yorkshire wapentakes of Staincross or Strafforth and Tickhill, for example. A full list of the places for which returns survive are given in the appendix to the Fifth Report of the *Historical Manuscripts Commission* (1876), pages 120–34, which may be consulted in a good reference library. The returns for some counties, such as Nottinghamshire and Lincolnshire, have been published with an index.

Lay Subsidies and Poll Taxes

Earlier taxation lists are much less complete than those of the seventeenth century. The reliability of these lists and the proportion of the population who were exempt from taxes are a matter for continued debate amongst historians. From the point of view of the family historian, however, they may at least provide early evidence for a family name in a particular area and may well offer some clues to the homes of many distinctive surnames.

Lay subsidies are so-called because the clergy was exempt from such taxes. The subsidies that were collected between 1290 and 1334 are some-times referred to as the tenths and fifteenths because of the practice of taxing one-tenth of the value of movable property of those who lived within a city, borough, or royal demesne and one-fifteenth of those who lived elsewhere. The names of taxpayers and the amount raised are arranged in the records under the vills (or townships) and boroughs. These returns are kept in the Exchequer division (E.179) of the Public Record Office, but some have been printed by record societies. Thus, in 1926 the Dugdale Society published *The Lay Subsidy Roll for Warwickshire of 6 Edward III (1332)*. The entry for the township of Wylye reads:

William son of Nicholas, 3*s.* 4*d.*, Wife of Thomas Daubeney, 3*s.* 6*d.*, Thomas Hiche, 2*s.* 0*d.*, William le Reue, 2*s.* 0*d.*, Executors of Robert le Clerke, 1*s.* 4*d.*, Thomas le Walshe, 1*s.* 6*d.*, Stephen le Whyte, 3*s.* 6*d.*, Peter the smith, 1*s.*, 0*d.*, Peter le Reue, 1*s.* 0*d.*, Richard de Kereslee, 4*s.* 0*d.*, Thomas Henry, 1*s.* 4*d.*, John de Morton, 2*s.* 0*d.*, Wife of Stephen atte Welle, 2*s.* 4*d.*, Nicholas le Walshe, 2*s.* 0*d.*, John atte Grene, 3*s.* 0*d.*, William the clerk, 1*s.* 0*d.*, Robert Lemon, 1*s.* 0*d.*

All the various categories of surname are represented here, at the period when some surnames were becoming hereditary.

From 1334 onwards the returns no longer give the names of the tax-payers. In the sixteenth century a fresh attempt was made to increase rev-enue by a new tax on either land or goods. Large numbers of people were exempt and many others managed to avoid payment. In southern and Midland England the lay subsidy of 1523 appears to be the fullest, but in the north and in Wales that of 1543 is the best. Some of the later subsidies are as detailed as these. A good idea of the range of returns available for this period can be obtained from *Early Tudor Craven: Subsidies and Assessments, 1510–1547*, edited by R. W. Hoyle.

An alternative method of taxation used by central government in medieval times was the poll tax, levied in 1377 on all over 14, in 1379 on all over 16, and in 1381 on all over 15. It is again debatable how many people evaded the tax and how many were exempt from payment, but generally the poll tax returns list far more people than do the lay sub-sidies. The returns of 1379, when payment was graded according to wealth, are usually the best for the family historian. They are kept with the lay subsidies under E.179 in the PRO and so far few have appeared in print. The returns of 1379 for the West Riding were published by the Yorkshire Archaeological and Topographical Association in 1882. They are an invaluable guide to the range of surnames that were just being formed at that time. In the thinly populated Pennine township of Langsett, for example, the following people were recorded:

Villata de Langside: Adam Cutter Cecilia *uxor ejus*, iiijd., Johanna *filia ejus*, iiijd., Willelmus Swan Johanna *ux. ejus*, iiijd., Agnes *filia*, iiijd., Henricus Draper, iiijd., Emma Draper, iiijd., Willelmus Drak' Agnes *ux. ejus*, iiijd., Robertus Sylbot Johanna *ux. ejus*, iiijd., Johannes Preest Matilda *ux. ejus*, iiijd., Agnes *filia*, iiijd., Adam Hatter Cecilia *ux. ejus*, iiijd., Elias del Strete Elena *ux.*, Berker, vjd., Johannes Sylbot Johanna *ux.*, Bakester, vjd., Robertus Amias Agnes *ux.*, iiijd., Adam de Sowthagh' Matilda *ux.*, iiijd., Alicia Robynwyf', Webster, vjd., Willelmus de Hatyrlay Elena *ux.*, Mercer, xijd., Johanna *ancilla*, iiijd., Amicia Hattirslay, Marschall', vjd., Alicia *ancilla*, iiijd., Johannes de Swyndene Cristiana *ux.*, iiijd., Johanna de Swyndene junior Matilda *ux.*, iiijd., Johanna Hattirslay mayden iiijd., *Summa* ixs.

The Latin forms—*uxor ejus* for 'his wife', *filia* for 'daughter', *ancilla* for 'servant'—do not present too much difficulty; nor do the Roman numerals. Married couples and single people each paid at the basic rate of 4*d.*, but craftsmen and traders were assessed at 6*d.* or 1*s.* Amongst the locative surnames recorded here is that of Hattersley, which originated across the Pennines and has since become common a few miles to the south, in and around Sheffield.

The revolt of 1381 convinced the government that personal taxation was extremely unpopular. There are therefore no comparable records for the fifteenth century, which is a difficult period for genealogical research. The poll tax was revived in 1641 and levied on seven occasions between 1660 and 1697. These returns may be found in the PRO or in local record offices. Some of the lists are long and detailed; the numbers who evaded payment were probably fewer than those who did not pay when the tax was revived in the late 1980s.

Reading Old Documents

The documents of the last 200 years are not usually difficult to read, unless the scribe has an idiosyncratic style. Words are normally spelt the same way as at present and letters are formed in a recognizable manner. The family historian who gets back to the sixteenth and seventeenth centuries, however, is faced with real problems of interpretation. The script is likely to be radically different from modern styles and much of it may be in Latin. The beginner has every reason to feel daunted by the sheer difficulty of reading a document, let alone understanding the information that it contains.

These are difficulties which must be admitted and faced honestly. There is no easy way out of the problem. Nevertheless, all hope should not be abandoned immediately. What seems impossible to read at first sight might be transcribed with practice. Several manuals provide guidance for the beginner. They include L. C. Hector, *The Handwriting of English Documents*, H. E. P. Grieve, *Examples of English Handwriting, 1150–1750*, C. T. Martin, *The Record Interpreter*, F. G. Emmison, *How to Read Local Archives, 1500–1700*, and K. C. Newton, *Medieval Local Records: A Reading Aid*. In addition to these, a number of similar guides are available from record offices, such as the *Borthwick Wallets* by A. Rycraft.

It is certainly possible with patience to teach oneself how to read Tudor and Stuart documents. The old adage 'practice makes perfect' is particularly appropriate here. Photocopies of documents should be obtained, if that is allowed, so that they can be examined at leisure. The trick is to recognize strange forms of letters in words which are obvious and to try these in the words that are proving difficult. It will be an encouragement to remember that even experienced researchers sometimes cannot read all the words in a document. Do not be embarrassed to ask for help; a fresh eye can often see the answer immediately and the helper will be pleased if he can read something that you cannot.

Half the battle is knowing what to expect. Wills can be read easily if the common form of the preamble is known and the usual way of proceeding is understood. That strange squiggle at the beginning of a probate inventory is soon recognized to be an abbreviated form of the Latin word *Imprimis*, meaning firstly. That list of names at the beginning of a manorial court roll will be seen to be a record of the jurors, whose first job will have been to choose the officers for the coming year. The more one knows about the ways that documents were drawn up and what they are likely to record, the easier is the task of deciphering the handwriting.

The ways in which documents written in Latin were set out are illustrated in a useful introductory guide, E. A. Gooder, *Latin for Local History*. Words that commonly appear in the records are translated in R. E. Latham (ed.), *Revised Medieval Latin Word List* and J. L. Fisher, *A Medieval Farming Glossary of Latin and English Words*. The beginner will therefore find plenty of guidance and can take heart that others have faced the same difficulties but have emerged triumphant.

Reference Section

Record Offices

1. The national record offices are as follows:

Public Record Office
Ruskin Avenue, Kew, Richmond TW9 4DU
British Library, Manuscript Collection
Great Russell Street, London WC1B 3DG
House of Lords Record Office
House of Lords, London SW1A 0PW
National Library of Wales, Department of Manuscripts and Records
Aberystwyth SY23 3BU
Scottish Record Office
HM General Register House, Edinburgh EH1 3YY
National Library of Scotland, Department of Manuscripts
George IV Bridge, Edinburgh EH1 1EW
The National Archives [Republic of Ireland]
Bishop Street, Dublin 7
Public Record Office of Northern Ireland
66 Balmoral Avenue, Belfast BT9 6NY

2. The major county and local record offices, arranged by modern counties, are:

England

Avon	Bath City Record Office, Guildhall, Bath BA1 5AW
	Bristol Record Office, 'B' Bond Warehouse, Smeaton Road, Bristol BS1 6XN
Bedfordshire	Bedfordshire Record Office, County Hall, Cauldwell Street, Bedford MK42 9AP
Berkshire	Berkshire Record Office, Shire Hall, Shinfield Park, Reading RG2 9XD
Buckinghamshire	Buckinghamshire Record Office, County Hall, Aylesbury HP20 1UA
Cambridgeshire	County Record Office, Cambridge, Shire Hall, Cambridge CB3 0AP
	County Record Office, Huntingdon, Grammar School Walk, Huntingdon PE18 6LF

Cheshire	Cheshire Record Office, Duke Street, Chester, CH1 1RL
	Chester City Record Office, Town Hall, Chester CH1 2HJ
Cleveland	Cleveland Archives Section, Exchange House, 6 Marton Road, Middlesbrough TS1 1DB
Cornwall	Cornwall Record Office, Truro, TR1 3AY
Cumbria	Cumbria Record Office, Carlisle, The Castle, Carlisle CA3 8UR
	Cumbria Record Office, Kendal, County Offices, Kendal LA9 4RQ
	Cumbria Record Office, Barrow, 140 Duke Street, Barrow-in-Furness, LA14 1XW
Derbyshire	Derbyshire Record Office, New Street, Matlock (correspondence to County Education Department, County Offices, Matlock DE4 3AG)
Devon	Devon Record Office, Castle Street, Exeter EX4 3PU
	North Devon Record Office, Tuly Street, Barnstaple EX32 7EJ
	West Devon Area Record Office, Unit 3, Clare Place, Coxside, Plymouth PL4 0JW
Dorset	Dorset Record Office, Bridport Road, Dorchester DT1 1RP
Durham	Durham County Record Office, County Hall, Durham DH1 5UK
Essex	Essex Record Office, PO Box 11, County Hall, Chelmsford CM1 1LX
	Essex Record Office, Colchester and North-East Essex Branch, Stanwell House, Stanwell Street, Colchester CO2 7DL
	Essex Record Office, Southend Branch, Central Library, Victoria Avenue, Southend-on-Sea SS2 6EX
Gloucestershire	Gloucestershire Record Office, Clarence Row, Alvin Street, Gloucester GL1 3DW
Hampshire	Hampshire Record Office, 20 Southgate Street, Winchester SO23 9EF
	Portsmouth City Records Office, 3 Museum Road, Portsmouth PO1 2LE
	Southampton City Records Office, Civic Centre, Southampton SO9 4XR
Hereford and Worcester	Hereford and Worcester Record Office, County Hall, Spetchley Road, Worcester WR5 2NP

Hereford Record Office, The Old Barracks, Harold Street, Hereford HR1 2QX

Worcester (St Helen's) Record Office, Fish Street, Worcester WR1 2HN

Hertfordshire   Hertfordshire Record Office, County Hall, Hertford SG13 8DE

Humberside   Humberside County Archive Office, County Hall, Beverley HU17 9BA

South Humberside Area Archive Office, Town Hall Square, Grimsby DN31 1HX

Kingston upon Hull City Record Office, 79 Lowgate, Kingston upon Hull HU1 2AA

Kent   Centre for Kentish Studies, County Hall, Maidstone ME14 1XQ

Canterbury City and Cathedral Archives, The Precincts, Canterbury CT1 2EG

Shepway Branch Archives Office, Central Library, Grace Hill, Folkestone CT20 1HD

Thanet Branch Archives Office, Ramsgate Library, Guildford Lawn, Ramsgate CT11 9AI

Medway Area Archives Office, Civic Centre, Strood, Rochester ME2 4AW

Sevenoaks Branch Archives Office, Central Library, Buckhurst Lane, Sevenoaks TN13 1LQ

Lancashire   Lancashire Record Office, Bow Lane, Preston PR1 2RE

Leicestershire   Leicestershire Record Office, 57 New Walk, Leicester LE1 7JB

Lincolnshire   Lincolnshire Archives, St Rumbold Street, Lincoln LN2 5AB

Greater London   Greater London Record Office and History Library, 40 Northampton Road, London EC1R 0HB

Corporation of London Records Office, PO Box 270, Guildhall, London EC2P 2EJ

Guildhall Library, Aldermansbury, London EC2P 2EJ

Barnet Archives and Local Studies Centre, Hendon Catholic Social Centre, Chapel Walk, Egerton Gardens, London NW4 4BE

Bexley Libraries and Museums Department, Local Studies Centre, Hall Place, Bourne Road, Bexley DA5 1PQ

Bromley Public Libraries, Archives Section,

Central Library, High Street, Bromley BR1 1EX

Camden Leisure Services, Swiss Cottage Library, Local Studies Library, 88 Avenue Road, London NW3 3HA

Camden Leisure Services, Holborn Library, Local Studies Library, 32–38 Theobalds Road, London WC1X 8PA

Greenwich Local History Library, Woodlands, 90 Mycenae Road, Blackheath, London SE3 7SE

Hackney Archives Department, Rose Lipman Library, De Beauvoir Road, London N1 5SQ

Hammersmith and Fulham Archives, The Lilla Huset, 191 Talgarth Road, London W6 8BJ

Haringey Community Information, Bruce Castle Museum, Lordship, London N17 8NU

Kensington and Chelsea Libraries and Arts Service, Central Library, Phillimore Walk, London W8 7RX

Lambeth Archives Department, Minet Library, 52 Knatchbull Road, London SE5 9QY

Lewisham Local History Centre, The Manor House, Old Road, Lee, London SE13 5SY

Redbridge Central Library, Local History Room, Clements Road, Ilford IG1 1EA

Southwark Local Studies Library, 211 Borough High Street, London SE1 1JA

Tower Hamlets Local History Library and Archives, Central Library, 277 Bancroft Road, London E1 4DQ

Waltham Forest Archives, Vestry House Museum, Vestry Road, Walthamstow, London E17 9NH

Westminster City Archives, Victoria Library, 160 Buckingham Palace Road, London SW1W 9UD

Westminster City Archives, Marylebone Library, Marylebone Road, London NW1 5PS

Greater Manchester   Greater Manchester County Record Office, 56 Marshall Street, New Cross, Manchester M4 5FU

Bolton Archive Service, Central Library, Civic Centre, Le Mans Crescent, Bolton BL1 1SE

Bury Archive Service, Derby Hall Annexe, Edwin Street, Bury BL9 0AS

Manchester Central Library, Local Studies Unit, St Peter's Square, Manchester M2 5PD

	Rochdale Libraries, Local Studies Department, Area Central Library, Esplanade, Rochdale OL16 1AS
	Salford Archives Centre, 658–662 Liverpool Road, Irlam, Manchester M30 5AD
	Stockport Archive Service, Central Library, Wellington Road South, Stockport SK1 3RS
	Tameside Archive Service, Tameside Local Studies Library, Astley Cheetham Public Library, Trinity Street, Stalybridge SK15 2BN
	Wigan Archives Service, Wigan Record Office, Town Hall, Leigh WN7 2DY
Merseyside	Merseyside Record Office, Cunard Building (4th Floor), Pier Head, Liverpool L3 1EG
	Liverpool Record Office, City Libraries, William Brown Street, Liverpool L3 8EW
	St Helens Local History and Archives Library, Central Library, Gamble Institute, Victoria Square, St Helens WA10 1DY
	Wirral Archives Service, Birkenhead Reference Library, Borough Road, Birkenhead L41 2XB
West Midlands	Birmingham Central Library, Archives Division, Chamberlain Square, Birmingham B3 3HQ
	Coventry City Record Office, Mandela House, Bayley Lane, Coventry CV1 5RG
	Dudley Archives and Local History Service, Mount Pleasant Street, Coseley, Dudley WV14 9JR
	Sandwell District Libraries, Local Studies Centre, Smethwick Library, High Street, Smethwick, Warley B66 1AB
	Walsall Archives Service, Local History Centre, Essex Street, Walsall WS2 7AS
	Wolverhampton Borough Archives, Central Library, Snow Hill, Wolverhampton WV1 3AX
Norfolk	Norfolk Record Office, Central Library, Norwich NR2 1NJ
Northamptonshire	Northamptonshire Record Office, Wootton Hall Park, Northampton NN4 9BQ
Northumberland	Northumberland Record Office, Melton Park, North Gosforth, Newcastle upon Tyne NE3 5QX
	Berwick upon Tweed Record Office, Council Offices, Wallace Green, Berwick upon Tweed TD15 1ED

274

Nottinghamshire	Nottinghamshire Archives Office, County House, Castle Meadow Road, Nottingham NG2 1AG
Oxfordshire	Oxfordshire Archives, County Hall, New Road, Oxford OX1 1ND
Shropshire	Shropshire Record Office, Shirehall, Abbey Foregate, Shrewsbury SY2 6ND
	Shropshire Local Studies Library, Castle Gates, Shrewsbury SY1 2AS
Somerset	Somerset Archive and Record Service, Obridge Road, Taunton TA2 7PU
Staffordshire	Staffordshire Record Office, County Buildings, Eastgate Street, Stafford ST16 2LZ
	William Salt Library, Eastgate Street, Stafford ST16 2LZ
	Lichfield Joint Record Office, Lichfield Library, The Friary, Lichfield WS13 6QG
Suffolk	Suffolk Record Office, Ipswich Branch, Gatacre Road, Ipswich IP1 2LQ
	Suffolk Record Office, Bury St Edmunds Branch, Raingate Street, Bury St Edmunds IP33 1RX
	Suffolk Record Office, Lowestoft Branch, Central Library, Clapham Road, Lowestoft NR32 1DR
Surrey	Surrey Record Office, County Hall, Penrhyn Road, Kingston upon Thames KT1 2DN
	Surrey Record Office, Guildford Muniment Room, Castle Arch, Guildford GU1 3SX
East Sussex	East Sussex Record Office, The Maltings, Castle Precincts, Lewes BN7 1YT
West Sussex	West Sussex Record Office, Sherburne House, 3 Orchard Street, Chichester (correspondence to County Hall, Chichester PO19 1RN)
Tyne and Wear	Tyne and Wear Archives Service, Blandford House, Blandford Square, Newcastle upon Tyne NE1 4JA
	Gateshead Central Library, Local Studies Collection, Prince Consort Road, Gateshead NE8 4LN
Warwickshire	Warwickshire County Record Office, Priory Park, Cape Road, Warwick CV34 4JS
Isle of Wight	Isle of Wight County Record Office, 26 Hillside, Newport PO30 2EB
Wiltshire	Wiltshire Record Office, County Hall, Trowbridge BA14 8JG

North Yorkshire	Borthwick Institute of Historical Research, St Anthony's Hall, York YO1 2PW
	North Yorkshire County Record Office, Malpas Road, Northallerton DL7 8TB
	York City Archives Department, Art Gallery Building, Exhibition Square, York YO1 2EW
	York Minster Archives, Dean's Park, York YO1 2JD
South Yorkshire	Barnsley Archive Service, Central Library, Shambles Street, Barnsley S70 2JF
	Doncaster Archives Department, King Edward Road, Balby, Doncaster DN4 0NA
	Rotherham Archives and Local Studies Section, Brian O'Malley Central Library, Walker Place, Rotherham S65 1JH
	Sheffield Archives, 52 Shoreham Street, Sheffield S1 4SP
West Yorkshire	West Yorkshire Archive Service, Wakefield Headquarters, Registry of Deeds, Newstead Road, Wakefield WF1 2DE
	West Yorkshire Archive Service, Bradford, 15 Canal Road, Bradford BD1 4AT
	West Yorkshire Archive Service, Calderdale, Central Library, Northgate House, Halifax HX1 1UN
	West Yorkshire Archive Service, Kirklees, Central Library, Princess Alexandra Walk, Huddersfield HD1 2SU
	West Yorkshire Archive Service, Leeds, Chapeltown Road, Sheepscar, Leeds LS7 3AP
	West Yorkshire Archive Service, Yorkshire Archaeological Society, Claremont, 23 Clarendon Road, Leeds LS2 9NZ

Wales

Clwyd	Clwyd Record Office, Hawarden Branch, The Old Rectory, Hawarden, Deeside CH5 3NR
	Clwyd Record Office, Ruthin Branch, 46 Clwyd Street, Ruthin LL15 1HP
Dyfed	Dyfed Archives Service, Carmarthenshire Area Record Office, County Hall, Carmarthen SA31 1JP
	Dyfed Archives Service, Cardiganshire Area Record Office, County Office, Marine Terrace, Aberystwyth, SY23 2DE

	Dyfed Archive Service, Pembrokeshire Area Record Office, The Castle, Haverfordwest SA61 2EF
Mid and South Glamorgan	Glamorgan Record Office, County Hall, Cathays Park, Cardiff CF1 3NE
West Glamorgan	West Glamorgan Record Office, County Hall, Oystermouth Road, Swansea SA1 3SN
Gwent	Gwent County Record Office, County Hall, Cwmbran NP44L 2XH
Gwynedd	Gwynedd Archives, Caernarfon Area Record Office, Victoria Dock, Caernarfon (correspondence to County Offices, Shirehall Street, Caernarfon LL55 1SH)
	Gwynedd Archives, Dolgellau Area Record Office, Cae Penarlag, Dolgellau LL40 2YB
	Gwynedd Archives, Llangefni Area Record Office, Shire Hall, Llangefni LL77 7TW
Powys	Powys County Archives Office, County Hall, Llandrindod Wells LD1 5LD

Scotland

Borders	Borders Region Archive and Local History Centre, Regional Library Headquarters, St Mary's Mill, Selkirk TD7 5EW
Central	Central Regional Council Archives Department, Unit 6, Burghmuir Industrial Estate, Stirling FK7 7PY
Dumfries and Galloway	Dumfries and Galloway Regional Library Service, Ewart Public Library, Catherine Street, Dumfries DG1 1JB
	Dumfries Archive Centre, 33 Burns Street, Dumfries DG1 2PS
Grampian	Grampian Regional Archives, Old Aberdeen House, Dunbar Street, Aberdeen AB2 1UE
	Moray District Record Office, Tolbooth, High Street, Forres IV36 0AB
	Aberdeen City Archives, The Charter Room, The Town House, Aberdeen AB9 1AQ
Highland	Highland Regional Archive, Inverness Branch Library, Farraline Park, Inverness IV1 1NH
Lothian	City of Edinburgh District Council Archives, Department of Administration, City Chambers, High Street, Edinburgh EH1 1YJ

Orkney	Orkney Archives, Orkney Library, Laing Street, Kirkwall, KW15 1NW
Shetland	Shetland Archives, 44 King Harald Street, Lerwick ZE1 0EQ
Strathclyde	Strathclyde Regional Archives, Mitchell Library, North Street, Glasgow G3 7DN
	Argyll and Bute District Archives, Kilmory, Lochgilphead PA31 8RT
Tayside	Dundee District Archive and Record Centre, 14 City Square, Dundee DD1 3BY
	Perth and Kinross District Archive, Sandeman Library, 16 Kinnoul Street, Perth PH1 5ET

3. Special collections of national interest are housed at the following:

Centre for Rural History, University of Reading, Whiteknights Park, PO Box 229, Reading RG6 2AG

Cambridge University Library, Department of Manuscripts and University Archives, West Road, Cambridge CB3 9DR

British Architectural Library, Royal Institute of British Architects, Manuscripts and Archives Collection, 66 Portland Place, London W1N 4AD

Dr Williams's Library, 14 Gordon Square, London WC1H 0AG

Bodleian Library, Department of Western Manuscripts, Broad Street, Oxford OX1 3BG

Further information is available in Jeremy Gibson and Pamela Peskett, *Record Offices: How to Find Them* (1985), Jean Cole and Rosemary Church, *In and Around Record Offices in Great Britain* (1990), J. Foster and J. Shepherd, *British Archives: A Guide to Archive Resources in the United Kingdom* (2nd edn., 1989), and A. Morton and G. Donaldson, *British National Archives and the Local Historian* (1983), which is a guide to official record publications.

Regnal years

William I	14 Oct. (crowned 25 Dec.) 1066–9 Sept. 1087
William II	26 Sept. 1087–2 Aug. 1100
Henry I	5 Aug. 1100–1 Dec. 1135
Stephen	26 Dec. 1135–25 Oct. 1154
Henry II	19 Dec. 1154–6 July 1189
Richard I	3 Sept. 1189–6 April 1199
John	27 May 1199–19 Oct. 1216
Henry III	28 Oct. 1216–16 Nov. 1272
Edward I	20 Nov. 1272–7 July 1307

Edward II	8 July 1307–20 Jan. 1327
Edward III	25 Jan. 1327–21 June 1377
Richard II	22 June 1377–29 Sept. 1399
Henry IV	30 Sept. 1399–20 March 1413
Henry V	21 March 1413–31 Aug. 1422
Henry VI	1 Sept. 1422–4 March 1461 (and 9 Oct. 1470–14 April 1471)
Edward IV	4 March 1461–9 April 1483
Edward V	9 April 1483–25 June 1483
Richard III	26 June 1483–22 Aug. 1485
Henry VII	22 Aug. 1485–21 April 1509
Henry VIII	22 April 1509–28 Jan. 1547
Edward VI	28 Jan. 1547–6 July 1553
Mary	6 July 1553–24 July 1554
Philip and Mary	25 July 1554–17 Nov. 1558
Elizabeth I	17 Nov. 1558–24 March 1603
James I	24 March 1603–27 March 1625
Charles I	27 March 1625–30 Jan. 1649
Interregnum	30 Jan. 1649–29 May 1660
Charles II	29 May 1660–6 Feb. 1685 (but reckoned from 30 Jan. 1649)
James II	6 Feb. 1685–11 Dec. 1688
Interregnum	12 Dec. 1688–12 Feb. 1689
William and Mary	13 Feb. 1689–27 Dec. 1694
William III	28 Dec. 1694–8 March 1702
Anne	8 March 1702–1 Aug. 1714
George I	1 Aug. 1714–11 June 1727
George II	11 June 1727–25 Oct. 1760
George III	25 Oct. 1760–29 Jan. 1820
George IV	29 Jan. 1820–26 June 1830
William IV	26 June 1830–20 June 1837
Victoria	20 June 1837–22 Jan. 1901
Edward VII	22 Jan. 1901–6 May 1910
George V	6 May 1910–20 Jan. 1936
Edward VIII	20 Jan. 1936–11 Dec. 1936
George VI	11 Dec. 1936–6 Feb. 1952
Elizabeth II	6 Feb. 1952–

Prime Ministers

Britain/United Kingdom

The term was first used in a mocking way about the person who held the post of First Lord of the Treasury.

Sir Robert Walpole	Whig	1721–42
Earl of Wilmington	Whig	1742–3
Henry Pelham	Whig	1743–54
Duke of Newcastle	Whig	1754–6
Duke of Devonshire	Whig	1756–7
Duke of Newcastle	Whig	1757–62
Earl of Bute	Tory	1762–3
George Grenville	Whig	1763–5
Marquis of Rockingham	Whig	1765–6
Earl of Chatham	Whig	1766–8
Duke of Grafton	Whig	1768–70
Lord North	Tory	1770–82
Marquis of Rockingham	Whig	1782
Earl of Shelburne	Whig	1782–3
Duke of Portland	coalition	1783
William Pitt	Tory	1783–1801
Henry Addington	Tory	1801–4
William Pitt	Tory	1804–6
Lord William Grenville	Whig	1806–7
Duke of Portland	Tory	1807–9
Spencer Perceval	Tory	1809–12
Earl of Liverpool	Tory	1812–27
George Canning	Tory	1827
Viscount Goderich	Tory	1827–8
Duke of Wellington	Tory	1828–30
Earl Grey	Whig	1830–4
Viscount Melbourne	Whig	1834
Duke of Wellington	Tory	1834
Sir Robert Peel	Conservative	1834–5
Viscount Melbourne	Whig	1835–41
Sir Robert Peel	Conservative	1841–6
Lord John Russell	Whig	1846–52
Earl of Derby	Conservative	1852
Earl of Aberdeen	coalition	1852–5
Viscount Palmerston	Liberal	1855–8
Earl of Derby	Conservative	1858–9
Viscount Palmerston	Liberal	1859–65
Earl Russell	Liberal	1865–6

Earl of Derby	Conservative	1866–8
Benjamin Disraeli	Conservative	1868
William Ewart Gladstone	Liberal	1868–74
Benjamin Disraeli	Conservative	1874–80
William Ewart Gladstone	Liberal	1880–5
Marquis of Salisbury	Conservative	1885–6
William Ewart Gladstone	Liberal	1886
Marquis of Salisbury	Conservative	1886–92
William Ewart Gladstone	Liberal	1892–4
Earl of Rosebery	Liberal	1894–5
Marquis of Salisbury	Conservative	1895–1902
Arthur James Balfour	Conservative	1902–5
Sir Henry Campbell-Bannerman	Liberal	1905–8
Herbert Henry Asquith	Liberal	1908–16
David Lloyd George	coalition	1916–22
Andrew Bonar Law	Conservative	1922–3
Stanley Baldwin	Conservative	1923–4
James Ramsay MacDonald	Labour	1924
Stanley Baldwin	Conservative	1924–9
James Ramsay MacDonald	Labour	1929–31
James Ramsay MacDonald	coalition	1931–5
Stanley Baldwin	Conservative	1935–7
Neville Chamberlain	Conservative	1937–40
Winston Spencer Churchill	coalition	1940–5
Clement Richard Attlee	Labour	1945–51
Sir Winston Spencer Churchill	Conservative	1951–5
Sir Anthony Eden	Conservative	1955–7
Harold Macmillan	Conservative	1957–63
Sir Alec Douglas-Home	Conservative	1963–4
Harold Wilson	Labour	1964–70
Edward Heath	Conservative	1970–4
Harold Wilson	Labour	1974–6
James Callaghan	Labour	1976–9
Margaret Thatcher	Conservative	1979–90
John Major	Conservative	1990–

Northern Ireland

Sir James Craig (1927 Viscount Craigavon)	Unionist	1921–40
John M. Andrews	Unionist	1940–3
Sir Basil Brooke (1952 Viscount Brookeborough)	Unionist	1943–63
Terence O'Neil	Unionist	1963–9

| James Chichester-Clark | Unionist | 1969–71 |
| Brian Faulkner | Unionist | 1971–2 |

The office was suspended on 30 March 1972.

Republic of Ireland

William T. Cosgrave (1922–32) and Eamon De Valera (1932–7) held the office of President of the Executive Council of the Irish Free State. The term Prime Minister was used from 1937, under the remodelled constitution.

Many Irish governments have been coalitions; the political party noted here was that of the Prime Minister.

Eamon De Valera	Fianna Fáil	1937–48
John A. Costello	Fine Gael	1948–51
Eamon De Valera	Fianna Fáil	1951–4
John A. Costello	Fine Gael	1954–7
Eamon De Valera	Fianna Fáil	1957–9
Sean Lemass	Fianna Fáil	1959–66
Jack Lynch	Fianna Fáil	1966–73
Liam Cosgrave	Fine Gael	1973–7
Jack Lynch	Fianna Fáil	1977–9
Charles J. Haughey	Fianna Fáil	1979–81
Dr Garret Fitzgerald	Fine Gael	1981–2
Charles J. Haughey	Fianna Fáil	1982
Dr Garret Fitzgerald	Fine Gael	1982–7
Charles J. Haughey	Fianna Fáil	1987–92
Albert Reynolds	Fianna Fáil	1992–4
John Bruton	Fine Gael	1994–

Saints' Days

6 January	Epiphany
2 February	Candlemas (Purification of the Blessed Virgin Mary)
24 February	St Matthias
1 March	St David
17 March	St Patrick
25 March	Lady Day (Annunciation of the Blessed Virgin Mary)
23 April	St George
25 April	St Mark
1 May	St Philip and St James the Less
24 June	St John the Baptist (Midsummer)

29 June	St Peter
30 June	St Paul
25 July	St James the Apostle
1 August	Lammas Day (changed in 1752 to August 13)
24 August	St Bartholomew
21 September	St Matthew
29 September	Michaelmas (St Michael and All Angels)
18 October	St Luke
28 October	St Simon and St Jude
1 November	All Saints (All Hallows)
2 November	All Souls
11 November	Martinmas (St Martin)
30 November	St Andrew and St Nicholas
21 December	St Thomas the Apostle
25 December	Christmas
26 December	St Stephen
27 December	St John the Evangelist
28 December	Holy Innocents
29 December	St Thomas Becket

For a fuller list, see David H. Farmer (ed.), *The Oxford Dictionary of Saints* (1978).

Weights and Measures

1. British and American, with metric equivalents

LINEAR MEASURE

1 inch	= 25.4 millimetres exactly
1 foot = 12 in.	= 0.3048 metre exactly
1 yard = 3 ft.	= 0.9144 metre exactly
1 (statute) mile = 1,760 yd.	= 1.609 kilometres

SQUARE MEASURE

1 square inch	= 6.45 sq. centimetres
1 square foot = 144 sq. in.	= 9.29 sq. decimetres
1 square yard = 9 sq. ft.	= 0.836 sq. metre
1 acre = 4,840 sq. yd.	= 0.405 hectare
1 square mile = 640 acres	= 259 hectares

CUBIC MEASURE

1 cubic inch	= 16.4 cu. centimetres
1 cubic foot = 1,728 cu. in	= 0.0283 cu. metre
1 cubic yard = 27 cu. ft.	= 0.765 cu. metre

CAPACITY MEASURE

British
1 pint = 29 fluid oz.	= 0.568 litre
= 34.68 cu. in.	
1 quart = 2 pints	= 1.136 litres
1 gallon = 4 quarts	= 4.546 litres
1 peck = 2 gallons	= 9.092 litres
1 bushel = 4 pecks	= 36.4 litres
1 quarter = 8 bushels	= 2.91 hectolitres

American dry
1 pint = 33.60 cu. in.	= 0.550 litre
1 quart = 2 pints	= 1.101 litres
1 peck = 8 quarts	= 8.81 litres
1 bushel = 4 pecks	= 35.3 litres

American liquid
1 pint = 16 fluid oz.	= 0.473 litre
= 28.88 cu. in.	
1 quart = 2 pints	= 0.946 litre
1 gallon = 4 quarts	= 3.785 litres

AVOIRDUPOIS WEIGHT
1 grain	= 0.065 gram
1 dram	= 1.772 grams
1 ounce = 16 drams	= 28.35 grams
1 pound = 16 ounces	= 0.4536 kilogram
= 7,000 grains	(0.45359237 exactly)
1 stone = 14 pounds	= 6.35 kilograms
1 quarter = 2 stones	= 12.70 kilograms
1 hundredweight = 4 quarters	= 50.80 kilograms
1 (long) ton = 20 hundredweight	= 1.016 tonnes
1 (short) ton = 2,000 pounds	= 0.907 tonne

2. Metric, with British equivalents

LINEAR MEASURE
1 millimetre	= 0.039 inch
1 centimetre = 10 mm	= 0.394 inch
1 decimetre = 10 cm	= 3.94 inches
1 metre = 10 dm	= 1.094 yards
1 decametre = 10 m	= 10.94 yards
1 hectometre = 100 m	= 109.4 yards
1 kilometre = 1,000 m	= 0.6214 mile

SQUARE MEASURE

1 square centimetre	= 0.155 sq. inch
1 square metre = 10,000 sq. cm	= 1.196 sq. yards
1 are = 100 sq. m	= 119.6 sq. yards
1 hectare = 100 ares	= 2.471 acres
1 square kilometre = 100 hectares	= 0.386 sq. mile

CUBIC MEASURE

1 cubic centimetre	= 0.061 cu. inch
1 cubic metre = 1,000,000 cu. cm	= 1.308 cu. yards

CAPACITY MEASURE

1 millilitre	= 0.002 pint (British)
1 centilitre = 10 ml	= 0.018 pint
1 decilitre = 10 cl	= 0.176 pint
1 litre = 10 dl	= 1.76 pints
1 decalitre = 10 l	= 2.20 gallons
1 hectolitre = 100 l	= 2.75 bushels
1 kilolitre = 1,000 l	= 3.44 quarters

WEIGHT

1 milligram	= 0.015 grain
1 centigram = 10 mg	= 0.154 grain
1 decigram = 10 cg	= 1.543 grains
1 gram = 10 dg	= 15.43 grains
1 decagram = 10 g	= 5.64 drams
1 hectogram = 100 g	= 3.527 ounces
1 kilogram = 1,000 g	= 2.205 pounds
1 tonne (metric ton) = 1,000 kg	= 0.984 (long) ton

The conversion factors are not exact unless so marked. They are given only to the accuracy likely to be needed in everyday calculations

Further Reading

Family History: Sources and Approaches

Begley, Donal (ed.), *Irish Genealogy: A Record Finder* (1981)

Bell, Robert, *The Book of Ulster Surnames* (1988)

Bevan, A. and Duncan, A., *Tracing Your Ancestors in the Public Record Office* (1991)

Camp, A. J., *Wills and Their Whereabouts* (1974)

Colwell, Stella, *Dictionary of Genealogical Sources in the Public Record Office* (1992)

—— *Tracing Your Family Tree* (1984)

Finnegan, Ruth and Drake, Michael (eds.), *From Family Tree to Family History* (1994)

—— —— and Eustace, Jacqueline (eds.), *Sources and Methods for Family and Community Historians: A Handbook* (1994)

Fitzhugh, T. V. H., *The Dictionary of Genealogy* (1985)

Gibson, J. S. W., *Wills and Where to Find Them* (1974)

—— *Guides for Genealogists, Family and Local Historians* (various booklets, Federation of Family History Societies)

Golby, John (ed.), *Communities and Families* (1994)

Grenham, John, *Tracing Your Irish Ancestors* (1992)

Guppy, H. B., *Homes of Family Names in Great Britain* (1890)

Hanks, Patrick and Hodges, Flavia, *The Oxford Dictionary of Surnames* (1989)

—— —— *A Dictionary of First Names* (1990)

Hawkings, David T., *Criminal Ancestors: A Guide to Historical Criminal Records in England and Wales* (1992)

—— *Railway Ancestors: A Guide to the Staff Records of the Railway Companies of England and Wales, 1822–1947* (1995)

Hey, David, *Family History and Local History in England* (1987)

—— *The Oxford Guide to Family History* (1993)

McKinley, Richard, *A History of British Surnames* (1990)

MacLysaght, Edward, *The Surnames of Ireland* (1980)

Maxwell, F. C. and Saul, P., *The Family Historian's Enquire Within* (1988)

Mitchell, Brian, *A New Genealogical Atlas of Ireland* (1986)

Moody, David, *Scottish Family History* (1988)

Morgan, T. J. and Morgan, Prys, *Welsh Surnames* (1985)

Pryce, Rees (ed.), *From Family History to Community History* (1994)

Reaney, P. H., *The Origins of English Surnames* (1967)

—— and Wilson, R. M., *A Dictionary of English Surnames* (1991)

Rogers, C. D., *The Family Tree Detective* (1983)

—— *The Surname Detective* (1995)

—— and Smith, J. H., *Local Family History in England* (1992)

Rowlands, John, *et al.* (eds.), *Welsh Family History: A Guide to Research* (1993)

Sinclair, Cecil, *Tracing Your Scottish Ancestors: A Guide to Ancestry Research in the Scottish Record Office* (1990)

Steel, D. J. (ed.), *The National Index of Parish Registers, xii: Sources for Scottish Genealogy and Family History* (1970)

—— (ed.), *Sources for Roman Catholic and Jewish Genealogy and Family History* (1974)

—— *General Sources of Births, Marriages and Deaths before 1837* (1976)

—— *Discovering Your Family History* (1980)

Steel, Don, and Taylor, Lawrence, *Family History in Focus* (1984)

Wagner, A. R., *English Genealogy* (3rd edn., 1983)

Withycombe, E. G., *The Oxford Dictionary of English Christian Names* (1977)

Woodcock, Thomas and Robinson, John Martin, *The Oxford Guide to Heraldry* (1988)

Local History: Sources and Approaches

Alcock, N. W., *Old Title Deeds: A Guide for Local and Family Historians* (1986)

Bettey, J. H., *Church and Parish: An Introduction for Local Historians* (1987)

Caunce, Stephen, *Oral History and the Local Historian* (1994)

Dymond, D. P., *Writing Local History* (1981)

Edwards, Peter, *Farming Sources for Local Historians* (1991)

—— *Rural Life: Guide to Local Records* (1993)

Ellis, Mary, *Using Manorial Records* (1994)

English, Barbara and Saville, John, *Strict Settlement: A Guide for Historians* (1983)

Evans, G. E., *Ask the Fellows Who Cut the Hay* (1956)

—— *Where Beards Wag All* (1977)

—— *Spoken History* (1987)

Foster, Janet and Sheppard, Julia, *British Archives: A Guide to Archive Resources in the United Kingdom* (3rd edn., 1995)

Gibson, Jeremy, Rogers, Colin, and Webb, Cliff, *Poor Law Union Records, parts 1–4* (1992)

Ginter, Donald E., *A Measure of Wealth: The English Land Tax in Historical Analysis* (1992)

Guy, Susanna, *English Local Studies Handbook* (1993)

Further Reading

Harvey, P. D. A., *Manorial Records* (1984)

Haythornthwaite, J. A., *Scotland in the Nineteenth Century: An Analytical Bibliography of Material relating to Scotland in Parliamentary Papers, 1800–1900* (1993)

Hoskins, W. G., *Local History in England* (3rd edn., 1984)

Hoyle, Richard, *Tudor Tax Records: A Guide for Users* (1994)

Humphrey-Smith, C. (ed.), *The Phillimore Atlas and Index of Parish Registers* (2nd edn., 1994)

Kain, Roger, *An Atlas and Index of the Tithe Files of Mid-Nineteenth-Century England and Wales* (1986)

—— and Prince, Hugh, *The Tithe Surveys of England and Wales* (1985)

—— and Oliver, Richard, *The Tithe Maps of England and Wales: A Cartographic Analysis and County-by-County Catalogue* (1995)

MacFarlane, Alan, *et. al.*, *Reconstructing Historical Communities* (1977)

Martin, G. H. and Spufford, Peter (eds.), *The Records of the Nation: The Public Record Office, 1838–1988; The British Record Society, 1888–1988* (1990)

Milward, Rosemary, *A Glossary of Household and Farming Terms from Sixteenth-Century Probate Inventories* (1977)

Moody, David, *Scottish Local History: An Introductory Guide* (1986)

Nolan, William, *Tracing the Past: Sources for Local Studies in the Republic of Ireland* (1985)

Norton, Jane E., *A Guide to National and Provincial Directories* (1984)

Olney, R. J., *Manuscript Sources for British History: Their Nature, Location and Use* (1995)

Phythian-Adams, Charles, *Re-thinking English Local History* (1987)

—— (ed.), *Societies, Cultures and Kinship, 1580–1850: Cultural Provinces and English Local History* (1993)

Riden, Philip, *Local History: A Handbook for Beginners* (1983)

—— *Record Sources for Local History* (1987)

Royal Commission on Historical Manuscripts, *Record Repositories in Great Britain: A Geographical Directory* (1992)

Shaw, Gareth and Tipper, Allison, *British Directories: A Bibliography and Guide to Directories Published in England and Wales, 1850–1950, and Scotland, 1775–1950* (1988)

Sinclair, Cecil, *Tracing Scottish Local History: A Guide to Local History Records in the Scottish Record Office* (1994)

Stephens, W. B., *Sources for English Local History* (3rd edn., 1994)

Stuart, Denis, *Manorial Records: An Introduction to their Transcription and Translation* (1992)

Tarver, Ann, *Church Court Records* (1994)

Tiller, Kate, *English Local History: An Introduction* (1992)

Upton, Clive, *et al.*, *Survey of English Dialects: The Dictionary and the Grammar* (1994)

Wakelin, Martyn F., *English Dialects: An Introduction* (1977)

Williams, Michael A., *Researching Local History: The Human Journey* (1996)

Youngs, F. A., Jr., *Guide to the Local Administrative Units of England* (2 vols, 1980–91)

Reading Old Documents

Barrett, John and Iredale, David, *Discovering Old Handwriting* (1995)

Emmison, F. G., *How to Read Local Archives, 1500–1700* (1967)

Fisher, J. L., *A Medieval Farming Glossary of Latin and English Words* (1968)

Gooder, Eileen A., *Latin for Local History* (1978)

Grieve, H. E. P., *Examples of English Handwriting, 1150–1750* (1978)

Hector, L. C., *The Handwriting of English Documents* (1979)

Latham, R. E., *Revised Medieval Latin Word List* (1965)

Martin, C. T., *The Record Interpreter* (1982)

Munby, Lionel, *Reading Tudor and Stuart Handwriting* (1987)

Newton, K. C., *Medieval Local Records: A Reading Aid* (1971)

Demography

Anderson, Michael, *Family Structure in Nineteenth-Century Lancashire* (1971)

Appleby, A. P., *Famine in Tudor and Stuart England* (1978)

Baines, Dudley, *Emigration from Europe, 1815–1930* (1991)

Canny, Nicholas (ed.), *Europeans on the Move: Studies on European Migration, 1500–1800* (1995)

Clark, Peter and Souden, David (eds.), *Migration and Society in Early Modern England* (1987)

Coldham, P. W., *The Complete Book of Emigrants in Bondage, 1614–1775* (1987)

Devine, T. M., *The Great Highland Famine* (1988)

Hawkings, David T., *Bound for Australia* (1987)

Higgs, Edward, *Making Sense of the Census: The Manuscript Returns for England and Wales, 1801–1901* (1988)

Holmes, Colin, *John Bull's Island: Immigration and British Society, 1871–1971* (1988)

Houston, R. A., *The Population History of Britain and Ireland, 1500–1750* (1992)

Merriman, Nick, ed., *The Peopling of London: Fifteen Thousand Years of Settlement from Overseas* (1993)

O Grada, Cormac, *The Great Irish Famine* (1989)

Schurer, Kevin and Arkell, Tom (eds.), *Surveying the People: The Interpretation and Use of Document Sources for the Study of Population in the Later Seventeenth Century* (1992)

Further Reading

Slack, Paul, *The Impact of Plague in Tudor and Stuart England* (1985)

Swift, Roger and Gilley, Sheridan (eds.), *The Irish In Britain, 1815–1939* (1989)

Whiteman, Anne (ed.), *The Compton Census of 1676: A Critical Edition* (1986)

Wrigley, E. A. and Schofield, R. S., *The Population History of England, 1541–1871: A Reconstruction* (1981)

Landscape History

Albert, W., *The Turnpike Road System in England, 1663–1840* (1972)

Aston, M., Austin, D., and Dyer, C. (eds.), *The Rural Settlements of Medieval England: Studies Dedicated to Maurice Beresford and John Hurst* (1989)

Baker, Alan R. H. and Butlin, Robin A. (eds.), *Studies of Field Systems in the British Isles* (1973)

Beresford, Maurice, *History on the Ground* (1957)

—— *New Towns of the Middle Ages* (1967)

—— *Time and Place: Collected Essays* (1984)

—— and Hurst, John, *Deserted Medieval Villages* (1971)

Beresford, M. W. and St Joseph, J. K. S., *Medieval England: An Aerial Survey* (1979)

Colyer, Richard, *Roads and Trackways of Wales* (1984)

Crossley, David, *Post-Medieval Archaeology in Britain* (1990)

Dyer, Christopher, *Hanbury: Settlement and Society in a Woodland Landscape* (1991)

Evans, E. E., *The Personality of Ireland: Habitat, Heritage and History* (1973)

Everitt, Alan, *Landscape and Community in England* (1985)

—— *Continuity and Colonization: The Evolution of Kentish Settlement* (1986)

Field, John, *A History of English Field-Names* (1993)

Gelling, Margaret, *Place-Names in the Landscape* (1984)

Haldane, A. R. B., *The Drove Roads of Scotland* (1973)

Harley, J. B. and Phillips, C. W., *The Historian's Guide to Ordnance Survey Maps* (1984)

Hey, David, *Packmen, Carriers and Packhorse Roads: Trade and Communications in North Derbyshire and South Yorkshire* (1980)

Hindle, B. P., *Maps for Local History* (1988)

—— *Roads, Tracks and their Interpretation* (1993)

Hoskins, W. G., *The Making of the English Landscape* (1955)

—— *Fieldwork in Local History* (1967)

Morris, Richard, *Churches in the Landscape* (1989)

Rackham, Oliver, *Trees and Woodland in the British Landscape* (1976)

—— *The History of the Countryside* (1986)

Salway, Peter, *The Oxford Illustrated History of Roman Britain* (1993)

Taigel, A. and Williamson, T., *Parks and Gardens* (1993)

Taylor, Christopher, *Fields in the English Landscape* (1975)
—— *Village and Farmstead: A History of Rural Settlement in England* (1983)
Trinder, Barrie, *The Making of the Industrial Landscape* (1988)
Warner, Peter, *Greens, Commons and Clayland Colonization: The Origins and Development of Greenside Settlement in East Suffolk* (1987)
Winchester, Angus, *Discovering Parish Boundaries* (1990)

The Hodder and Stoughton county landscape history series

Allison, K. J., *The East Riding of Yorkshire Landscape* (1976)
Balchin, W. G. V., *Cornwall* (1955)
Bigmore, Peter, *The Bedfordshire and Huntingdonshire Landscape* (1979)
Brandon, Peter, *The Sussex Landscape* (1974)
Dymond, David, *The Norfolk Landscape* (1985)
Emery, Frank, *The Oxfordshire Landscape* (1974)
Finberg, H. P. R., *Gloucestershire* (1955)
Havinden, Michael, *The Somerset Landscape* (1981)
Hoskins, W. G., *Leicestershire* (1955)
Millward, Roy, *Lancashire* (1955)
Munby, Lionel, *The Hertfordshire Landscape* (1977)
Newton, Robert, *The Northumberland Landscape* (1972)
Palliser, David, *The Staffordshire Landscape* (1976)
Raistrick, Arthur, *West Riding of Yorkshire* (1955)
Reed, Michael, *The Buckinghamshire Landscape* (1979)
Rowley, Trevor, *The Shropshire Landscape* (1972)
Scarfe, Norman, *The Suffolk Landscape* (1972)
Steane, John, *The Northamptonshire Landscape* (1974)
Taylor, Christopher, *Dorset* (1970)
—— *The Cambridgeshire Landscape* (1973)
Williams, Moelwyn, *The South Wales Landscape* (1975)

The Longman Regional History of England

Beckett, J. V., *The East Midlands from AD 1000* (1988)
Bettey, J. H., *Wessex from AD 1000* (1986)
Brandon, Peter and Short, Brian, *The South-East from AD 1000* (1990)
Cunliffe, Barry, *Wessex to AD 1000* (1993)
Drewett, Peter, *et al.*, *The South-East to AD 1000* (1988)
Hey, David, *Yorkshire from AD 1000* (1986)
Higham, Nick, *The Northern Counties to AD 1000* (1986)
Phillips, C. B. and Smith, J. H., *Lancashire and Cheshire from AD 1540* (1994)
Rowlands, Marie B., *The West Midlands from AD 1000* (1987)
Todd, Malcolm, *The South-West to AD 1000* (1987)

Further Reading

Buildings

Airs, Malcolm, *The Making of the English Country House, 1500–1640* (1975)

Alcock, N. W., *People At Home: Living in a Warwickshire Village, 1500–1800* (1993)

Barley, Maurice, *Houses and History* (1986)

Borsay, Peter, *The English Urban Renaissance: Culture and Society in the Provincial Town, 1660–1770* (1989)

Brunskill, R. W., *Illustrated Handbook of Vernacular Architecture* (1970)

Butler, Lionel and Given-Wilson, Chris, *Medieval Monasteries of Great Britain* (1979)

Clifton-Taylor, Alec, *The Pattern of English Building* (1972)

Colvin, H. M., *English Architectural History: A Guide to the Sources* (2nd edn., 1976)

Coppack, Glynn, *Abbeys and Priories* (1990)

Daunton, M., *House and Home in the Victorian City: Working-Class Housing, 1850–1914* (1983)

Gilbert, Christopher, *English Vernacular Furniture, 1750–1900* (1991)

Giles, Colum, *Rural Houses of West Yorkshire, 1400–1830* (1986)

Girouard, Mark, *Life in the English Country House* (1978)

Harrison, Barry and Hutton, Barbara, *Vernacular Houses in North Yorkshire and Cleveland* (1984)

Harvey, John, *The Perpendicular Style, 1330–1485* (1978)

Linstrum, Derek, *West Yorkshire: Architects and Architecture* (1978)

Mercer, Eric, *English Vernacular Houses* (1975)

Parker, Vanessa, *The Making of King's Lynn* (1971)

Pearson, Sarah, *Kentish Houses in the Later Middle Ages: An Historical Analysis* (1994)

Quiney, A. P., *The Traditional Buildings of England* (1990)

Richardson, Ruth and Thorne, Robert, *The Builder: Illustrations Index, 1843–1883* (1995)

Smith, Peter, *Houses of the Welsh Countryside* (1975)

Wight, Jane A., *Brick Building in England* (1972)

Local Studies

Atkinson, J. C., *Forty Years in a Moorland Parish* (1891)

Beckett, J. V., *Laxton: England's Last Open-Field Village* (1989)

Binfield, Clyde, *et al.*, *The History of the City of Sheffield, 1843–1993* (3 vols, 1993)

Chartres, John and Honeyman, Katrina (eds.), *Leeds City Business, 1893–1993* (1993)

Dyer, Alan D., *Worcester in the Sixteenth Century* (1973)

Dyos, H. J., *Victorian Suburb: A Study of Camberwell* (1961)

Everitt, Alan, *The Community of Kent and the Great Rebellion, 1640–60* (1966)

Goodacre, John, *The Transformation of a Peasant Economy: Townspeople and Villagers in Lutterworth, 1500–1700* (1994)

Hey, David, *An English Rural Community: Myddle under the Tudors and Stuarts* (1974)

—— (ed.), *Richard Gough: The History of Myddle* (1981)

—— *The Fiery Blades of Hallamshire: Sheffield and its Neighbourhood, 1660–1740* (1991)

Hoskins, W. G., *The Midland Peasant: The Economic and Social History of a Leicestershire Village* (1957)

—— *Provincial England: Essays in Social and Economic History* (1964)

Howell, Cecily, *Land, Family and Inheritance in Transition: Kibworth Harcourt, 1280–1700* (1983)

Jenkins, David, *The Agricultural Community in South-West Wales at the Turn of the Twentieth Century* (1971)

Levine, David and Wrightson, Keith, *The Making of an Industrial Society: Whickham, 1560–1765* (1991)

Marshall, J. D. and Walton, J. K., *The Lake Counties from 1830 to the Mid-Twentieth Century: A Study in Regional Change* (1981)

Obelkevich, James, *Religion and Society: South Lindsey, 1825–1875* (1976)

Palliser, David, *Tudor York* (1979)

Phythian-Adams, Charles, *Desolation of a City: Coventry and the Urban Crisis of the Later Middle Ages* (1979)

Poos, L. R., *A Rural Society after the Black Death: Essex, 1350–1525* (1991)

Prior, Mary, *Fisher Row: Fishermen, Bargemen and Canal Boatmen in Oxford, 1500–1900* (1982)

Robin, Jean, *Elmdon: Continuity and Change in a North-West Essex Village, 1861–1964* (1980)

Spufford, Margaret, *Contrasting Communities: English Villagers in the Sixteenth and Seventeenth Centuries* (1974)

Thompson, Flora, *Lark Rise to Candleford* (1945)

Thompson, F. M. L., *Hampstead: Building of a Borough, 1650–1964* (1974)

Wrightson, Keith and Levine, David, *Poverty and Piety in an English Village: Terling, 1525–1700* (2nd edn., 1975)

Zell, Michael, *Industry in the Countryside: Wealden Society in the Sixteenth Century* (1994)

General Works: The Middle Ages and Early Modern Period

Beier, A. L., *Masterless Men: The Vagrancy Problem in England, 1560–1640* (1965)

Britnell, R. H., *The Commercialisation of English Society, 1000–1500* (1993)

Chartres, John and Hey, David (eds.), *English Rural Society, 1500–1700: Essays in Honour of Joan Thirsk* (1990)

Clark, Peter and Slack, Paul, *Crisis and Order in English Towns, 1500–1700* (1972)

Cressy, David, *Literacy and the Social Order: Reading and Writing in Tudor and Stuart England* (1980)

Duffy, Eamon, *The Stripping of the Altars: Traditional Religion in England, 1400–1580* (1992)

Earle, Peter, *The Making of the English Middle Class: Business, Society and Family Life in London, 1660–1730* (1989)

Erickson, Amy Louise, *Women and Property in Early Modern England* (1993)

Fletcher, Anthony, *Reform in the Provinces: The Government of Stuart England* (1986)

Gelling, Margaret, *Signposts to the Past: Place-Names and the History of England* (2nd edn., 1988)

Gittings, Clare, *Death, Burial and the Individual in Early Modern England* (1984)

Horrox, Rosemary, *The Black Death* (1994)

Houlbrooke, Ralph A., *The English Family, 1450–1700* (1984)

Hutton, Ronald, *The Rise and Fall of Merry England: The Ritual Year, 1400–1700* (1994)

Ingram, Martin, *Church Courts, Sex and Marriage in England, 1570–1640* (1987)

Kent, Joan R., *The English Village Constable* (1986)

Kussmaul, Anne, *Servants in Husbandry in Early Modern England* (1981)

Litten, Julian, *The English Way of Death: The Common Funeral Since 1450* (1991)

MacFarlane, Alan, *The Family Life of Ralph Josselin, a Seventeenth-Century Clergyman* (1970)

Malcolmson, Robert W., *Popular Recreations in English Society, 1700–1850* (1973)

—— —— *Medieval England: Rural Society and Economic Change, 1086–1348* (1978)

Miller, Edward and Hatcher, John, *Medieval England: Towns, Commerce and Crafts, 1086–1348* (1995)

Neeson, Jean M., *Commoners: Common Right, Enclosure and Social Change in England, 1700–1820* (1993)

Newman, Peter, *A Companion to the English Civil Wars* (1990)

O'Day, Rosemary, *Education and Society, 1500–1800: The Social Foundations of Education in Early Modern England* (1982)

Palliser, David, *The Age of Elizabeth: England under the later Tudors, 1547–1603* (2nd edn., 1992)

Ramsay, G. D., *The English Woollen Industry* (1982)

Sharpe, J. A., *Early Modern England: A Social History* (1987)

Slack, Paul, *The English Poor Law, 1531–1782* (1990)

Smith, Lucy Toulmin (ed.), *John Leland: The Itinerary* (5 vols, 1964)

Spufford, Margaret, *Small Books and Pleasant Histories: Popular Fiction and its Readership in Seventeenth-Century England* (1981)

—— *The Great Reclothing of Rural England: Petty Chapmen and their Wares in the Seventeenth Century* (1984)

—— (ed.), *The World of Rural Dissenters, 1520–1725* (1995)

Thirsk, Joan, *Economic Policy and Projects: The Development of a Consumer Society in Early Modern England* (1978)

—— *The Rural Economy of England: Collected Essays* (1984)

—— *England's Agricultural Regions and Agrarian History, 1500–1750* (1987)

Thomas, Keith, *Religion and the Decline of Magic* (1971)

Thompson, E. P., *Whigs and Hunters: The Origins of the Black Act* (1975)

—— *Customs in Common* (1991)

Underdown, David, *Revel, Riot and Rebellion: Popular Politics and Culture in England, 1603–1660* (1985)

Weatherill, Lorna, *Consumer Behaviour and Material Culture in Britain, 1600–1760* (1988)

Whyte, Ian D., *Scotland Before the Industrial Revolution: An Economic and Social History, c.1050–c.1750* (1995)

Wrightson, Keith, *English Society, 1580–1680* (1982)

General Works: The Modern Period

Armytage, W. H. G., *Four Hundred Years of English Education* (1964)

Benson, John, *The Working Class in Britain, 1850–1939* (1989)

—— *British Coalminers in the Nineteenth Century: A Social History* (1993)

Boyes, Georgina, *The Imagined Village: Culture, Ideology and the English Folk Revival* (1993)

Brailsford, David, *Sport, Time and Society: The British at Play* (1991)

Bushaway, Bob, *By Rite: Custom, Ceremony and Community in England, 1700–1880* (1982)

Caunce, Stephen, *Amongst Farm Horses: The Horse Lads of East Yorkshire* (1991)

Chapman, John, *A Guide to Parliamentary Enclosures in Wales* (1992)

Cullen, Louis, *The Emergence of Modern Ireland* (1981)

Devine, T. M., *Clanship to Crofters' War: The Social Transformation of the Scottish Highlands* (1994)

Dewey, Peter, *Britain, 1914–1945: An Economic and Social History* (1996)

Driver, Felix, *Power and Pauperism: The Workhouse System, 1834–1864* (1993)

Hobsbawm, Eric and Ranger, Terence (eds.), *The Invention of Tradition* (1983)

Jenkins, Philip, *A History of Modern Wales, 1536–1990* (1992)

Further Reading

Jones, David J. V., *Rebecca's Children: A Study of Rural Society, Crime and Protest* (1989)

Lamb, H. H., *Climate, History and the Modern World* (2nd edn., 1995)

Lowerson, John, *Sport and the English Middle Classes, 1870–1914* (1993)

Mingay, G. E. (ed.), *The Victorian Countryside* (2 vols., 1981)

Roach, John, *A History of Secondary Education in England, 1800–1870* (1986)

—— *Secondary Education in England, 1870–1902* (1991)

Rose, M. E., *The Relief of Poverty, 1834–1914* (1972)

Rule, John, *The Labouring Classes in Early Industrial England, 1750–1850* (1986)

—— *Albion's People: English Society, 1714–1815* (1992)

Samuel, Raphael (ed.), *Village Life and Labour* (1975)

—— (ed.), *Miners, Quarrymen and Saltworkers* (1977)

Short, Brian (ed.), *The English Rural Community: Images and Analysis* (1992)

Simmons, Jack, *The Railways of Britain: An Historical Introduction* (3rd edn., 1986)

Snell, K. D. M., *Church and Chapel in the North Midlands: Religious Observance in the Nineteenth Century* (1991)

Tate, W. E. (ed. Michael Turner), *A Domesday of English Enclosure Acts and Awards* (1978)

Thompson, E. P., *The Making of the English Working Class* (2nd edn., 1968)

Thompson, F. M. L., *The Rise of Suburbia* (1982)

—— *The Rise of Respectable Society: A Social History of Victorian Britain, 1830–1900* (1988)

Turner, Michael, *Enclosures in Britain, 1750–1830* (1984)

Vincent, David, *Poor Citizens: The State and the Poor in Twentieth-Century Britain* (1991)

Walton, John K., *The English Seaside Resort* (1983)

The Agrarian History of England and Wales

I.1   Piggott, S. and Fowler, P. J. (eds.), *Prehistory* (1981)

I.2   Finberg, H. P. R. (ed.), *AD 43–1042* (1972)

II   Hallam, H. E. (ed.), *1042–1350* (1988)

III   Miller, Edward (ed.), *1350–1500* (1991)

IV   Thirsk, Joan (ed.), *1500–1640* (1967)

V.1   Thirsk, Joan (ed.), *1640–1750: Regional Farming Systems* (1984)

V.2   Thirsk, Joan (ed.), *1640–1750: Agrarian Change* (1984)

VI   Mingay, G. E. (ed.), *1750–1850* (1989)

VII   Collins, E. J. T. (ed.), *1850–1914* (forthcoming)

VIII   Whetham, E. H. (ed.), *1914–1939* (1978)

Academic Journals

The following national journals contain articles of interest to family and local historians:

Agricultural History Review
Archaeological Journal, The
Ecclesiastical History
Economic History Review
Family Tree
Folk Life
Folklore
Garden History
Genealogists' Magazine
Historical Geography
History Workshop Journal
Industrial Archaeology
Local and Regional Studies, Journal of
Local Historian, The
Local History Magazine
Local Population Studies
Medieval Archaeology
Midland History
Northern History
Oral History
Past and Present
Post-Medieval Archaeology
Recusant History
Rural History: Economy, Society, Culture
Southern History
Tools and Trades
Transport History, Journal of
Urban History